GEOProcessing 2025

The Seventeenth International Conference on Advanced Geographic Information Systems, Applications, and Services

May 18 - 22, 2025

Nice, France

GEOProcessing 2025 Editors

Lidia M. Ortega Alvarado, University of Jaén, Spain

Roger Tilley, Sandia National Laboratories, USA

Printed from e-media with permission by:

Curran Associates, Inc.
57 Morehouse Lane
Red Hook, NY 12571

Some format issues inherent in the e-media version may also appear in this print version.

International Academy, Research, and Industry Association (IARIA)
412 Derby Way
Wilmington, DE 19810

Phone: (408) 893-6407
Fax: (408) 527-6351

petre@iaria.org

Additional copies of this publication are available from:

Curran Associates, Inc.
57 Morehouse Lane
Red Hook, NY 12571 USA
Phone: 845-758-0400
Fax: 845-758-2633
Email: curran@proceedings.com
Web: www.proceedings.com

Table of Contents

GEOProcessing 2025

Forward

The Seventeenth International Conference on Advanced Geographic Information Systems, Applications, and Services (GEOProcessing 2025), held between May 18th, 2025, and May 22nd, 2025, in Nice, France, continued a series of events addressing various aspects of managing geographical information and web services. The goal of the GEOProcessing 2025 conference was to bring together researchers from the academia and practitioners from the industry in order to address fundamentals of advances in geographic information systems and the new applications related to them using the Web Services. Such systems can be used for assessment, modeling, and prognosis of emergencies.

The event provided a forum where researchers were able to present recent research results and new research problems and directions related to them. The topics covered aspects from fundamentals to more specialized topics such as 2D & 3D information visualization, web services and geospatial systems, geoinformation processing, and spatial data infrastructure.

We would like to warmly thank all the members of the GEOProcessing 2025 technical program committee, as well as all the reviewers. The creation of such a high-quality conference program would not have been possible without their involvement. We also kindly thank all the authors who dedicated much of their time and effort to contribute to GEOProcessing 2025. Thanks to all these efforts, the final conference program consisted of top-quality contributions. We also thank the members of the GEOProcessing 2025 organizing committee for their help in handling the logistics of this event.

We hope that GEOProcessing 2025 was a successful international forum for the exchange of ideas and results between academia and industry for the promotion of progress in the field of geographical information systems, applications, and services.

GEOProcessing 2025 Chairs

GEOProcessing 2025 Steering Committee Chair
Claus-Peter Rückemann, Universität Münster / DIMF / Leibniz Universität Hannover, Germany

GEOProcessing 2025 Steering Committee
Thomas Ritz, FH Aachen, Germany
Yerach Doytsher, Technion - Israel Institute of Technology, Haifa, Israel
Roger Tilley, Sandia National Laboratories, USA
Alexey Cheptsov, Information Service Center of the University of Stuttgart (TIK), Germany
Jui-Hsin (Larry) Lai, Ping-An Technology - Research Lab, USA

GEOProcessing 2025 Publicity Chairs
José Miguel Jiménez, Universitat Politècnica de València, Spain
Francisco Javier Díaz Blasco, Universitat Politècnica de València, Spain
Ali Ahmad, Universitat Politècnica de València, Spain
Sandra Viciano Tudela, Universitat Politècnica de València, Spain
Laura Garcia, Universidad Politécnica de Cartagena, Spain

GEOProcessing 2025
Committee

GEOProcessing 2025 Steering Committee Chair

Claus-Peter Rückemann, Universität Münster / DIMF / Leibniz Universität Hannover, Germany

GEOProcessing 2025 Steering Committee

Thomas Ritz, FH Aachen, Germany
Yerach Doytsher, Technion - Israel Institute of Technology, Haifa, Israel
Roger Tilley, Sandia National Laboratories, USA
Alexey Cheptsov, Information Service Center of the University of Stuttgart (TIK), Germany
Jui-Hsin (Larry) Lai, Ping-An Technology - Research Lab, USA

GEOProcessing 2025 Publicity Chairs

José Miguel Jiménez, Universitat Politècnica de València, Spain
Francisco Javier Díaz Blasco, Universitat Politècnica de València, Spain
Ali Ahmad, Universitat Politècnica de València, Spain
Sandra Viciano Tudela, Universitat Politècnica de València, Spain
Laura Garcia, Universidad Politécnica de Cartagena, Spain

GEOProcessing 2025 Technical Program Committee

Mahdi Abdelguerfi, University of New Orleans, USA
Alia I. Abdelmoty, Cardiff University, Wales, UK
Danial Aghajarian, Georgia State University, USA
Nuhcan Akçit, Middle East Technical University, Turkey
Zaher Al Aghbari, University of Sharjah, UAE
Hoda Allahbakhshi, UZH | Digital Society Initiative, Switzerland
Bharath H. Aithal, IIT Kharagpur, India
Rajendran Shobha Ajin, Resilience Development Initiative (RDI), Bandung, Indonesia
Md Mahbub Alam, Dalhousie University, Canada
Heba Aly, University of Maryland, College Park, USA
Oussama Annad, Higher School of Advanced Technologies (Ecole Nationale Supérieure des Technologies Avancées ENSTA), Algeria
Francisco Javier Ariza López, Escuela Politécnica de Jaén - Universidad de Jaén, Spain
Thierry Badard, Centre de Recherche en Géomatique (CRG) | Université Laval, Canada
Fabian Barbato, UDELAR-School of Engineering, Uruguay
Melih Basaraner, Yildiz Technical University, Turkey
Peter Baumann, rasdaman GmbH Bremen / Jacobs University Bremen, Germany
Mikael Brunila, McGill University, Canada
Lorenzo Carnevale, University of Messina, Italy
Mete Celik, Erciyes University, Turkey
Aizaz Chaudhry, Carleton University, Canada
Wei Chen, University of Birmingham, UK

Dickson K.W. Chiu, The University of Hong Kong, Hong Kong
Alexey Cheptsov, Information Service Center of the University of Stuttgart (TIK), Germany
Daniel Enrique Constantino Recillas, TESE, Mexico
Giuliano Cornacchia, University of Pisa / Institute of Information Science and Technologies, National Research Council of Italy (ISTI-CNR), Italy
Mehmet Ali Çullu, Harran University, Türkiye
Clodoveu Davis, Universidade Federal de Minas Gerais, Brazil
Giacomo De Carolis, CNR-IREA, Italy
Monica De Martino, CNR-IMATI (National research Council, Institute of applied Mathematics and Information technology), Italy
Cláudio de Souza Baptista, University of Campina Grande, Brazil
Subhadip Dey, Indian Institute of Technology Bombay, India
Yerach Doytsher, Technion - Israel Institute of Technology, Haifa, Israel
Suzana Dragicevic, Simon Fraser University, Canada
Surya Durbha, IIT Bombay, India
Emre Eftelioglu, Amazon, USA
Süleyman Eken, Kocaeli University, Turkey
Salah Er-Raki, Université Cadi Ayyad, Morocco
Javier Estornell, Universitat Politècnica de València, Spain
Jamal Ezzahar, Université Cadi Ayyad, Morocco
Zhiwen Fan, University of Texas at Austin, USA
Francisco R. Feito, University of Jaén, Spain
Anabella Ferral, Instituto de Altos Estudios Espaciales Mario Gulich | Centro Espacial Teófilo Tabanera - CONAE, Córdoba, Argentina
John Fillwalk, Ball State University, USA
Kaiqun Fu, South Dakota State University, USA
Nir Fulman, Heidelberg University, Germany
Erica Goto, University of Michigan, USA
Jayant Gupta, Oracle Inc., USA
Mohd Helmy Abd Wahab, Universiti Tun Hussein Onm Malaysia, Malaysia
Arif Hidayat, Monash University, Australia / Brawijaya University, Indonesia
Masaharu Hirota, Okayama University of Science, Japan
Qunying Huang, University of Wisconsin, Madison, USA
Xin Huang, Towson University, USA
Chih-Cheng Hung, Kennesaw State University - Marietta Campus, USA
Sergio Ilarri, University of Zaragoza, Spain
Ge-Peng Ji, Wuhan University (WHU) & Inception Institute of Artificial Intelligence (IIAI), China
Jehn-Ruey Jiang, National Central University, Taiwan
Joaquim João Sousa, INESC TEC, Portugal
Katerina Kabassi, Ionian University, Greece
Hassan A. Karimi, University of Pittsburgh, USA
Baris M. Kazar, Oracle America Inc., USA
Saïd Khabba, Université Cadi Ayyad, Marrakech, Morocco
Kyoung-Sook Kim, National Institute of Advanced Industrial Science and Technology (AIST), Tokyo, Japan
Mel Krokos, University of Portsmouth, UK
Anoop Kumar Shukla, Manipal Academy of Higher Education, India
Piyush Kumar, Florida State University, USA
Jui-Hsin (Larry) Lai, Ping-An Technology - Research Lab, USA

Robert Laurini, INSA Lyon | University of Lyon, France
Dan Lee, Esri Inc.,USA
José Luis Lerma, Universitat Politècnica de València, Spain
Lei Li, University of Copenhagen, Denmark
Jonathan Li, University of Waterloo, Canada
Arika Ligmann-Zielinska, Michigan State University, USA
Jugurta Lisboa-Filho, Federal University of Viçosa, Brazil
Zhiguo Long, School of Computing and Artificial Intelligence | Southwest Jiaotong University, China
Ying Lu, DiDi Research America, Mountain View, USA
Giovanni Ludeno, Institute for the Electromagnetic Sensing of the Environment | National Research Council of Italy, Napoli, Italy
Dandan Ma, Northwestern Polytechnic University, China
Ali Mansourian, Lund University, Sweden
Jesús Martí Gavilá, Research Institute for Integrated Management of Coastal Areas (IGIC) | Universitat Politècnica de València, Spain
Giovanni Mauro, University of Pisa / IMT School for Advanced Studies, Lucca / Institute of Information Science and Technologies, National Research Council of Italy (ISTI-CNR), Italy
Sara Migliorini, University of Verona, Italy
Sobhan Moosavi, The Ohio State University, USA
Hanan Muhajab, Cardiff University, UK / Jazan University, Saudi Arabia
Tathagata Mukherjee, The University of Alabama in Huntsville, USA
Beniamino Murgante, University of Basilicata, Italy
Ahmed Mustafa, The New School University, New York, USA
Purevtseren Myagmartseren, National University of Mongolia, Mongolia
Aldo Napoli, MINES ParisTech - CRC, France
Maurizio Napolitano, Fondazione Bruno Kessler, Trento, Italy
Rayan Nas, Yüksel Proje Inc., Ankara, Turkey
Rouhollah Nasirzadehdizaji, Istanbul University - Cerrahpaşa, Turkey
Alexey Noskov, Philipps University of Marburg, Germany
Hadj Sahraoui Omar, Algerian Space Agency | Space Techniques Centre, Algeria
Lidia Ortega Alvarado, University of Jaén, Spain
Xiao Pan, Shijiazhuang Tiedao University, China
Shray Pathak, School of Geographic Sciences | East China Normal University, Shanghai, China
Akshay Patil, AiDASH.inc, India
Kostas Patroumpas, Athena Research Center, Greece
Davod Poreh, Università degli Studi di Napoli "Federico II", Italy
Viktor Prasanna, University of Southern California, USA
Kuldeep Purohit, Michigan State University, USA
Honggang Qi, University of Chinese Academy of Sciences, China
María Isabel Ramos Galán, Universidad de Jaén, Spain
Thomas Ritz, FH Aachen, Germany
Ricardo Rodrigues Ciferri, Federal University of São Carlos (UFSCar), Brazil
Armanda Rodrigues, Universidade NOVA de Lisboa | NOVA LINCS, Portugal
Claus-Peter Rückemann, Universität Münster / DIMF / Leibniz Universität Hannover, Germany, Germany, Germany
André Sabino, Universidade Europeia, Portugal
Arpan Sainju, Middle Tennessee State University, USA
Raja Sengupta, McGill University, Montreal, Canada

Elif Sertel, Istanbul Technical University, Turkey
Arun Sharma, University of Minnesota, Twin Cities, USA
Shih-Lung Shaw, University of Tennessee, Knoxville, USA
Yosio E. Shimabukuro, Brazilian Institute for Space Research - INPE, Brazil
Rajat Shinde, Indian Institute of Technology Bombay, India
Dericks Praise Shukla, IIT Mandi, India
Spiros Skiadopoulos, University of the Peloponnese, Greece
Srushti Rashmi Shirish, Woven planet holdings, Tokyo, Japan
Francesco Soldovieri, Istituto per il Rilevamento Elettromagnetico dell'Ambiente - Consiglio Nazionale delle Ricerche (CNR), Italy
Katia Stankov, University of British Columbia, Canada
Behnam Tahmasbi, University of Maryland, College Park, USA
Ergin Tari, Istanbul Technical University, Turkey
Brittany Terese Fasy, Montana State University, USA
Roger Tilley, Sandia National Laboratories, USA
Goce Trajcevski, Iowa State University, USA
Linh Truong-Hong, Delft University of Technology, Netherlands
Taketoshi Ushiama, Kyushu University, Japan
Munazza Usmani, Fondazione Bruno Kessler, Trento, Italy
Marlène Villanova-Oliver, Univ. Grenoble Alpes - Grenoble Informatics Lab, France
Massimo Villari, University of Messina, Italy
Tin Vu, Microsoft Corporation, USA
Hong Wei, University of Maryland, College Park, USA
John P. Wilson, University of Southern California, USA
Jianhong Cecilia Xia, Curtin University, Australia
Ningchuan Xiao, The Ohio State University, USA
Yanan Xin, Institute of Cartography and Geoinformation | ETH Zurich, Switzerland
Daisuke Yamamoto, Nagoya Institute of Technology, Japan
Xiaojun Yang, Florida State University, USA
Zhaoming Yin, Google LLC, USA
Qiangqiang Yuan, School of Geodesy and Geomatics | Wuhan University, China
F. Javier Zarazaga-Soria, University of Zaragoza, Spain
Bingyi Zhang, University of Southern California, USA
Zenghui Zhang, Shanghai Jiao Tong University, China
Shenglin Zhao, Tencent, Shenzhen, China
Qiang Zhu, University of Michigan - Dearborn, USA
Rui Zhu, Institute of High Performance Computing - A*STAR, Singapore
Alexander Zipf, Heidelberg University, Germany

Copyright Information

Geospatial Modelling for the Optimal Location of Solar Panels for Agrivoltaic Systems - A Case Study in Olive Groves

Andressa Cardoso and María Isabel Ramos
Department of Cartographic, Geodetic and Photogrammetric Engineering
University of Jaén
Jaén, Spain
Email: asousa@ujaen.es/miramos@ujaen.es

Francisco Feito and Juan Manuel Jurado
Department of Computer Science
University of Jaén
Jaén, Spain
Email: ffeito@ujaen.es/jjurado@ujaen.es

Abstract— **Agrivoltaic systems represent an innovative strategy to improve sustainability in agriculture by integrating solar energy production with food cultivation. In the province of Jaén, Spain, where olive cultivation is key, the implementation of these systems could optimise land use and increase farmers' profitability. This study uses Geographic Information Systems (GIS) and Multi-Criteria Decision Analysis (MCDA), specifically the Analytic Hierarchy Process (AHP) method to identify the most suitable sites for the installation of agrivoltaics. The results indicate that 19% of the area studied (33,840 km^2) is highly suitable for agrivoltaic systems, with solar radiation and terrain slope being the most influential factors. This paper contributes a reproducible GIS-MCDM methodology for agrivoltaic site selection using expert- weighted criteria and spatial layers. The novelty lies in applying these techniques specifically to olive groves in Jaén, integrating solar potential with crop viability to support land- use optimization.**

Keywords - Agrivoltaics; Geographic Information System; Agriculture; Geospatial analysis.

I. INTRODUCTION

The growing demand for energy and food intensifies competition for land use, making agrivoltaic systems a strategic solution for integrating agricultural production with solar energy generation. Photovoltaic energy has been expanding globally, and in Spain, after a period of stagnation, its capacity more than doubled between 2019 and 2021, driven by lower technology costs and high solar radiation levels [1] [2].

Agrivoltaic systems allow for dual land use, enabling both agricultural production and electricity generation, providing environmental and economic benefits, such as improved soil quality, reduced water consumption, and increased biodiversity [3]. Additionally, studies show that this system can increase farmers' income, especially in low- margin crops. However, poorly positioned solar panels may compromise the productivity of the solar plant.

To address this challenge, GIS and MCDA are widely used to select optimal locations for renewable energy projects [4]. AHP, in particular, is effective in weighting different criteria without complex calculations, ensuring more consistent decision-making [5].

Previous research has demonstrated the effectiveness of GIS and MCDA, specifically the AHP method, in the selection of ideal sites for solar power plants. Studies in Morocco [8], Turkey [9], and Indonesia [6] have shown that between 16% and 19% of the analyzed areas are highly suitable for photovoltaic installations. In addition to MCDA, methods such as Weighted Linear Combination (WLC), Fuzzy AHP, and Technique for Order Preference by Similarity to Ideal Solution (TOPSIS) have also been employed to evaluate multiple criteria [12].

This study focuses on Jaén province, Spain, the world's largest olive oil producer, where agrivoltaics is not yet widely implemented. The methodology combines GIS, MCDA, and 3D modeling to assess the impact of shading.

The results indicate that 19% of the study area is highly suitable for agrivoltaic projects, allowing clean energy generation without compromising agricultural productivity. This proposed approach can be replicated in other agricultural regions, promoting food and energy security in a sustainable way.

The remainder of this paper is structured as follows: Section 2 describes the study area and data collection process. Section 3 explains the MCDA methodology based on the Analytic Hierarchy Process (AHP). Section 4 presents the results of the spatial analysis, while Section 5 discusses the implications of the findings. Finally, Section 6 outlines conclusions and future research directions.

II. RELATED WORKS

Recent studies have applied Geographic Information Systems (GIS) and Multi-Criteria Decision Analysis (MCDA) methods, particularly the Analytic Hierarchy Process (AHP), to identify optimal locations for photovoltaic (PV) energy projects. In Saudi Arabia [7][13], Morocco [8], Turkey [9], and Egypt [10], GIS-AHP frameworks have successfully classified between 16% and 19% of their territories as highly suitable for solar energy installations, primarily based on criteria such as solar radiation, slope, land use, and proximity to infrastructure. Additionally, alternative decision techniques such as Weighted Linear Combination (WLC), Fuzzy AHP [14], and TOPSIS [12] have been introduced to enhance evaluation accuracy.

However, although these approaches have been effective in optimizing site selection for energy purposes, they often overlook the agricultural context, particularly the preservation of existing crops and rural heritage. In Spain, olive groves cover more than 2.5 million hectares, representing not only a key agricultural product but also an important cultural and environmental asset. The rapid expansion of large-scale photovoltaic plants has raised concerns about the loss of olive cultivation areas, threatening food production, local economies, and traditional landscapes.

Addressing this gap, the present study proposes a GIS-MCDA framework specifically adapted for the development of agrivoltaic systems within existing olive groves, aiming to optimize land use by integrating solar energy production without displacing agricultural activities. By focusing on the specific conditions of Jaén province—the leading olive oil-producing region globally—this work contributes a reproducible methodology that balances renewable energy deployment with agricultural preservation and sustainability.

III. MATERIALS AND METHODS

A. *Study Area*

The study area consists of 22 towns in Jaén, Andalusia, Spain, covering 2,700 km², a region with high solar radiation (2,625 kWh/m² annually) and extensive olive cultivation (550,000 ha). Jaén is the world's largest olive oil producer and has 219 MW of installed solar capacity, enough to power 100,000 homes. The region's long sunshine hours and available land make it highly suitable for agrivoltaic systems, allowing farmers to integrate solar energy with agriculture, improving land productivity and income while promoting sustainable energy generation.

B. *Definition criteria*

Identifying the factors used to evaluate site suitability is essential for optimizing solar power plant performance and cost efficiency. Common factors include Global Horizontal Irradiance (GHI), slope, and land cover, though variations exist depending on the study area and expert knowledge.

The criteria are divided into two types:

- Evaluation Criteria – Factors that influence site suitability.
- Constraints – Factors that exclude unsuitable areas.

The constraints were selected based on previous research on optimal PV plant siting [4][9][10][11]. These include permanent water bodies, restricted zones (airports, military sites), protected areas (e.g., Natura 2000, cultural heritage sites), and urban centers. These restricted areas and their buffer zones were identified following the Guide for Environmental Impact Studies for Photovoltaic Projects. In this study, the evaluation criteria were grouped into three categories: Climatology, Orography, and Location (Figure 1). The selection was based on previous studies and expert evaluations in PhotoVoltaic (PV) energy.

- Selected Criteria:

C1 - Slope (%): Steep slopes complicate solar panel installation and reduce sunlight exposure. Research indicates that areas with slopes less than 5° are ideal for maximizing PV system efficiency [13] [14].

C2 - Aspects (Orientation): The orientation of the land influences solar energy capture. In the Northern Hemisphere, south-facing panels receive the most sunlight, whereas in the Southern Hemisphere, north-facing ones are optimal. Non-optimal orientations may require adjustments to improve efficiency [15].

C3 - Global Horizontal Irradiance (GHI) (kWh/m²): Solar radiation is the most critical factor in PV site selection. High GHI values ensure continuous and effective energy generation.

C4 - Average Temperature (°C): High temperatures negatively impact photovoltaic cell performance. Efficiency drops when temperatures exceed 25°C, making it essential to consider temperature variations when selecting sites.

- Distance-Based Criteria:

C5 - Distance to Roads (m): Sites close to roads ensure easy transportation, installation, and maintenance of solar panels. Proximity minimizes infrastructure costs and environmental impacts [15].

C6 - Distance to Transmission Lines (m): PV plants should be near power lines to reduce energy losses and avoid the high costs of new transmission infrastructure. Efficient connection to the grid ensures profitability [15].

C7 - Distance to Residential Areas (m): Closeness to urban centers affects land availability, costs, and energy distribution. While proximity reduces grid connection expenses, buffer zones are necessary to minimize social and environmental impacts.

These criteria were validated by PV energy experts and integrated into GIS and MCDA to determine the most suitable locations for agrivoltaic systems. The evaluation criteria, such as climate, topography, and location, were prioritized according to expert judgment and literature of 100,000 homes. The region's long sunshine hours and available land make it highly suitable for agrivoltaic systems, allowing farmers to integrate solar energy with agriculture, improving land productivity and income while promoting sustainable energy generation.

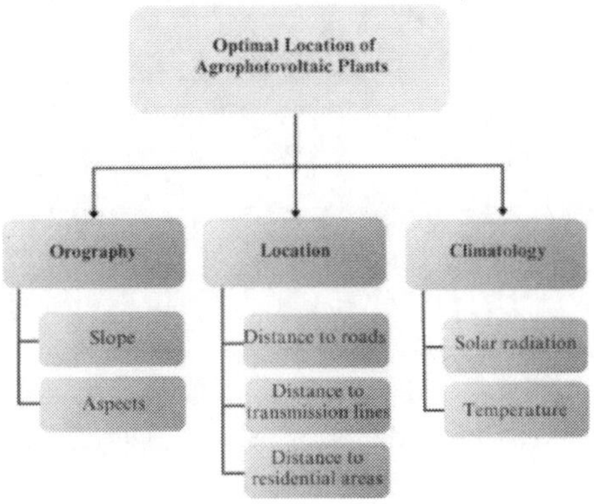

Figure 1. Criteria for optimal location of agrivoltaic plants.

C. *Obtaining Thematic Layers*

After defining the criteria, thematic layers were created through geoprocessing in Quantum Geographic Information System (QGIS) to analyze the suitability of sites for agrivoltaic plants. This involved combining GIS and MCDA techniques to assess the installation sites for solar panels. The process began with the collection of data, followed by spatial analysis using tools like surface, geometric, and distance operations.

A filtering step was performed on the Cadastral Parcels layer, focusing on olive grove farms identified by SIGPAC land use codes: OV (Olive groves), VO (Olive grove–Vineyard), OF (Olive grove–Fruit trees), FL (Shell fruit trees–Olive grove), and OC (Olive grove–Citrus). These categories correspond to different types of agricultural land where olive cultivation is predominant, either alone or in combination with other crops. Only parcels larger than 1,000 m² were selected, as smaller plots are not suitable for photovoltaic installations.

For each evaluation criterion, relevant data layers were generated:

- Criterion C1 - Slope (%): Calculated using Digital Elevation Model (DEM) with the QGIS Slope tool to identify flatter areas.
- Criterion C2 - Aspects: Orientation of the terrain calculated using DEM and the QGIS Aspect tool, with south-facing areas considered ideal for solar panels.
- Criterion C3 - Global Horizontal Irradiation (kWh/m²): Solar irradiance data from the Global Solar Atlas [16], downloaded as raster layers and clipped to the study area. Data was transformed using QGIS to align with the study's spatial resolution and suitability classification.
- Criterion C4 - Average Temperature (°C): Temperature data from the Global Solar Atlas, also clipped to the study area.
- Criterion C5, C6, C7 - Distance to Roads, Transmission Lines, and Residential Areas (m): Distances calculated using QGIS Euclidean distance tool for proximity analysis.

Once all layers were created, they were standardized on a common scale. Each layer was reclassified into 10 classes (1 = most suitable, 10 = least suitable), with special restrictions applied for Aspect (south-facing = 1) and Slope (slopes greater than 5° = 1). This reclassification allowed for integration into a unified suitability map for agrivoltaic plant siting. The processing results can be seen in the maps presented in Figure 2.

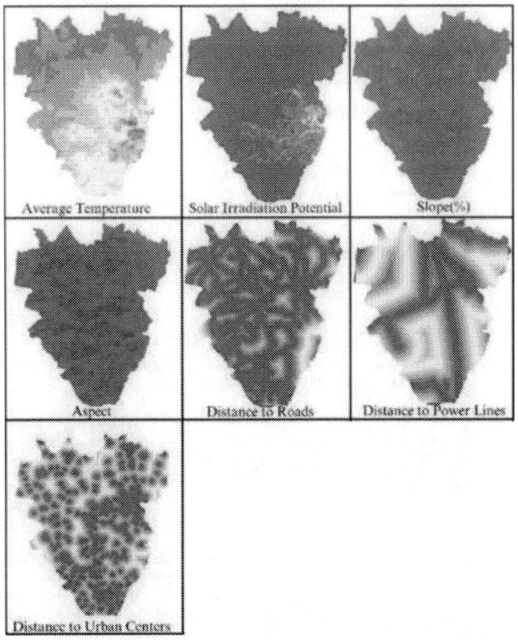

Figure 2. Maps of the geoprocessed and classified criteria.

Figure 2 presents the raster layers classified for each evaluation criterion. The slope and aspect maps reveal that south-facing land with gentle slopes-ideal for solar panel efficiency-are concentrated in the southern and southwestern regions of the study area. The solar radiation layer indicates higher irradiance values in these same areas, reinforcing their suitability. In addition, proximity-based criteria, such as distance to roads and power lines, highlight the advantage of the central and western municipalities in terms of access to infrastructure.

IV. MCDA Using an AHP Approach

This study employs the Analytic Hierarchy Process (AHP) within a Geographic Information System (GIS)- based Multi-Criteria Decision Analysis (MCDA) framework to identify optimal sites for agrivoltaic systems in Jaén, Spain. The AHP method is particularly suitable for renewable energy applications due to its ability to incorporate multiple qualitative and quantitative factors through structured expert judgment.

The AHP process follows structured steps, as shown in Figure 3 (decision-making flowchart). The process begins with problem definition, followed by hierarchical structuring of criteria and sub-criteria, and then constructing the Pairwise

Comparison Matrix (PCM). Experts evaluate the importance of each criterion using pairwise comparisons, and the results are normalized before computing the overall weight. A critical step is checking the Consistency Ratio (CR), which should be less than or equal to 10% to ensure the reliability of the decision matrix. If CR exceeds this threshold, adjustments are required before proceeding with the GIS mapping.

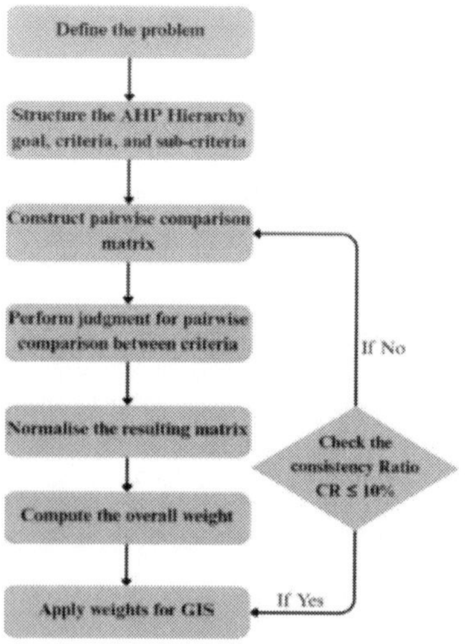

Figure 3. Steps for applying the AHP multi-criteria decision method.

AHP relies on expert pairwise comparisons, using a numerical scale from 1 (equal importance) to 9 (extreme importance). Table I presents the scale used to assess the relative importance of each criterion.

TABLE I. JUDGEMENT OF THE PAIRWISE COMPARISONS

N	Importance
Ci is equally as important as Cj	1
Ci is slightly more important than Cj	3
Ci is strongly more important than Cj	5
Ci is very strongly more important than Cj	7
Ci is extremely more important than Cj	9
Intermediate values	2, 4, 6, 8

After defining the importance levels, a PCM is constructed using a numerical grade scale (using Table I). Each criterion is compared with the others based on expert judgment. The reciprocal property is applied: if one criterion is considered much more important than another (e.g., C1 is 6 times more important than C6), the inverse value (1/6) is assigned to the opposite comparison (C6 compared to C1).

TABLE II. PAIRWISE COMPARISON MATRIX (PCM)

Criteria	C1	C2	C3	C4	C5	C6	C7
C1	1	2	3	4	7	6	5
C2	1/2	1	2	3	6	5	4
C3	1/3	1/2	1	2	5	4	3
C4	1/4	1/3	1/2	1	4	3	2
C5	1/7	1/6	1/5	1/4	1	1/2	1/3
C6	1/6	1/5	1/4	1/3	2	1	1/2
C7	1/5	1/4	1/3	1/2	3	2	1

Each entry a_{ij} in the pairwise comparison matrix was normalized by dividing it by the sum of its respective column, as shown in Equation (1):

$$s_{ij} = \frac{a_{ij}}{\sum_{i=1}^{n} a_{ij}} \quad (1)$$

This transformation ensures that all criteria are expressed in relative terms, making them directly comparable. To determine the criterion weight vector (W_j), Equation (2) was applied. The relative weight of each criterion was obtained by averaging the normalized values across each row, where n is the number of elements in the row:

$$W_j = \frac{\sum_{j=1}^{n} s_{jk}}{n-1} \quad (2)$$

Then, the CI was divided by the Random Consistency Index (RI), a reference value that varies depending on the number of criteria (3):

$$CR = \frac{CI}{RI} \quad (3)$$

The resulting weights are presented in Table III, with slope (C1) and aspect (C2) emerging as the most influential criteria for site selection.

TABLE III. FINAL RESULT OF THE AHP APPLICATION

Criterion	Valor	Percentage
C1	0.354	35.44%
C2	0.240	24.00%
C3	0.159	15.85%
C4	0.104	10.36%
C5	0.031	3.11%
C6	0.045	4.49%
C7	0.068	6.75%

To ensure the reliability of expert judgments, a Consistency Ratio (CR) was calculated. First, the Consistency Index (CI) is determined by comparing the maximum eigenvalue of the matrix with the number of criteria.

$$CI = \frac{\lambda max - n}{m} \quad (4)$$

Then, the CI is divided by a Random Consistency Index (RI), a reference value that depends on the number of criteria in the matrix. The RI values used for reference are presented in Table IV.

TABLE IV. RANDOM CONSISTENCY INDEX (RI) VALUES

N	1	2	3	4	5	6	7
RI	0	0	0.58	0.90	1.12	1.24	1.32

A CR $\leqslant$ 10% indicates acceptable consistency, ensuring that expert evaluations are logically consistent. In this study, the calculated CR was 0.03, confirming that the matrix is reliable.

Once the normalized weights were established, a final suitability map was created using a weighted linear combination method (Figure 4). Each criterion was represented as a raster layer previously standardized on a 1–10 suitability scale, and each layer was multiplied by its corresponding weight. The weighted layers were then summed to produce a composite suitability score for each cell in the study area.

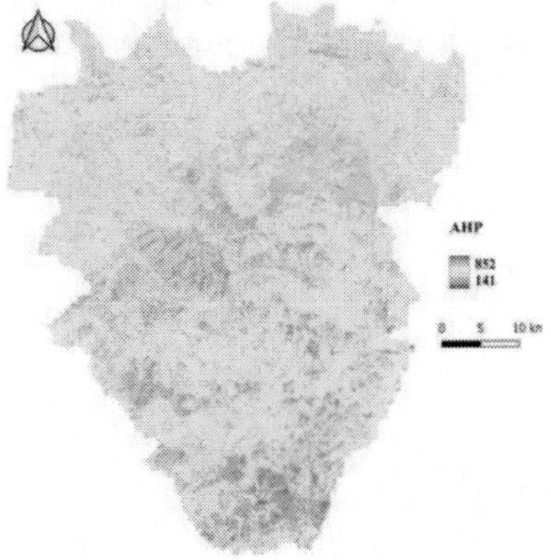

Figure 4. AHP Map.

In this step, spatial constraints previously defined — such as steep slopes or protected zones — were applied to mask out unsuitable areas. The result is a continuous raster map highlighting the most favorable locations for agrivoltaic development. To refine the results, areas deemed unsuitable for agrivoltaics—such as protected zones, urban regions, and bodies of water—were excluded from the final map.

The analysis revealed that 19% of the studied area is highly suitable for agrivoltaic projects, effectively balancing solar energy generation with agricultural productivity.

In sumary, using the MCDA-AHP technique, weighted values were assigned, and QGIS was used for spatial analysis. The results indicate that 33,840 km² of the study area are highly suitable, with a suitability level exceeding 80%. To simplify interpretation, the results were classified using the Land Suitability Index (LSI), as shown in Table V.

TABLE V. LAND SUITABILITY INDEX (LSI)

Suitability Level	Suitability Percentage	Area (km²)
Most Suitable	> 80%	33,840
Highly Suitable	70% – 80%	899,710
Moderately Suitable	60% – 70%	1,416,590
Marginally Suitable	50% – 60%	257,810
Least Suitable	< 50%	2,320

After classification, restricted areas (e.g., protected lands, urban zones, and bodies of water) were excluded using the QGIS clipping tool (Figure 5).

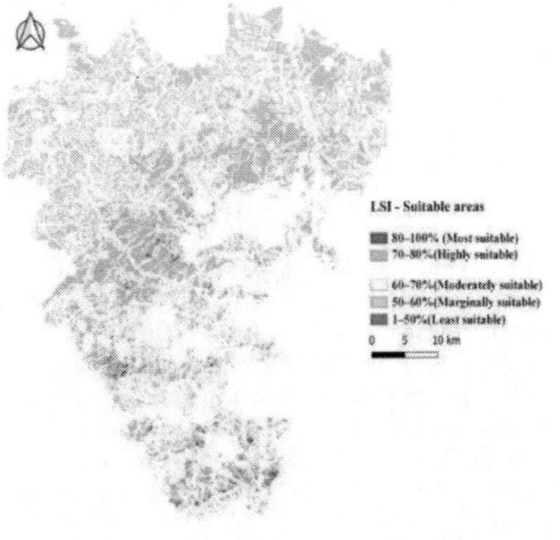

Figure 5. LSI with Restrictions excluded.

The most highly suitable areas are mainly in the south and west, benefiting from lower temperatures, high solar radiation, and accessibility to roads and power infrastructure. In contrast, northwestern areas are less suitable due to lower irradiation and infrastructure density. This solar site suitability analysis provides a data-driven approach to support decision-makers in selecting optimal agrivoltaic locations in Andalusia, whether for small or large-scale PV systems.

IV. CONCLUSION AND FUTURE WORKS

This study proposed a spatial framework based on GIS and Multi-Criteria Decision Analysis (MCDA) to identify optimal locations for agrivoltaic installations in olive-growing areas of Jaén province, Spain. By combining environmental, topographic, and infrastructure-related criteria using the Analytic Hierarchy Process (AHP), the study generated a spatial suitability map indicating that 33,840 km² — mainly in the south and west — are highly suitable for agrivoltaic systems, with an overall suitability level above 80%.

These results demonstrate that the integration of GIS and AHP methodologies enables informed land-use decision-making, promoting both energy transition and agricultural productivity. The spatial framework developed is replicable and adaptable to other contexts, making it a valuable tool for planners and policymakers.

However, this study is not without limitations. Agronomic variables such as crop yield under shading or irrigation needs were not included, and they could significantly influence the final suitability of the sites. Additionally, the results rely on static environmental datasets and expert-derived weights, which may vary over time or across regions.

Future work should consider the integration of dynamic agronomic models, real-time data, and alternative decision-making techniques such as the Fuzzy AHP algorithm. In addition, developing an intuitive and user-friendly interface would enhance accessibility and enable stakeholders to interact with spatial data and suitability maps more effectively, thereby supporting informed decision-making and encouraging broader public engagement. Finally, expanding this methodology to other agricultural regions of Spain or the Mediterranean could provide a more generalized understanding of sustainable dual land use.

ACKNOWLEDGMENT

This research has been partially funded through the research projects HORIZON-MISS-2021-SOIL-02-03 and HORIZON-MISS-2023-SOIL-01, which are financed with the European Union's Horizon Europe research and innovation programme. We are also grateful for the support provided by the Ministry of Innovation and Science of the Government of Spain through the research projects TED2021- 132120B-I00, PID2021-126339OB-I00, PID2022- 137938OA-I00 and GOPO-JA-23-0008. Finally, the research project GOPO-JA-23-0008 which is financed by the European Union FEDER funds has also contributed to the financing of this work.

REFERENCES

[1] I. Mauleón, "Optimising the spatial allocation of photovoltaic investments: Application to the Spanish case", *Energy Conversion and Management*, vol. 291, pp. 117292, 2023.

[2] M. Šúri, T. A. Huld, E. D. Dunlop, and H. A. Ossenbrink, "Potential of solar electricity generation in the European Union member states and candidate countries", *Solar Energy*, vol. 81, no. 10, pp. 1295–1305, 2007.

[3] H. Marrou, L. Guilioni, L. Dufour, C. Dupraz, and J. Wery, "Microclimate under agrivoltaic systems: Is crop growth rate affected in the partial shade of solar panels?", *Agricultural and Forest Meteorology*, vol. 177, pp. 117–132, 2013.

[4] L. Albraheem and L. Alabdulkarim, "Geospatial analysis of solar energy in Riyadh using a GIS-AHP-based technique", *ISPRS International Journal of Geo-Information*, vol. 10, no. 5, pp. 291, 2021.

[5] K. Ioannou, G. Tsantopoulos, and G. Arabatzis, "A decision support system methodology for selecting wind farm installation locations using AHP and TOPSIS: Case study in Eastern Macedonia and Thrace region, Greece", *Energy Policy*, vol. 132, pp. 232–246, 2019.

[6] H. S. Ruiz, A. Sunarso, K. Ibrahim-Bathis, S. A. Murti, and I. Budiarto, "GIS-AHP Multi Criteria Decision Analysis for the optimal location of solar energy plants at Indonesia", *Energy Reports*, vol. 6, pp. 3249–3263, 2020.

[7] H. Z. Al Garni and A. Awasthi, "Solar PV power plant site selection using a GIS-AHP based approach with application in Saudi Arabia", *Applied Energy*, vol. 206, pp. 1225–1240, 2017.

[8] A. A. Merrouni, F. E. Elalaoui, A. Mezrhab, A. Mezrhab, and A. Ghennioui, "Large scale PV sites selection by combining GIS and Analytical Hierarchy Process. Case study: Eastern Morocco", *Renewable Energy*, vol. 119, pp. 863–873, 2018.

[9] H. E. Colak, T. Memisoglu, and Y. Gercek, "Optimal site selection for solar photovoltaic (PV) power plants using GIS and AHP: A case study of Malatya Province, Turkey", *Renewable Energy*, vol. 149, pp. 565–576, 2020.

[10] J. R. Doorga, S. D. V. Rughooputh, and R. Boojhawon, "Multi-criteria GIS-based modelling technique for identifying potential solar farm sites: A case study in Mauritius", *Renewable Energy*, vol. 133, pp. 1201–1219, 2019.

[11] S. Zambrano-Asanza, J. Quiros-Tortos, and J. F. Franco, "Optimal site selection for photovoltaic power plants using a GIS-based multi-criteria decision making and spatial overlay with electric load", *Renewable and Sustainable Energy Reviews*, vol. 143, pp. 110853, 2021.

[12] J. M. Sánchez-Lozano, M. S. García-Cascales, and M. T. Lamata, "Evaluation of suitable locations for the installation of solar thermoelectric power plants", *Computers & Industrial Engineering*, vol. 87, pp. 343–355, 2015.

[13] I. Guaita-Pradas, I. Marques-Perez, A. Gallego, and B. Segura, "Analyzing territory for the sustainable development of solar photovoltaic power using GIS databases", *Environmental Monitoring and Assessment*, vol. 191, no. 12, pp. 764, 2019.

[14] S. Wang, L. Zhang, D. Fu, X. Lu, T. Wu, and Q. Tong, "Selecting photovoltaic generation sites in Tibet using remote sensing and geographic analysis", *Solar Energy*, vol. 133, pp. 85–93, 2016.

[15] G. Rediske, J. C. Mairesse Siluk, N. G. Gastaldo, P. D. Rigo, and C. B. Rosa, "Determinant factors in site selection for photovoltaic projects: A systematic review", *International Journal of Energy Research*, vol. 43, no. 5, pp. 1689–1701, 2019.

[16] The World Bank, ESMAP, "Global Solar Atlas", *The World Bank Group*, Washington, DC, 2020. [Online]. Available: https://globalsolaratlas.info.

Development of a Geospatial Predictive System of Crop Yield in Vineyards - A Case Study in Spain

Juan J. Cubillas
Dept. Information and Communication Technologies applied to Education.
International University of La Rioja
Logroño, Spain
e-mail: {juanjose.cubillas}@unir.net
Francisco Feito, Juan M. Jurado, David Jurado, J.Roberto Jiménez, Lidia Ortega
Dept. Computer Science.
University of Jaen
Jaen, Spain
e-mail: {ffeito|jjurado|djurado|rjimenez|lidia}@ujaen.es
Carlos Enríquez, Antonio Garrido, M.Isabel Ramos
Dept. Cartographic, Geodetic and Photogrammetric Engineering.
University of Jaen
Jaen, Spain
e-mail: {cenrique|agarrido|miramos}@ujaen.es

***Abstract*—This project aims to develop an Artificial Intelligence (AI)-based system for early crop yield prediction in vineyards. The objective is to provide farmers with a reliable tool that allows them to optimize resource planning, reduce risks, and enhance crop sustainability. The methodology integrates multi-source and multi-scale data, including historical yield information, multispectral satellite images, and climatic variables, such as temperature, humidity and precipitation, obtained from MODIS and ERA5, from Copernicus services. It employs advanced AI techniques, such as image processing and regression models. A key phase is validating and adjusting the model using high-resolution data captured by drones. The expected impact is outstanding accuracy in harvest prediction, which will lead to a significant reduction in uncertainty, greater operational efficiency, and improved grape quality, transforming viticulture into a more predictive and sustainable discipline.**

Keywords-Artificial intelligence; agriculture; crop yield prediction; remote sensing.

I. INTRODUCTION

The early estimation of crop yields for a specific crop is essential for all actors involved, including farmers, intermediaries, insurance companies, administrations and, of course, the consumer himself. Since time immemorial, good or bad harvests have brought both prosperity and famine to populations and thus determined their livelihoods and subsistence. Today, they still generate major imbalances in the economies of many families and areas of the planet, mainly because there are still no effective tools to make accurate forecasts sufficiently in advance. In this field, the most significant advances are determined by Information and Communication Technologies (ICT) at the service of Precision Agriculture (PA). This field also includes Remote Sensing for capturing images of the terrain and their advanced processing using Machine Learning techniques to forecast possible problems, such as diseases, and above all those related to crop yields [1] and [2].

It is the focus of most of the scientific community's efforts to try to identify the variables that mainly determine the behaviour of harvests. Undoubtedly, one of the most determining factors is climate [3], [4]. Although the wine sector has a somewhat more stable production than other traditional crops, such as olives, weather conditions are the main reason for the variability between the harvests of 2013 (7,500 tonnes) and 2017 (5,400 tonnes) at regional level [5]. Another important aspect related to climate is the quality of the grapes and, therefore, of the resulting wines [6], .

In order to be able to determine future behaviour, it is usually necessary to know what happened in the past. In the case of crop prediction, it is important to make this correlation between climatological variables and harvest results. The use of satellite data offers great advantages for working with medium and large-scale territories, such as municipalities, provinces or other types of geographical demarcations. However, their greatest capacity is to provide data with a certain frequency, providing historical data [7], [8]. Although they do not provide the same resolution as sensors attached to drones, they can cover large areas of land and provide data from the past that can also be correlated with data from previous harvests. In addition, different satellites provide images of different types: optical, multispectral, hyperspectral, thermal or LiDAR (Light Detection and Ranging), which are widely used in precision agriculture.

Most of the works developed for harvest forecasting differ in methodology depending on the type of crop. The importance of its forecasting in the field of wine production is pointed out in some works to determine the desired quantity and quality of grapes, which is crucial for winemakers [9], [10], [11]. However, the methodology of data capture, data cleaning and pre-processing can be considered a common task. Although each crop needs to adjust a different model based on its specific characteristics, a common methodology can be established for many crop types. In each case, the importance of data collection at different times of the year both at the climatological level and using specific vegetation indices for each case is considered.

Crop yield prediction is definitely one of the challenging problems in precision agriculture; however, as Xu et al. [12] point out, it is not a trivial task. Nowadays, crop yield prediction models can reasonably estimate actual values, but better performance in yield prediction is still desirable [6]. Numerous authors have emphasised the importance of quantitative crop yield prediction for years, considering it as a valuable tool to support farmers [13]. The close relationships between pollen emission and fruit production are extensively studied in this research. However, final fruit production is influenced by various climatic and agronomic conditions both in the pre-flowering period and in the period between flowering and harvest, such as water deficit, temperature extremes and phytopathological problems.

The structure of the paper has 4 sections: Section I is the Introduction where the crucial importance of early yield estimation in vineyards is highlighted for all actors in the sector. Section II, Methodology, proposes the implementation of a geospatial vineyard yield prediction system using AI and remote sensing, by integrating multi-source and multi-scale data. Section III describes the expected results and, finally, Section IV presents the incipient conclusions of this work.

II. Methodology

The implementation of a vintage prediction system for vineyards using AI and remote sensing involves the integration of multi-source and multi-scale data, the design of a geospatial database in the cloud and the creation of a predictive model validated with field data. Success lies in efficient data management and analysis, accuracy of predictions and accessibility for winegrowers, as shown in 1 . A phased implementation is proposed.

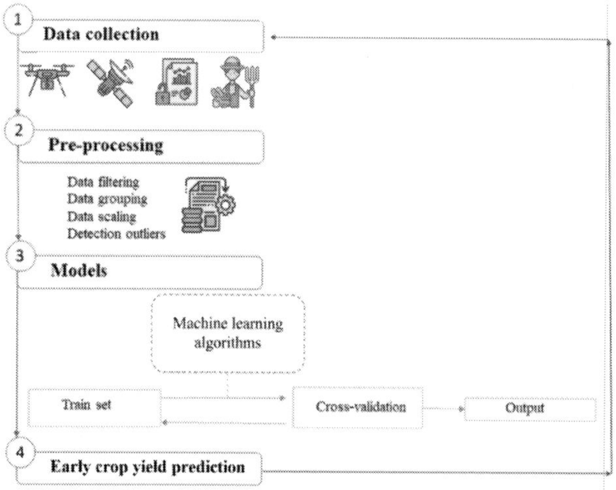

Figure 1. Methodology workflow.

A. *System architecture planning and design*

The first step will be to design a system architecture that allows data to be managed, processed and analysed in an efficient and scalable way. Three main sources of data will be considered:

1) Public data:: Satellite imagery providing multispectral information on vine cultivation.

2) Project-specific data:: High-resolution images, both satellite and captured from drone-mounted sensors.

3) Meteorological data:: Real-time weather information from local stations and historical bases, as well as products derived from remote sensing.

A geospatial database will be designed to efficiently store and manage geolocated information, and a cloud infrastructure will be implemented to ensure remote access, scalability and data security.

B. *Data acquisition and processing*

This phase includes the collection of the multi-source data and the processing of the data. The different origin and nature of the data requires a specific treatment of the data, both to be integrated homogeneously in the database without affecting the coherence of the data and to generate the derived products necessary for the implementation of the predictive model itself.

C. *Implementation of the geospatial database*

The geospatial database will be used to store and manage spatial data, allowing complex queries based on vineyard locations and associated variables. In addition, geospatial visualisation tools will be integrated to provide users with a visual representation of the data and to facilitate the interpretation of the information. Furthermore, being cloud-based, the database will be scalable, allowing new datasets to be incorporated as more data is obtained, without affecting the performance of the system. The cloud will also facilitate collaboration by allowing multiple users to access the system from different locations, which is essential when working with a technology transfer project involving multiple stakeholders.

D. *Design and implementation of the predictive system in the cloud*

The next step is the design and implementation of the predictive system in the cloud. This system will use advanced Machine Learning (ML) techniques capable of integrating diverse data sources and learning complex patterns that allow early estimation of the harvest. Once the model is trained, it will be implemented on Oracle's cloud platform. This cloud platform should also be accessible from mobile devices, facilitating remote access for users, so that it can also serve as a means of capturing data on harvest quantity (in the first instance) and other information on farming practices to feed back and retrain the predictive system.

E. Design and development of graphical interface for system use

Using Oracle Application Express, a system will be developed that will allow authorised users to visualise the harvest prediction and allow them to analyse the actual harvest and prediction data. This will allow non-expert users and from home to access and use the machine learning models, allowing to interpret and apply predictions in an intuitive and efficient way.

F. Validation and adjustment of the model with drone data

A fundamental part of the implementation of the system is the validation of the predictions generated by the predictive model. For this purpose, data collected directly with drones in the vineyards will be used as a reference point to verify the accuracy of the system's predictions from satellite images. The drone data, due to its high resolution and ability to capture fine details of the vineyard, will allow validation of the harvest predictions and adjustment of the model as needed. In order to ensured statistically robust validation it shall be adopted a sufficient number of sampling points covering a representative range of conditions within the study vineyards. Also, the timing of data collection will be directly related to the vegetative cycle of the vineyard.

This validation process is iterative and will progressively improve the accuracy of the system as more drone data is collected and more experience is gained with the system.

G. Scalability and maintenance of the system

Once the predictive system has been validated and fine-tuned, the focus will be on ensuring its long-term scalability and maintainability. As technology and data will continue to evolve, the system must be flexible and able to adapt to new data sources and predictive algorithms. The cloud platform must have tools that allow for continuous updating of the model, incorporation of new data, and enhancement of the system without interrupting service to users. This also includes the implementation of a monitoring system to ensure optimal performance of the infrastructure, detect possible errors and ensure the accuracy of the system.

H. Knowledge transfer and training

Training programmes will be designed to teach winegrowers how to use the platform, interpret forecasts and make informed harvesting decisions. This training will be crucial to ensure technology adoption and maximise the impact of the system on improving productivity in the vineyards.

III. Preliminary Results and Expectations

In a machine learning study focused on early grape harvest prediction, results are anticipated that will transform vineyard management. The primary goal is to achieve outstanding accuracy in harvest date prediction, minimising the discrepancy between model estimate and reality. Regression algorithms, trained on historical data, climatological data and multispectral images, are expected to reveal complex and non-linear patterns, overcoming the limitations of traditional methods. This accuracy would translate into more efficient harvest planning, allowing growers to optimise resource allocation and coordinate labour in advance.

The model is expected to reveal the relative importance of the variables analysed, from climatic fluctuations to vegetation indices captured by satellites and drones. This information will allow winegrowers to better understand the influence of various factors on their vineyards, adapting to the particularities of each vintage and mitigating the effects of climate change.

Rigorous validation of the model is crucial to ensure its robustness and applicability in different scenarios. The integration of drone data, with its high spatial resolution, is expected to complement satellite information, refining predictions and allowing accurate assessment at the plot scale. In terms of metrics, high R^2 values, close to 1, and low RMSE (Root Mean Square Error) and MAE (Mean Absolute Error) values are aspired, reflecting the high accuracy and low error of the predictions.

IV. Conclusions

The implementation of machine learning models for early grape harvest prediction represents a significant advance in precision viticulture. The expected results, based on the integration of multi-source data and regression algorithms, promise not only to improve the accuracy of predictions, but also to deepen our understanding of the factors influencing grapevine phenology. The ability to accurately anticipate harvest yields months in advance will allow grape growers to optimise the planning of their activities, from resource allocation to grape quality management. In addition, the identification of the most influential variables, such as climatic conditions and vegetation indices, will provide valuable information for informed decision-making.

Ultimately, this approach has the potential to transform viticulture into a more predictive and sustainable discipline. Rigorous validation of the models, using high-resolution drone and satellite data, will ensure their robustness and applicability in different contexts. Quantification of model performance through metrics, such as R^2, RMSE and MAE will provide an objective basis for assessing their accuracy and reliability. The implementation of these models is expected to lead to a significant reduction of uncertainty in wine crop management, resulting in increased efficiency and improved grape quality. In addition, the ability to capture and analyse complex patterns in the data will allow researchers and viticulturists to gain new insights into grapevine physiology and its response to environmental conditions.

References

[1] N. Bali and A. Singla, "Emerging Trends in Machine Learning to Predict Crop Yield and Study Its Influential Factors: A Survey," *Archives of Computational Methods in Engineering*, vol. 29, no. 1, pp. 95–112, Jan. 2022, ISSN: 1886-1784. DOI: 10.1007/s11831-021-09569-8.

[2] P. Nevavuori, N. Narra, and T. Lipping, "Crop yield prediction with deep convolutional neural networks," *Computers and Electronics in Agriculture*, vol. 163, p. 104 859, Aug. 2019, ISSN: 0168-1699. DOI: 10.1016/j.compag.2019.104859.

[3] S. Quiroga and A. Iglesias, "A comparison of the climate risks of cereal, citrus, grapevine and olive production in Spain," en, *Agricultural Systems*, vol. 101, no. 1, pp. 91–100, Jun. 2009, ISSN: 0308-521X. DOI: 10.1016/j.agsy.2009.03. 006.

[4] A. Barriguinha, B. Jardim, M. de Castro Neto, and A. Gil, "Using NDVI, climate data and machine learning to estimate yield in the Douro wine region," *International Journal of Applied Earth Observation and Geoinformation*, vol. 114, 2022, DOI: 10.1016/j.jag.2022.103069.

[5] S. Miovska, C. M. Bande, and N. Stojkovik, "Predicting Wine Properties Based on Weather Conditions Using Machine Learning Techniques," in *2024 47th ICT and Electronics Convention, MIPRO 2024 - Proceedings*, 2024, pp. 140–145. DOI: 10.1109/MIPRO60963.2024. 10569756.

[6] G. Canavera *et al.*, "A sensorless, Big Data based approach for phenology and meteorological drought forecasting in vineyards," *Scientific Reports*, vol. 13, no. 1, 2023. DOI: 10.1038/s41598-023-44019-4.

[7] M. F. Aslan, K. Sabanci, and B. Aslan, "Artificial Intelligence Techniques in Crop Yield Estimation Based on Sentinel-2 Data: A Comprehensive Survey," *Sustainability (Switzer-land)*, vol. 16, no. 18, 2024. DOI: 10.3390/su16188277.

[8] S. Pancholi and A. Kumar, "Investigating the Capability of DOVE Satellite Temporal Data for Mapping Harvest Dates of Sugarcane Crop Types Using Fuzzy Model," *Journal of the Indian Society of Remote Sensing*, vol. 52, no. 10, pp. 2127–2142, 2024, Type: DOI: 10.1007/s12524-024-01927-w.

[9] F. Palacios, M. P. Diago, P. Melo-Pinto, and J. Tardaguila, "Early yield prediction in different grapevine varieties using computer vision and machine learning," *Precision Agriculture*, vol. 24, no. 2, pp. 407–435, 2023. DOI: 10.1007/s11119-022-09950-y.

[10] C. Laurent *et al.*, "A review of the issues, methods and perspectives for yield estimation, prediction and forecasting in viticulture," *European Journal of Agronomy*, vol. 130, p. 126 339, 2021, ISSN: 1161-0301. DOI: https://doi.org/10.1016/j.eja.2021.126339.

[11] J. A. Taylor, B. Tisseyre, and C. Leroux, "A simple index to determine if within-field spatial production variation exhibits potential management effects: Application in vineyards using yield monitor data," *Precision Agriculture*, vol. 20, no. 5, pp. 880–895, Oct. 2019, ISSN: 1573-1618. DOI: 10.1007/s11119-018-9620-3.

[12] X. Xu *et al.*, "Design of an integrated climatic assessment indicator (ICAI) for wheat production: A case study in Jiangsu Province, China," en, *Ecological Indicators*, vol. 101, pp. 943–953, Jun. 2019, ISSN: 1470-160X. DOI: 10.1016/j.ecolind.2019.01.059.

[13] O. Fabio *et al.*, "Yield modelling in a Mediterranean species utilizing cause–effect relationships between temperature forcing and biological processes," en, *Scientia Horticulturae*, vol. 123, no. 3, pp. 412–417, Jan. 2010, Number: 3, ISSN: 0304-4238. DOI: 10.1016/j.scienta.2009.09.015.

Optimizing Picual Olive Variety Recognition through Deep Learning and Hyperspectral Imaging in Precision Agriculture

Alba Gómez Liébana, Ruth M. Córdoba Ortega
Researcher at the University of Jaén, Paraje Las Lagunillas Jaén, Spain
e-mail: aglieban@ujaen.es | rcortega@ujaen.es
Juan J. Cubillas
Dept. Information and Communication Technologies applied to Education.
International University of La Rioja, Logroño, Spain
e-mail: juanjose.cubillas@unir.net
Lidia M. Ortega
Dept. Computer Science. University of Jaén Jaén, Spain
e-mail: lidia@ujaen.es

Abstract—**The automated classification of olive varieties plays a crucial role in *Precision Agriculture*, enabling optimized resource allocation, improved irrigation strategies, and enhanced olive oil quality. This study explores the integration of *Hyperspectral Imaging (HSI)* and *Deep Learning (DL)* to classify olive varieties, focusing on *Picual*. Utilizing drone-acquired hyperspectral data, a *Convolutional Neural Network (CNN)* was employed to analyze leaf reflectance and extract spectral-spatial features with high accuracy. The Unmanned Aerial Vehicle (UAV)-based *HSI* system captures high-resolution spectral data, allowing for the detection of subtle differences in reflectance patterns that are imperceptible to traditional sensors. The study demonstrates that the proposed deep learning approach achieves an accuracy of approximately 90% in classifying olive varieties, significantly outperforming traditional machine learning methods. These findings highlight the potential of hyperspectral deep learning in agricultural applications, paving the way for scalable, efficient, and sustainable orchard management.**

Keywords-Hyperspectral Imaging (HSI); Deep Learning (DL); Convolutional Neural Networks (CNN); Precision Agriculture; Olive Variety Classification; UAV-based Imaging; Spectral-Spatial Analysis; Arbequina; Picual.

I. INTRODUCTION

Olive cultivation (Olea europaea) is a fundamental component of Mediterranean agriculture, contributing significantly to global olive oil production. The identification of olive varieties is crucial for optimizing agricultural management, ensuring efficient irrigation, and enhancing oil quality. However, traditional classification methods rely on manual expertise, which is labor-intensive and impractical for large-scale olive groves [1].

Spain, with the province of Jaén as its production heart, leads the olive grove sector worldwide, being the largest producer of olive oil and a benchmark for the quality and tradition of this crop. In this province, ***Picual*** and ***Arbequina*** varieties are the most prevalent, and it is a common practice to substitute ***Picual*** trees with ***Arbequina*** due to the significant problem of Verticillium wilt. This substitution results in a high prevalence of mixed-variety groves, significantly affecting agricultural management. Specifically, irrigation, pruning, fertilization, and pest control strategies vary based on the type of variety. From a cooperative perspective, cultivar identification is crucial; ***Picual*** oil is characterized by an intense profile, high polyphenol content, and a bitter, pungent flavor. The identification of this variety is important to control the mixture with other varieties, such as ***Arbequina***. This justifies the projects that accurately identify different tree specimens within groves.

This automatic species identification is now possible. ***HSI*** has emerged as a powerful tool in ***Precision Agriculture***, enabling the detailed spectral analysis of plant species. Unlike multispectral imaging, ***HSI*** captures narrow and continuous spectral bands, allowing for the detection of subtle differences in reflectance properties between varieties [2]. This technology has been widely applied in tasks, such as vegetation monitoring, disease detection, and yield estimation [2][3]. However, conventional analysis techniques often struggle with the high-dimensional nature of hyperspectral data.

To address these challenges, Artificial Intelligence (AI) and ***Deep Learning (DL)*** methods have been increasingly integrated with ***HSI*** for agricultural applications. Deep learning techniques, particularly ***CNNs***, have demonstrated significant improvements in classification accuracy for various crops, including wheat, rice, and maize [4]. ***CNNs*** effectively extract spectral-spatial features from hyperspectral data, reducing the need for manual feature engineering and improving classification efficiency [5].

Recent studies have highlighted the advantages of ***DL*** over traditional machine learning approaches in handling complex hyperspectral datasets [2]. Traditional models, such as k-Nearest Neighbors (k-NN) and Support Vector Machines (SVMs), often struggle with the curse of dimensionality and require extensive preprocessing. In contrast, ***CNNs*** automatically learn hierarchical feature representations, enabling superior performance in hyperspectral classification tasks [6].

Despite these advancements, limited research has been conducted on the application of deep learning for ***Olive Variety Classification***. The spectral differences between olive varieties, such as ***Arbequina*** and ***Picual***, are often subtle, making traditional classification approaches less effective [3]. Leveraging ***UAV-based*** hyperspectral imaging combined with

CNNs offers a promising solution for automating and scaling olive variety identification [4].

This study aims to develop a deep learning-based approach for ***Olive Variety Classification*** using drone-acquired hyperspectral imagery. By applying ***CNN*** architectures optimized for hyperspectral data, this research seeks to improve classification accuracy and provide a scalable solution for ***Precision Agriculture***.

Section 2 provides an overview of related work and describes the methodology used, including data acquisition and preprocessing. Section 3 reports the experimental results, focusing on model training and performance evaluation. Section 4 discusses and interprets the findings. Finally, Section 5 presents the conclusions and outlines potential directions for future research.

II. Related work | Methods

The research took place in Mengíbar, Jaén, on land owned by the Andalusian Institute of Agricultural and Fisheries Research and Training (IFAPA) at the Venta del Llano Center. This agricultural research facility operates under the research instituteian Regional Government and is dedicated to research and development in the agricultural sector, with a focus on olive cultivation [7]. The center is located in Jaén, which provides convenient access to a variety of olive plantations for conducting field studies and experiments. The study was carried out on a plot of land that offers optimal conditions for examining different olive varieties in a real-world agricultural setting.

The research area consists of rows of olive trees planted specifically for experimental purposes, allowing for the assessment of various olive cultivars. The experimental design includes 14 rows, each with around 24 trees. Within each row, groups of four trees from the same variety are planted, followed by a shift to a different variety. The row selected for the study can be seen in Figure 1, seeing that there are 8 ***Picual*** olive trees and the rest of other varieties.

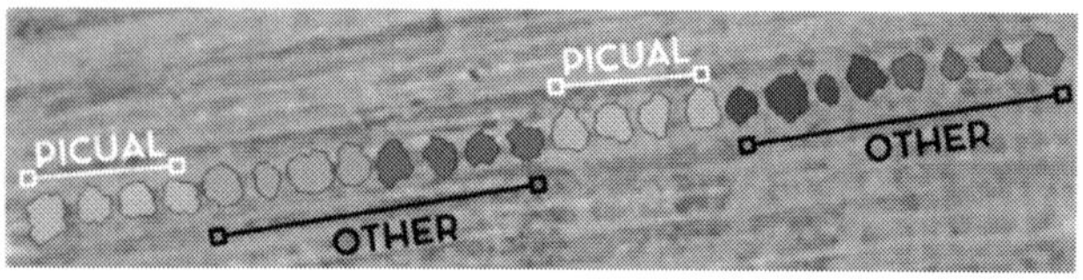

Figure 1. Row selected for the study.

Most of the other varieties are hybrids under investigation and are not widely cultivated. The random arrangement of these varieties within each block ensures comprehensive data collection and reduces bias. This structure enables IFAPA to gather important insights into the adaptability, productivity, and characteristics of different olive cultivars in the specific environmental conditions of Jaén.

A. Hyperspectral data capture and preparation

This study utilized a ***UAV*** equipped with a NanoHyperspec camera and Light Detection and Ranging (LiDAR) sensor to acquire hyperspectral imagery of olive trees. Flight parameters were optimized for high-quality data capture, including a 30-meter altitude, 5 m/s speed, and specific overlap percentages to ensure comprehensive coverage. The hyperspectral data, capturing 270 spectral bands from 400 to 1000 nm, was processed using Headwall SpectralView™ software, involving reflectance calibration and geometric correction using a high-resolution DEM (Digital Elevation Model) generated from LiDAR data. This process resulted in a dataset of 24 olive trees, showcasing spectral variations after applying necessary corrections.

Subsequent steps focused on refining the hyperspectral data for accurate classification. Tree canopy segmentation was performed using the Enhanced Vegetation Index (EVI) and Density-Based Spatial Clustering of Applications with Noise (DBSCAN) clustering to delineate individual trees, creating a vector mask with unique identifiers and variety classifications. To further improve data quality, noisy pixels, particularly those affected by shadows, were removed through a filtering process based on Near Infrared (NIR) reflectance and standard deviation. This filtering ensured that only spectrally stable pixels were used for analysis, enhancing the consistency and reliability of the data for subsequent classification methods. The effectiveness of these filtering techniques was demonstrated through visual comparisons and spectral signature analyses, ultimately leading to a refined dataset suitable for precise olive tree characterization.

B. Train, test and validation subsets

This section outlines the methodology for creating the training, testing, and validation subsets for **Picual vs. non-Picual (PI - NO PI)** classification. The data comes from the IFAPA farm, where the fourth row was selected for data extraction.

After segmentation, all the ***Picual*** olive trees were selected, totalling 264. Similarly, another 264 of the other varieties were randomly selected so that both sets were balanced, as can be clearly seen in Table I. For the training set, approximately 80% of the above-mentioned set (180 olive trees for ***picual*** and 186 for Non-Picual) were chosen. On the other hand, for the validation set, the remaining 20% were chosen (49 and 43 respectively), reserving 35 of each class for a subsequent test of the model generated (see Table I).

TABLE I
Description and distribution of Picual dataset.

Dataset	Train Data	Validation Data	Test Data	Total
PI	180	49	35	264
NO PI	186	43	35	264

This partitioning ensures that the models are trained on diverse and representative samples, improving reliability, generalizability, and reducing bias, while the separate validation set helps prevent overfitting.

C. Justification for the Use of Deep Learning and Neural Networks

Deep learning models, such as Multi-Layer Perceptrons (MLP) and ***CNNs***, are particularly well-suited for handling the intricate nature of hyperspectral data. These models excel in identifying and learning hierarchical patterns directly from the data, allowing them to adapt to the complex relationships found in the numerous spectral bands of hyperspectral images. This capability is crucial when classifying olive varieties, as it enables the model to discover subtle, non-linear distinctions that might otherwise be overlooked.

Additionally, deep learning models offer the advantage of automated feature extraction, simplifying the overall process by eliminating the need for manual intervention in selecting key features. This not only streamlines the workflow but also ensures that the model can capture essential information more effectively. Combined with their ability to manage high-dimensional data, deep learning models are well-equipped to improve classification accuracy and address the challenges posed by the intricate structure of hyperspectral datasets.

D. CNN architecture

As mentioned above, ***CNNs*** are highly suited for this study due to the nature of hyperspectral data and the complexity of ***Olive Variety Classification***. A *one-dimensional (1D)* ***CNN*** *model* was developed specifically for the classification of ***Picual*** variety, using hyperspectral data. The model architecture consists of *four convolutional layers*, *two max-pooling layers*, a fully connected layer with *dropout*, and an *output layer* for binary classification. The structure of the model is illustrated in Figure 2. The input consists of the dataset depicted in Table I. The first convolutional layer (in dark blue) applies the Exponential Linear Unit (ELU) activation function, which improves learning and normalizes feature maps by introducing non-linearity [8]. These layers, shown in dark blue, vary in the number of filters, and their kernels scan the hyperspectral sequence to extract relevant features. Filters help capture important patterns from the data, while the kernel size remains consistent across all convolutional layers.

Following the convolutional layers, a MaxPooling layer (shown in light blue) reduces the dimensionality of the feature maps, using a pool size of 3. This step enhances the model's efficiency by focusing on the most prominent features, reducing computational complexity, and preventing overfitting. After every two convolutional layers, MaxPooling layers further reduce the dimensionality, allowing the model to retain key spectral features critical for classification.

Once the convolutional layers have extracted the necessary features, the feature maps are flattened into a one-dimensional vector and passed to a fully connected layer. This dense layer captures complex relationships between the features, applying the ReLU activation function to enhance learning by setting negative values to zero, which helps avoid issues like vanishing gradients. A dropout layer is then added to mitigate overfitting, and the final output layer uses a sigmoid function to classify the sample as either ***Picual*** or ***Non-Picual***.

E. Computational Environment

The calculations in this study were carried out using the Anaconda distribution with Python 3.9, together with the NumPy, Pandas, TensorFlow and Scikit-learn libraries. For Bayesian optimisation, the BayesianOptimization library was used. All calculations were run on a personal computer with the following specifications: Intel(R) Core(TM) i9-12900K 12th generation 3.20 GHz processor and 64 GB of RAM. The operating system used was 64-bit on an x64-based architecture.

III. RESULTS

By employing ***UAV***-based hyperspectral imaging, this study removes the necessity for manual sampling, allowing for real-time, high-throughput classification. This represents a major leap forward in ***Precision Agriculture***, enhancing the scalability and efficiency of identifying olive varieties.

In this section, the hyperparameters of the ***CNN*** model used for classifying olive varieties are further optimized. A combination of manual tuning and Bayesian optimization was utilized to determine the most effective configurations for the ***Picual*** variety classification.

A. Refining the Classification

This section details the process of adjusting the hyper-parameters of the ***CNN*** for the classification of olive tree varieties. Different configurations were explored to optimise the performance of the model, resulting in specific parameters for ***Picual*** variety.

Initially, hyperparameters were manually tested to improve model performance, but this approach proved to be time-consuming and inefficient. As a result, Bayesian optimization was chosen to streamline the process and systematically explore the hyperparameter space. Bayesian optimization employs a probabilistic surrogate model to approximate the objective function—in this case, classification accuracy. It iteratively refines its search by leveraging information from previous trials, making it particularly useful when computational resources are limited or evaluations are costly, as was the case in this study.

The optimized values, detailed in Table II, include the filters applied to the convolutional layers, the kernel size for the ELU layers, and the number of neurons in the dense layer. These parameters were fine-tuned through Bayesian optimization to enhance model performance.

TABLE II
RANGE OF CNN HYPERPARAMETERS USED FOR OPTIMIZATION IN THIS STUDY.

Hyperparameters	Range
Filter 1	[10,20]
Filter 2	[25,35]
Filter 3	[60,75]
Filter 4	[110,130]
Kernel size	[2,5]
Dense Neurons	[32,70]

After applying Bayesian optimisation, the optimal values for the hyperparameters are shown in Table III. In addition, we

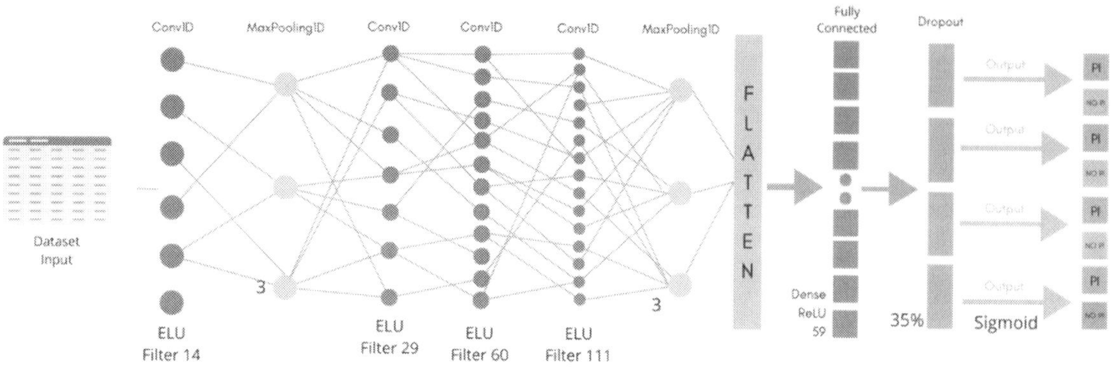

Figure 2. Neural Network CNN.

add the Pool Size, Epochs and Patience which were adjusted manually.

TABLE III
RANGE OF CNN HYPERPARAMETERS USED FOR PICUAL.

Picual	
Hyperparameters	**Value**
Filter 1	14
Filter 2	29
Filter 3	60
Filter 4	111
Kernel size	4
Dense Neurons	59
Pool Size	3
Batch Size	32
Epochs	50
Patience	10

B. Output of CNN

The application of ***CNNs*** for the classification of olive tree varieties has produced significant results, showcasing the capability of deep learning techniques to efficiently process hyperspectral data. By leveraging ***UAV***-based hyperspectral imaging, this study eliminates the need for manual sampling, enabling real-time, high-throughput classification. This represents a major advancement in ***Precision Agriculture***, making the identification of olive varieties more scalable and efficient. The models were evaluated based on their performance in classifying ***Picual*** **(PI)** and **non-Picual (NO PI)** varieties.

In addition to metrics, such as **accuracy**, **recall**, and **F1-score**, confusion matrices were generated to visualize the model's performance for each class, illustrating true positives, false positives, true negatives, and false negatives. During training, epoch plots were generated, showing the reduction in the loss function and the increase in accuracy over time, allowing for an assessment of model convergence and the detection of potential overfitting.

The ***CNN*** model for the ***Picual*** variety demonstrated robust performance:

- **Loss:** 0.4201
- **Accuracy:** 0.8804

Table IV presents the classification report for the ***Picual*** variety. The precision of the model shows that, when it predicts an olive tree as ***Picual***, it is correct 84% of the time, while predictions of Non-Picual olive trees are correct 94% of the time. The recall metric reveals that the model accurately identifies 96% of all actual Picual olive trees and 79% of the Non-Picual ones.

The F1-Score, which provides a balance between precision and recall, is 0.90 for the ***Picual*** class and 0.86 for the Non-Picual class. Overall, the model achieved an accuracy of 88% in classifying the 92 test olive trees. The macro average of the metrics (precision, recall, and F1-score) represents an unweighted average across all classes, while the weighted average accounts for the number of samples per class, ensuring a more representative performance evaluation.

TABLE IV
CLASSIFICATION REPORT FOR PICUAL VARIETY.

Class	Precision	Recall	F1-Score
Picual	0.84	0.96	0.90
No Picual	0.94	0.79	0.86
Accuracy		0.88	
Macro Avg	0.89	0.87	0.88
Weighted Avg	0.89	0.88	0.88

The results of this can also be seen in the graph in Figure 3.

The epoch chart in Figure 4 visualizes how the ***CNN*** model improves its performance during training for the classification of the ***Picual*** variety. In this graph, the horizontal axis represents the training epochs, while the vertical axis shows the loss and accuracy. The confusion matrix for the ***Picual*** variety shown in Figure 5 presents the performance of the ***CNN*** model in distinguishing between ***Picual*** and Non-Picual (NON-PI) olive trees.

The generalisability of the model was assessed using a new set of 70 trees, equally divided between ***Picual*** and Non-Picual varieties. The results are shown in Table V and demonstrate the model's ability to maintain a high level of accuracy on unseen data.

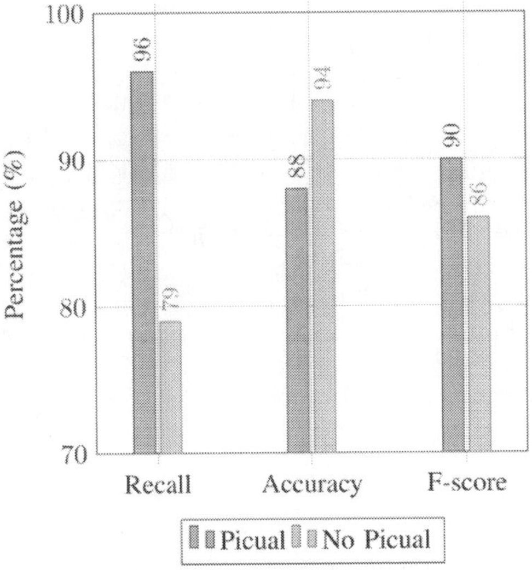

Figure 3. Comparison of Recall, Accuracy, and F-score between Picual and Non-Picual.

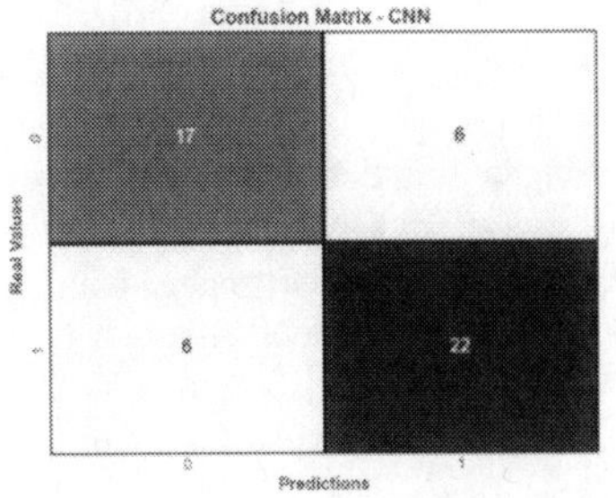

Figure 5. Confusion Matrix CNN.

TABLE V
CLASSIFICATION REPORT FOR NEW PICUAL DATA.

Class	**Precision**	**Recall**	**F1-Score**
Picual	0.78	0.91	0.84
No Picual	0.90	0.74	0.81
Accuracy	0.83 (70 instances)		
Macro Avg	0.84	0.83	0.83
Weighted Avg	0.84	0.83	0.83

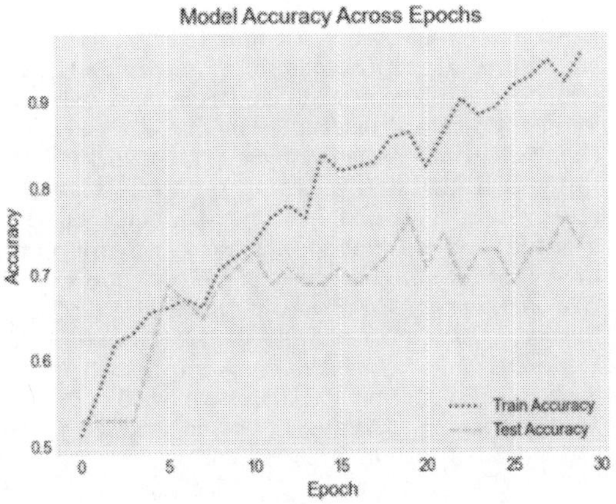

Figure 4. Model Accuracy Across Epochs.

IV. DISCUSSION AND EVALUATION

After presenting the results obtained from the neural network for the datasets, this section provides an interpretation of those outcomes. The overall performance of the ***CNN*** model applied to the ***Picual*** variety yields promising results in terms of classification, as detailed in Table IV. The model's loss value of 0.4201 is relatively low, indicating that the network makes few errors on average when classifying the ***Picual*** variety. Although this loss value is slightly higher than might be ideal, it still reflects the model's effective learning.

In terms of accuracy, the model achieves 88.04%, meaning it correctly classifies ***Picual*** trees in the majority of cases. This level of accuracy is a solid indication of the model's capability, correctly identifying ***Picual*** trees 88% of the time. Regarding recall for ***Picual*** (see Table IV), the model demonstrates an impressive 96%, meaning it successfully identifies 96% of all ***Picual*** trees in the dataset. This high recall indicates the model's strong sensitivity to the ***Picual*** variety, minimizing the number of ***Picual*** trees it misses. In contrast, the recall for Non-Picual trees is 79%, suggesting the model correctly identifies 79% of Non-Picual trees. Although lower, this value is still reasonable for distinguishing between these classes.

The F1 score, which balances precision and recall, reaches 0.90 for ***Picual*** and 0.86 for Non-Picual, as shown in Table IV. These high values confirm the model's strong performance across both classes, with slightly better performance for the ***Picual*** class. The epoch chart in Figure 4 illustrates the evolution of the model's performance during training. The gradual decrease in loss and the increase in accuracy with each epoch reflect the model's improvement over time. The curves stabilize towards the end of the training process, suggesting that the model has converged and is ready to generalize to new data.

The confusion matrix (Figure 5) offers further insight into the model's classification performance. Higher values along the diagonal indicate the model's success in correctly classifying most of the samples, while the lower off-diagonal values point to fewer misclassifications, reflecting a high level of classification reliability. To further validate the model, a new dataset of 70 trees, equally split between ***Picual*** and Non-Picual classes, was used. The model (see Table V) achieved an overall accuracy of 83% in this validation set, with a class-specific accuracy of 78% for ***Picual*** and 90% for Non-Picual. These results confirm the model's ability to generalize, although with slightly lower performance compared to the test set. The recall for ***Picual*** in the validation is 91%, while for Non-Picual it is 74%, indicating that the model is more adept at identifying ***Picual*** trees than Non-Picual ones. The F1 scores are 0.84 for ***Picual*** and 0.81 for non-Picual, demonstrating robust performance, particularly for the ***Picual*** variety.

V. Conclusion and Future Work

This study confirms that ***UAV***-based ***HSI***, combined with ***DL***, represents a highly effective solution for automated ***Olive Variety Classification***. The CNN-based approach demonstrated strong performance in classifying the ***Picual*** variety with high accuracy and reliability. Nevertheless, further refinements could improve the model's robustness, including expanding the dataset to incorporate additional olive varieties and exploring how this ***UAV***-based system adapts under various environmental conditions, such as changes in lighting and seasons. Addressing these factors would enhance the scalability and real-world application of this ***Precision Agriculture*** system. Unlike traditional multispectral methods, ***HSI*** enables precise differentiation of cultivars based on subtle spectral reflectance variations, significantly reducing the reliance on labor-intensive manual sampling. These findings reinforce the potential of AI-driven remote sensing for improving efficiency in ***Precision Agriculture***.

The process addressed for the processing of the hyperspectral imagery includes reflectance calibration, geometric correction, and individual tree segmentation, using techniques, such as the Enhanced Vegetation Index (EVI) and the DBSCAN clustering algorithm. In addition, spectral filtering was applied to remove pixels with low reflectance, reducing noise from shaded areas in the canopy and improving the accuracy of the analysis. Then, the use of 1D ***CNN*** proved to be suitable for processing spectral data, with an architecture consisting of convolutional layers, max-pooling, and a fully connected layer, allowing the automatic extraction of relevant features from the data. Optimization of the ***CNN*** hyperparameters was crucial to obtain accurate results, with Bayesian optimization being used for the ***Picual*** variety.

For the ***Picual*** variety, the ***CNN*** model showed solid performance with an accuracy of 88.04% and a loss of 0.4201 in the test set, also with good generalization to unseen data. Further validation on a fresh dataset showed a slightly lower performance with an accuracy of 83%. The findings confirm that deep learning models, particularly ***CNNs***, excel in extracting hierarchical spectral features from hyperspectral data, achieving significantly higher accuracy than traditional machine learning methods. Approaches, such as k-NN, Naïve Bayes, and Decision Trees struggle to handle the high-dimensional nature of hyperspectral imaging, reinforcing the superiority of data-driven feature extraction techniques in agricultural classification tasks.

Overall, the study concludes that the combination of hyperspectral imaging with deep learning is an effective tool for automated olive variety identification, which can improve agricultural practices and increase the competitiveness of olive products.

The experiments were conducted at only a single farm, so the robustness of the method should be checked on other farms as well. This limitation highlights the need to validate the proposed approach across different locations to ensure its general applicability. Also, it is suitable to verify whether the approach can be applied over longer periods and under various environmental conditions. Future research will focus on addressing the challenge of model generalization in diverse environmental conditions and crop varieties, ensuring robust performance in diverse agricultural landscapes. The evaluation of alternative ***CNN*** architectures, including 2D and 3D models tailored to specific data structures, will be explored. Expanding the scope to include a broader spectrum of olive varieties and integrating complementary sensor data, such as LiDAR, will improve classification accuracy and comprehensiveness. The ultimate goal would be to automatically catalog the majority species in a region using a single ***UAV*** flight. These advancements collectively aim to refine ***Precision Agriculture*** practices, promoting sustainable and efficient crop management.

Acknowledgments

This research has been partially funded through the research support provided by the Ministry of Innovation and Science of the Government of Spain through the research project PID2021-126339OB-I00.

References

[1] E. Sena-Moreno, M. Álvarez-Ortí, D. C. Zied, A. Pardo-Giménez, and J. E. Pardo, "Olive oils from Campos de Hellin (Spain) exhibit significant varietal differences in fatty acid composition, sterol fraction, and oxidative stability", *European Journal of Lipid Science and Technology*, vol. 117, pp. 967–975, 2015. DOI: 10.1002/EJLT.201400136.

[2] K. E. Karfi, S. E. Fkihi, L. E. Mansouri, and O. Naggar, "Classification of Hyperspectral Remote Sensing Images for Crop Type Identification: State of the Art", *Proceedings of the 2nd International Conference on Advanced Technologies for Humanity*, 2020. DOI: 10.5220/0010426600110018.

[3] P. Messina, *Side-looking Airborne Radar (SLAR) System Operations*, Publication Title: Paula Messina, 2025.

[4] M. Govender, K. Chetty, V. Naiken, and H. Bulcock, "A comparison of satellite hyperspectral and multispectral remote sensing imagery for improved classification and mapping of vegetation", *Water sa*, vol. 34, no. 2, pp. 147–154, 2008. DOI: 10.4314/wsa.v34i2.183634.

[5] L. Shuai, Z. Li, Z. Chen, D. Luo, and J. Mu, "A research review on deep learning combined with hyperspectral Imaging in multiscale agricultural sensing", *Computers and Electronics in Agriculture*, vol. 217, p. 108 577, Feb. 2024, ISSN: 0168-1699. DOI: 10.1016/j.compag.2023.108577.

[6] P. Marques, L. Pádua, J. J. Sousa, and A. A. Fernandes-Silva, "Advancements in Remote Sensing Imagery Applications for Precision Management in Olive Growing: A Systematic Review", *Remote. Sens.*, vol. 16, p. 1324, 2024. DOI: 10.3390/rs16081324.

[7] R. G. o. A. Andalusian Research Institute, *IFAPA Center "VENTA DEL LLANO" | Institute for Agricultural and Fisheries Research and Training (Instituto de Investigación y Formación Agraria y Pesquera)*, 2025.

[8] Z. Khan *et al.*, "Optimizing precision agriculture: A real-time detection approach for grape vineyard unhealthy leaves using deep learning improved YOLOv7 with feature extraction capabilities", *Computers and Electronics in Agriculture*, vol. 231, p. 109 969, Apr. 2025, ISSN: 0168-1699. DOI: 10.1016/j.compag.2025.109969.

Aerial Hyperspectral Analysis: Distinguishing Olive Varieties for Precision Agriculture

Ruth M. Córdoba Ortega, Alba Gómez Liébana
Researcher at the University of Jaén, Paraje Las Lagunillas Jaén, Spain
e-mail: rcortega@ujaen.es | aglieban@ujaen.es
M.Isabel Ramos
Dept. Cartographic, Geodetic and Photogrammetric Engineering.
University of Jaen
Jaen, Spain
e-mail: miramos@ujaen.es
Lidia M. Ortega, Juan M. Jurado
Researcher at the University of Jaén, Paraje Las Lagunillas Jaén, Spain
e-mail: lidia@ujaen.es | jjurado@ujaen.es

Abstract—**Distinguishing olive varieties is essential for optimizing orchard management and oil quality. Hyper-Spectral Imaging (HSI) captures subtle spectral differences in leaf reflectance, surpassing conventional sensors. This study explores the use of drone-acquired HSI to differentiate Arbequina and Picual olives, two predominant varieties. The high spectral resolution of HSI enables precise varietal mapping, supporting more efficient and sustainable agriculture.**

***Keywords-Hyperspectral*; *olive*; *drone*; *agriculture*.**

I. INTRODUCTION

The identification of olive varieties is essential for optimizing orchard management, irrigation strategies, and oil quality control. Traditionally, this process has relied on expert knowledge, morphological analysis, or genetic testing, which are time-consuming, costly, and impractical for large-scale plantations. A more efficient alternative is Hyper-Spectral Imaging (HSI), which captures the spectral reflectance of plants across a wide range of wavelengths, allowing for precise differentiation between varieties.

HSI has proven to be highly effective in agricultural applications due to its ability to detect subtle biochemical and structural differences in plant tissues. Unlike multispectral imaging, which captures only a limited number of spectral bands, hyperspectral sensors provide continuous spectral information, enabling a more detailed analysis of plant characteristics. In the case of olive cultivation, this technology offers a non-invasive method for distinguishing between varieties based on their unique spectral signatures.

In this study, we investigate the potential of Unmanned Aerial Vehicle (UAV)-mounted hyperspectral sensors to classify olive varieties in a high-throughput manner. We focus on Arbequina and Picual, two of the most widely cultivated varieties in southern Spain, which exhibit distinct agronomic and oil composition traits. By analyzing spectral differences in leaf reflectance, we aim to demonstrate the feasibility of HSI for precise varietal mapping, which can support more efficient and sustainable orchard management practices.

In Section 2, we present related work and describe the methods employed, including a brief review of similar studies and the workflow followed for data processing. Section 3 discusses the results obtained after applying the proposed classification methods for olive variety differentiation. Section 4 provides an evaluation and discussion of the results, while Section 5 concludes the study and outlines potential directions for future research.

II. RELATED WORK | METHODS

HSI has become a key technology in precision agriculture, providing a non-destructive and high-resolution method for crop monitoring and analysis [1]. Unlike multispectral imaging, it captures reflectance across numerous narrow spectral bands, detecting subtle differences often missed by traditional sensors [2]. Applications include soil erosion analysis, plant health assessment, and water stress monitoring [3], as well as inventory management, irrigation control, disease detection, and yield estimation in olive cultivation [4], contributing to sustainable practices by optimizing resources and reducing environmental impact [5].

HSI's detailed chemical and physical information makes it particularly effective for distinguishing crop varieties [6]. It has been used to identify crop types like wheat, maize, and rice [7] [8], and even different varieties within the same crop, such as wheat [9] and rice [10]. In olive cultivation, beyond variety identification, HSI has supported disease detection, maturity assessment, and yield estimation [11] [12].

Given the diversity of olive varieties, HSI-based classification is a growing research field. By capturing differences in pigment concentration, moisture, and cellular structure, hyperspectral sensors can distinguish varieties, although challenges remain due to spectral similarities and external factors. Recent studies have shown the feasibility of variety identification using lightweight models throughout the season [13] [14].

Gomes et al. [15] demonstrated that hyperspectral reflectance effectively differentiates olive varieties, emphasizing its value for sustainable orchard management. Unlike manual spectral acquisition, our approach uses UAV-mounted sensors for automated, large-scale mapping without laboratory sampling.

However, UAV-based HSI faces challenges such as the influence of shadows on vegetation indices [16] and the need for improved hyperspectral mosaicking methods [17]. Addressing these issues is crucial to fully exploit HSI for olive variety identification and precision agriculture.

Figure 1 shows the general workflow followed by the methodology.

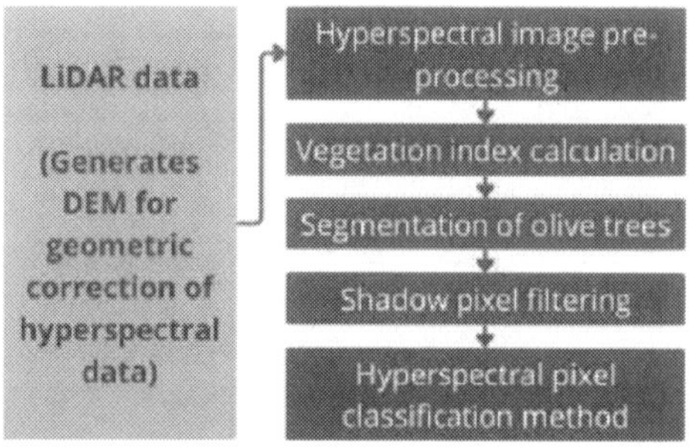

Figure 1. Methodology workflow.

The study was conducted in Mengíbar, Jaén, at the IFAPA Venta del Llano Center, a research facility focused on agricultural development, particularly olive cultivation. Its location is shown in Figure 2. The experimental plot consists of 14 rows of olive trees, each with approximately 24 trees, organized into blocks of four trees per variety. Among these, 21 different olive varieties are tested, including 'Arbequina' and 'Picual' as reference cultivars. The randomized distribution ensures representative data collection, aiding research on adaptability, productivity, and phenotypic characteristics.

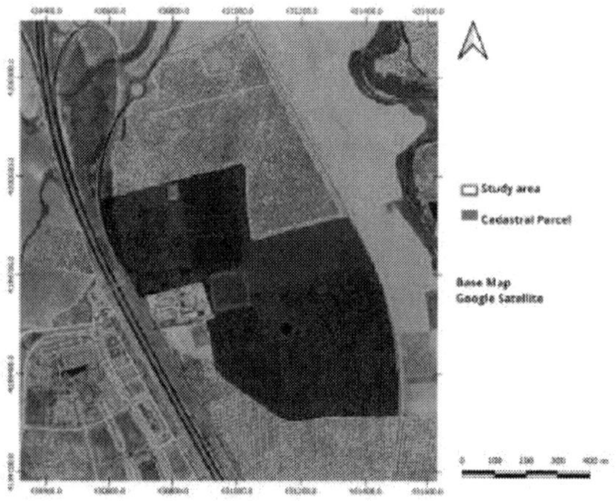

Figure 2. Geogrphic location for the study area.

A UAV equipped with a NanoHyperspec camera (Headwall) and a Light Detection And Ranging (LiDAR) sensor captured hyperspectral data across 270 spectral bands (400–1000 nm) at a 2 cm Ground Sample Distance (GSD). The flight was conducted at 30 meters AGL with a speed of 5 m/s, ensuring high data quality. Overlapping flight paths (1% longitudinal, 40% lateral) minimized gaps, while terrain adjustments maintained accuracy. Headwall SpectralView™ software processed the hyperspectral data, applying radiometric and geometric corrections using a Digital Elevation Model (DEM) derived from LiDAR data. The reflectance calibration was based on dark and white reference measurements. Figure 3 shows the processes required to properly correct the data taken with the hyperspectral sensor.

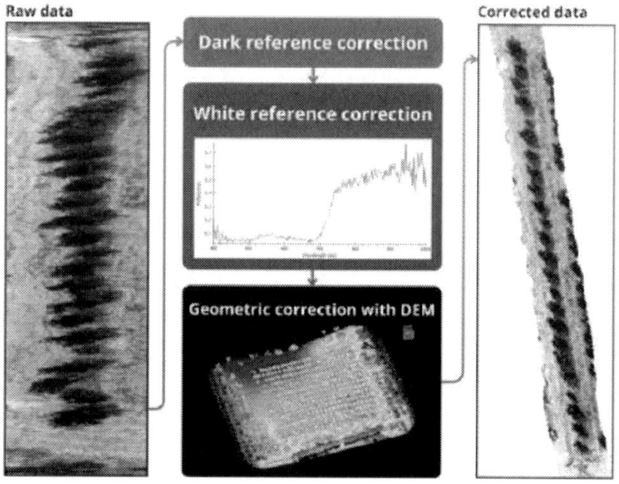

Figure 3. Spectral and geometric corrections applied to the hiperspectral data.

Once the hyperspectral data is properly adjusted, it is necessary to differenciate invidual olive trees, applying a tree canopy segmentation. Individual tree segmentation was essential for precise spectral analysis. Using the Enhanced Vegetation Index (EVI), vegetation was isolated, minimizing shadow effects. EVI was selected due to its effectiveness in distinguishing vegetation while minimizing shadow influence. The index's smoothing term (L) reduces soil background effects, which is particularly useful in olive orchards. By utilizing specific spectral bands (*Near-Infrared* (NIR), red, and blue), EVI is particularly well-suited for analyzing hyperspectral image data, where these bands are clearly defined [18].

The equation is as follows:

$$\text{EVI} = G \cdot \frac{\text{NIR} - \text{Red}}{\text{NIR} + C_1 \cdot \text{Red} - C_2 \cdot \text{Blue} + L}, \quad (1)$$

where:

- G: Gain factor, with a default value of 2.5
- C_1 y C_2: Atmospheric correction coefficients, with default values of 6.0 and 7.5, respectively.
- L: Smoothing term, with a default value of 1.0.

Once the pixels of interest are selected, the segmentation is refined by delineating olive trees more precisely using several geospatial processing techniques and clustering methods. The key method for this segmentation is the use of the *Density-Based Spatial Clustering of Applications with Noise* (DBSCAN) algorithm for grouping geometries into individual trees [19]. This process generates a vector mask with unique identifiers and variety classifications. The final segmentation was manually refined in the software *Quantum Geographic Information System* (QGIS) to ensure accuracy [20]. Figure 4 shows the steps taken to properly segment trees canopies.

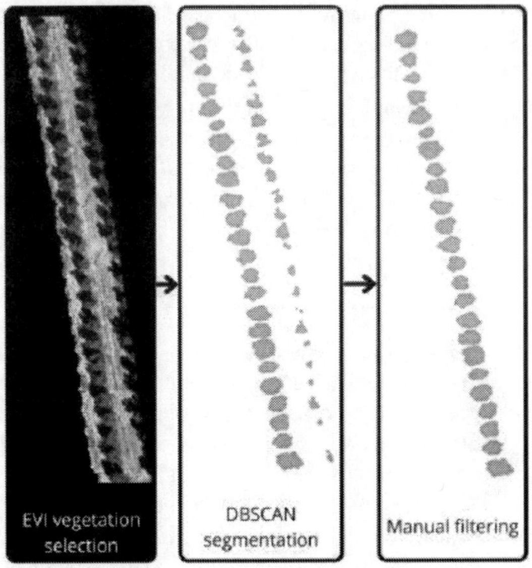

Figure 4. Segmentation process.

Once the olive canopy is identified, selecting relevant hyperspectral pixels is critical for improving classification accuracy. A two-step filtering process is applied: first, low-reflectance pixels, mainly from shadowed areas, are removed based on NIR reflectance thresholds; second, spectral stability is ensured by filtering out pixels with high variability across bands.

In the first step, pixels are assessed by their NIR reflectance, retaining only those exceeding a predefined threshold to exclude shadow-affected areas. The second step refines pixel selection by evaluating spectral variability. Two statistical parameters are computed for each band:

- **Spectral Relevance Threshold**: pixels are considered relevant if its reflectance value exceeds a dynamically calculated threshold:

$$\text{threshold}_{\text{mean}}[band] = \mu[band] + 0.5 \cdot \sigma[band]$$

- **Low Dispersion Criterion**: to ensure that selected pixels belong to bands with limited variability, an additional constraint is applied:

$$\sigma[band] < 0.75 \cdot \overline{\sigma}$$

where $\overline{\sigma}$ represents the global mean standard deviation across all bands. This condition excludes spectral bands with excessive variability, which may be less reliable for analysis.

Pixels meeting both criteria are retained, resulting in a binary mask that refines the dataset by eliminating spectral inconsistencies. As shown in Figure 5, these filters are applied to each tree to exclude pixels affected by shadows or extreme spectral responses, ensuring a more accurate and representative analysis.

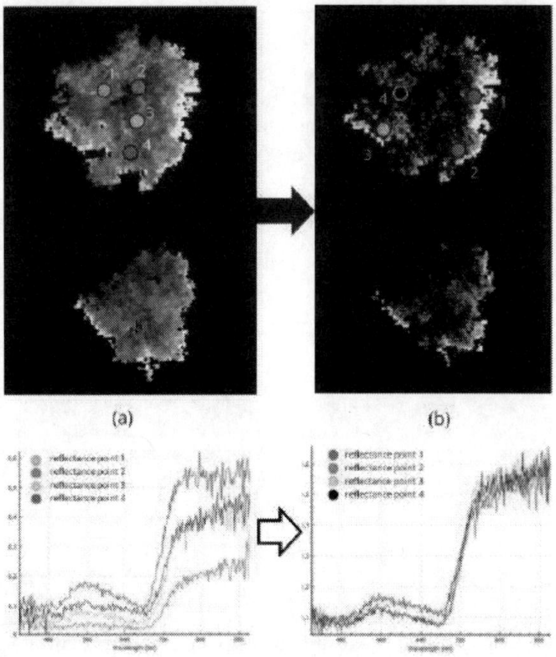

Figure 5. Before and after applying low reflectance filtering in the NIR and standard deviation. (a) Unfiltered view of Olive 401 and the reflectance response of randomly selected pixels. (b) View of Olive 401 after filtering and the reflectance response of randomly selected pixels.

To compare different olive trees and determine whether they exhibit similar spectral behaviour, a classification system based on spectral ranges was developed. This method operates at both the pixel and tree levels, calculating the percentage of pixels within each predefined range for each tree. To optimize computational efficiency, spectral bands were selectively sampled: one out of every ten bands, and one out of every five in the NIR region, where vegetation reflectance is most sensitive to variations. This resulted in a total selection of 27 bands.

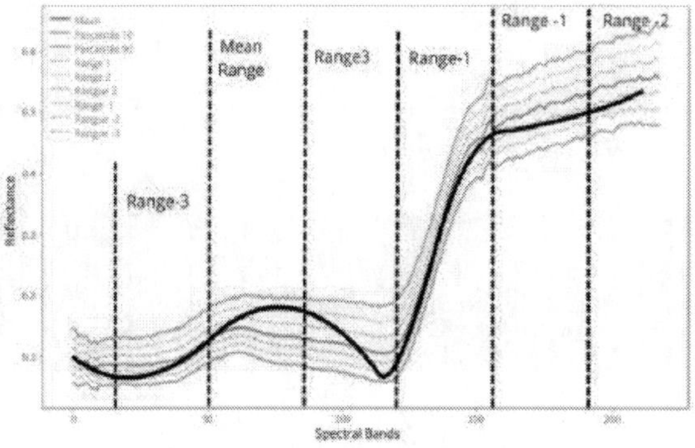

Figure 6. Comparison of any spectral response with the created ranges. Each spectral signature falls within a different range for each of the selected spectral bands.

The classification approach is based on a reference spectral signature constructed from the mean spectral response of all analysed olive trees. From this baseline, upper and lower thresholds are defined using the 90th and 10th percentiles, respectively. This ensures the exclusion of extreme pixel values that might distort classification results. Each pixel's spectral signature is compared against the baseline across the selected bands, classifying it into six ranges. Figure 6 illustrates a sample spectral reflectance response compared to the predefined ranges, indicating the corresponding range for each selected band. This information is then used to classify all pixels within the canopy of each tree.

TABLE I
VALUES BY ID_OLIVE AND THEIR RESPECTIVE RANGES.

ID_OLIVE	Variety	Range	10	20	30	...	217
401	36-41	Max range (Range 3 to 10.0)	19.86	18.29	18.92	...	3.10
401	36-41	Range 3 / Range 2	9.60	7.93	9.56	...	4.44
401	36-41	Range 2 / Range 1	13.31	10.50	10.14	...	8.91
401	36-41	Range 1 / Mean	16.25	16.19	15.32	...	14.06
401	36-41	Mean / Range -1	15.07	16.11	15.14	...	16.82
401	36-41	Range -1 / Range -2	12.12	13.34	14.71	...	17.41
401	36-41	Range -2 / Range -3	7.65	10.36	10.17	...	15.01
401	36-41	Min range (0.0 to Range -3)	6.13	7.29	6.04	...	20.27

The classification results are organized in a matrix where the x-axis represents the 27 spectral bands and the y-axis the defined ranges. Each cell shows the percentage of pixels falling within each range for a given band. For example, if all pixels of a band fall into range 2, it will account for 100% of the pixels, with the rest at 0%.

This classification enables the analysis of the pixel distribution across ranges for each tree, allowing comparative assessments of spectral behaviour between different olive trees and varieties. Results are systematically stored and analysed, providing a quantitative basis for evaluating varietal differences. As shown in Table I, the percentage distribution across ranges is displayed for each selected band, ensuring that the total per band sums to 100.

III. RESULTS

Following the implementation of the classification method for the hyperspectral image, numerical results were obtained, providing insights into the distribution of pixels within each olive tree across different predefined spectral ranges. By analyzing these proportions, comparisons were made between olive trees of similar and different varieties to identify potential differences in their spectral behaviour.

Given the complexity of interpreting numerical differences directly, graphical representations were employed. As shown in Figure 7, pixel proportions per spectral band were visualized for each created range, using olive tree 401 as an example. The graph is divided into six sections, each corresponding to a different range, illustrating the distribution of pixel proportions across spectral bands. A clear trend is observed, where most pixels are concentrated in intermediate ranges.

This graphical representation was extended to all 24 olive trees in the study row, with every four trees belonging to the same variety. The objective was to determine whether trees of the same variety exhibited similar trends in their spectral distributions. Figure 8 displays all graphical representations, where each set of four graphs corresponds to a specific variety.

Upon analysing the spectral distributions of the 24 olive trees, clear patterns emerged within each variety. Notably, Arbequina and Picual varieties exhibited consistent spectral trends, with similar curve shapes and peak amplitudes among trees of the same variety. These findings suggest that spectral characteristics, influenced by the biophysical and biochemical properties of the trees, are closely related to variety, reinforcing the idea that genetic and physiological factors impact spectral behaviour.

According to IFAPA farm organizers, the studied varieties originate from the same maternal lineage, implying genetic similarity. However, differences were observed between two groups of Picual trees, indicating variability despite belonging to the same variety. This discrepancy may be attributed to the fact that these groups do not share the same mother plant, potentially resulting in distinct genomes that explain the spectral differences. Consequently, trees within each subgroup

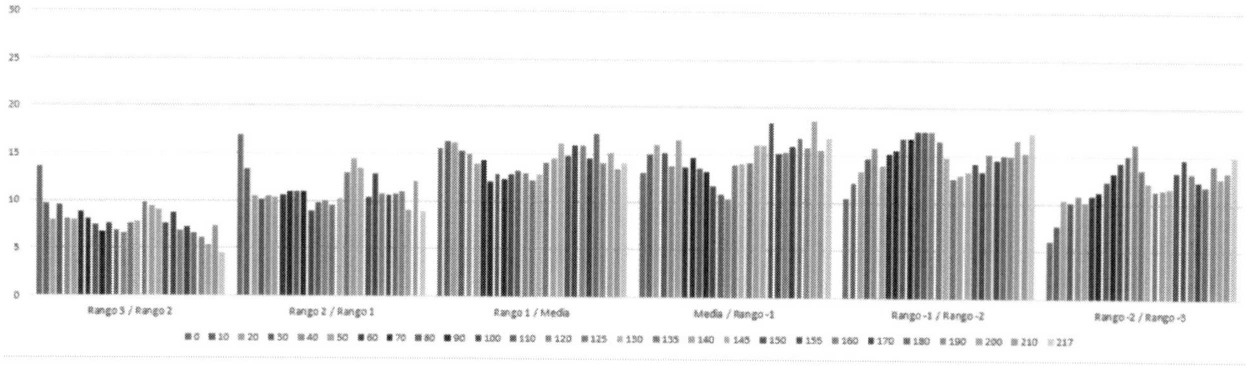

Figure 7. Graphical representation of the proportion of pixels in each range for a random olive tree.

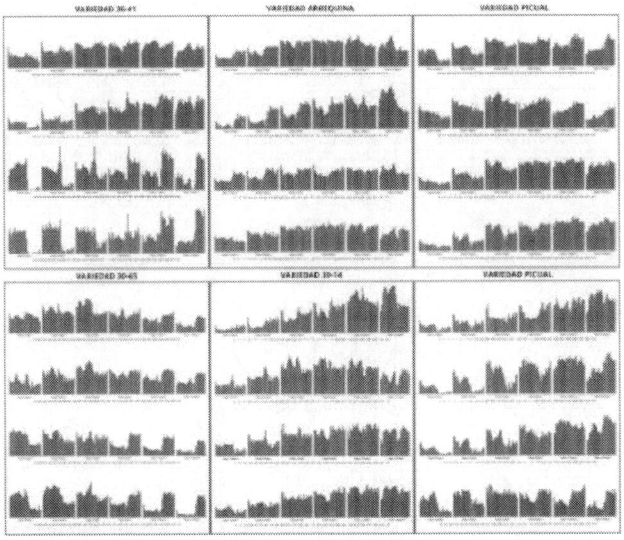

Figure 8. Representation of proportion graphs for each olive tree (24 in total).

are expected to be more similar to each other than to those in the other subgroup.

Additionally, minor variations were noted within each variety, likely influenced by external factors such as lighting conditions or localized environmental differences. These variations were more pronounced in the 36-41 variety, where certain spectral peaks displayed greater fluctuation. Despite these variations, the overall pattern remained consistent, reinforcing the potential of HSI as a reliable tool for olive variety differentiation, as is shown in Figure 8.

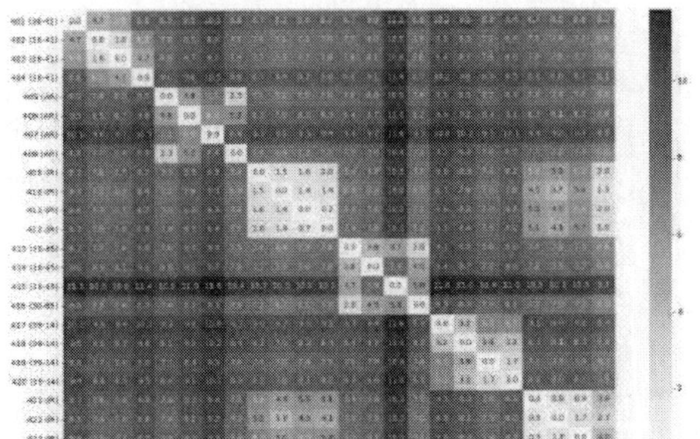

Figure 9. Heatmap of Euclidean distances between olive trees based on extracted features (mean, standard deviation, maximum, minimum, skewness, and kurtosis). Lighter colors (yellow) indicate smaller distances (higher similarity), and darker colors (red) indicate larger distances (lower similarity). Olive trees are labeled with their ID and variety (e.g., "401 (36-41)").

To further explore the similarities and differences among olive trees, a heatmap of pairwise Euclidean distances in a normalized feature space was generated, as is shown in Figure 9. Features including the mean, standard deviation, maximum, minimum, skewness, and kurtosis were extracted from the spectral data for each olive tree and standardized. The olive trees are compared to each other, generating this heat map, which visualizes these distances, with lighter colors (yellow) indicating higher similarity and darker colors (red) indicating greater dissimilarity. For instance, olive trees of the same variety, such as 403 and 404 (both "36-41"), show small distances, while trees from different varieties, such as 403 ("36-41") and 405 ("AR"), exhibit larger distances. A Random Forest classifier validated these features, achieving an accuracy of 1.0 across 5-fold cross-validation, confirming their effectiveness in distinguishing olive varieties. It is visible as well how the first four olives with variety PI (Picual) shown similarities with the last four olives of the same variety.

This analysis highlights the significance of Hyper-Spectral Imaging in varietal classification, as intra-varietal similarities were found to be substantial despite minor fluctuations. These findings support the use of spectral analysis for the classification and management of olive varieties in agricultural settings.

IV. Discussion | Evaluation

This study demonstrates the effectiveness of UAV-based Hyper-Spectral Imaging (HSI) for differentiating olive varieties based on spectral characteristics. The successful classification of Arbequina and Picual varieties highlights the potential of spectral analysis as a non-invasive tool for varietal identification.

Critical to this success were spectral filtering and advanced segmentation techniques, which minimized noise by removing shadow-affected pixels and applying spectral stability criteria. However, environmental factors such as illumination variability, atmospheric conditions, and leaf age remain challenges that can introduce inconsistencies.

Overall, the evaluation of the results obtained is positive. Not only was the spectral similarity between olive trees of the same variety intuited in the graphs shown in Figure 8, but the comparison of olive trees using the Euclidean distance calculation clearly shows the similarity between these varieties, clearly visualized in the matrix in Figure 9, taking into account the specific failures that are difficult to distinguish due to the environmental factors described above.

It can therefore be confirmed that UAV-based HSI offers valuable advantages for precision agriculture by enabling large-scale varietal monitoring, supporting more efficient orchard management, and promoting sustainable olive production.

V. Conclusion and Future Work

This work establishes UAV-based hyperspectral imaging as a scalable and effective method for olive variety classification, offering a promising alternative to traditional sampling approaches. Despite its success, environmental variability and computational demands must be addressed to fully unlock its potential.

Future research should focus on enhancing model robustness against external factors through advanced machine learning techniques, particularly deep learning models capable of capturing subtle spectral patterns. Improving computational efficiency using dimensionality reduction methods, such as autoencoders or a *Principal Component Analysis* (PCA), will be key to enabling real-time or near-real-time analysis.

Additionally, the fusion of hyperspectral data with other sensing modalities, like LiDAR or thermal imaging, presents a promising path for improving the differentiation of similar cultivars. Advances in these areas will drive the broader adoption of HSI in agriculture, fostering more precise, efficient, and sustainable orchard management.

Acknowledgments

This research has been partially funded through the research support provided by the Ministry of Innovation and Science of the Government of Spain through the research project PID2021-126339OB-I00 and from the European Union's Horizon Europe research and innovation programme under the grant agreements No. 101157502 (Soil Deal for Europe - HORIZON-MISS-2023-SOIL-01).

References

[1] L. Shuai, Z. Li, Z. Chen, D. Luo, and J. Mu, "A research review on deep learning combined with hyperspectral imaging in multiscale agricultural sensing", *Computers and Electronics in Agriculture*, vol. 217, p. 108 577, Feb. 1, 2024, ISSN: 0168-1699. DOI: 10.1016/j.compag.2023.108577.

[2] K. E. Karfi, S. E. Fkihi, L. E. Mansouri, and O. Naggar, "Classification of hyperspectral remote sensing images for crop type identification: State of the art", *Proceedings of the 2nd International Conference on Advanced Technologies for Humanity*, 2020. DOI: 10.5220/0010426600110018.

[3] G. Messina and G. Modica, "Twenty years of remote sensing applications targeting landscape analysis and environmental issues in olive growing: A review", *Remote. Sens.*, vol. 14, p. 5430, 2022. DOI: 10.3390/rs14215430.

[4] P. Marques, L. Pádua, J. J. Sousa, and A. A. Fernandes-Silva, "Advancements in remote sensing imagery applications for precision management in olive growing: A systematic review", *Remote. Sens.*, vol. 16, p. 1324, 2024. DOI: 10.3390/rs16081324.

[5] M. Govender, K. Chetty, V. Naiken, and H. Bulcock, "A comparison of satellite hyperspectral and multispectral remote sensing imagery for improved classification and mapping of vegetation", *Water sa*, vol. 34, no. 2, pp. 147–154, 2008. DOI: 10.4314/wsa.v34i2.183634.

[6] M. R. R. d. Oliveira, S. G. Ribeiro, J.-F. Mas, and A. d. S. Teixeira, "Advances in hyperspectral sensing in agriculture: A review", *revista ciencia agronomica*, 2020. DOI: 10.5935/1806-6690.20200096.

[7] R. N. Sahoo, S. Ray, and K. Manjunath, "Hyperspectral remote sensing of agriculture", *Current science*, pp. 848–859, 2015.

[8] F. Zhang *et al.*, "Hyperspectral imaging combined with CNN for maize variety identification", *Frontiers in Plant Science*, vol. 14, p. 1 254 548, 2023. DOI: 10.3389/fpls.2023.1254548.

[9] A.-K. Mahlein *et al.*, "Development of spectral indices for detecting and identifying plant diseases", *Remote Sensing of Environment*, vol. 128, pp. 21–30, 2013. DOI: 10.1016/j.rse.2012.09.019.

[10] B. Jin *et al.*, "Identification of rice seed varieties based on near-infrared hyperspectral imaging technology combined with deep learning", *ACS omega*, vol. 7, no. 6, pp. 4735–4749, 2022. DOI: 10.1021/acsomega.1c04102.

[11] T. Poblete *et al.*, "Discriminating xylella fastidiosa from verticillium dahliae infections in olive trees using thermal-and hyperspectral-based plant traits", *ISPRS Journal of Photogrammetry and Remote Sensing*, vol. 179, pp. 133–144, 2021. DOI: 10.1016/j.isprsjprs.2021.07.014.

[12] C. Riefolo *et al.*, "Assessment of the hyperspectral data analysis as a tool to diagnose xylella fastidiosa in the asymptomatic leaves of olive plants", *Plants*, vol. 10, no. 4, p. 683, 2021. DOI: 10.3390/plants10040683.

[13] G. Moreda, J. Ortiz-Cañavate, F. J. García-Ramos, and M. Ruiz-Altisent, "Non-destructive technologies for fruit and vegetable size determination–a review", *Journal of Food Engineering*, vol. 92, no. 2, pp. 119–136, 2009. DOI: 10.1016/j.jfoodeng.2008.11.004.

[14] S. Domínguez-Cid *et al.*, "Identification of olives using in-field hyperspectral imaging with lightweight models", *Sensors (Basel, Switzerland)*, vol. 24, 2024. DOI: 10.3390/s24051370.

[15] L. Gomes, T. Nobre, A. M. O. Sousa, F. T. Rei, and N. Guiomar, "Hyperspectral reflectance as a basis to discriminate olive varieties—a tool for sustainable crop management", *Sustainability*, 2020. DOI: 10.3390/su12073059.

[16] L. Zhang, X. Sun, T. Wu, and H. Zhang, "An analysis of shadow effects on spectral vegetation indexes using a ground-based imaging spectrometer", *IEEE Geoscience and Remote Sensing Letters*, vol. 12, no. 11, pp. 2188–2192, Nov. 2015, ISSN: 1558-0571. DOI: 10.1109/LGRS.2015.2450218.

[17] J. M. Jurado, L. Pádua, J. Hruška, F. R. Feito, and J. J. Sousa, "An efficient method for generating UAV-based hyperspectral mosaics using push-broom sensors", *IEEE Journal of Selected Topics in Applied Earth Observations and Remote Sensing*, vol. 14, pp. 6515–6531, 2021, ISSN: 2151-1535. DOI: 10.1109/JSTARS.2021.3088945.

[18] B. D. Wardlow, S. L. Egbert, and J. H. Kastens, "Analysis of time-series MODIS 250 m vegetation index data for crop classification in the US central great plains", *Remote sensing of environment*, vol. 108, no. 3, pp. 290–310, 2007, Publisher: Elsevier.

[19] M. Ester, H. P. Kriegel, J. Sander, and X. Xiaowei, "A density-based algorithm for discovering clusters in large spatial databases with noise", in *Proceedins of the international conference on knowledge discovery and data mining*, AAAI Press, Menlo Park, CA (United States), Dec. 1996.

[20] QGIS Development Team, *QGIS Geographic Information System*. Open Source Geospatial Foundation, 2009.

Extra Virgin Olive Oil Price Prediction from Multi-source Variables and Machine Learning

Juan J. Cubillas
Dept. Information and Communication Technologies applied to Education.
International University of La Rioja
Logroño, Spain
e-mail: {juanjose.cubillas}@unir.net

Ángel Calle
Dept. Computer Science.
University of Jaen
Jaen, Spain
e-mail: {acalle}@ujaen.es

M.Isabel Ramos, Ruth Córdoba
Dept. Cartographic, Geodetic and Photogrammetric Engineering.
University of Jaen
Jaen, Spain
e-mail: {miramos}@ujaen.es

***Abstract*—This research underscores the vital need for accurate Extra Virgin Olive Oil (EVOO) price prediction, especially in Andalusia, Spain, given its significant economic and social impact on inflation, trade, and stability. Anticipating price fluctuations benefits producers, distributors, consumers, and governments for improved planning. The complexity arises from diverse influencing factors like climate, global markets, energy costs, and policies, highlighted by recent price surges due to adverse conditions. The study aims to develop a Machine Learning (ML) approach using historical and current data from official sources, processed with ML algorithms and Oracle Data Mining. The promising results demonstrate the feasibility of enhancing prediction accuracy, potentially stabilizing markets, optimizing distribution, and improving agricultural budgeting. Furthermore, this work contributes to advancing predictive modeling research within the agricultural sector.**

Keywords-EVOO Price; Machine Learning Algorithms; Multi-source Data.

I. INTRODUCTION

The close relationship between the economy and the food industry is evidenced by macroeconomic indicators that directly affect the food supply chain, and vice versa, fluctuations in food prices influence price stability and purchasing power, in turn affecting macroeconomic indicators through inflation. In addition, recent global events such as the pandemic, the war in Ukraine and climate change have generated significant disruptions in global fuel and food prices, underlining the critical importance of food stability for economies and societies [1] and [2]. Predicting food prices is a crucial economic objective, as fluctuations affect inflation, trade and economic stability. Forecasting stabilises markets, enables informed decisions for producers and consumers, and facilitates the formulation of government policies on trade, subsidies and food security. It also helps mitigate food crises and plan distribution in emergencies, allowing consumers to manage their budgets.

Predictive modelling, an application of Machine Learning (ML), is revolutionizing price prediction and economic behaviour. Using algorithms and historical data, these models identify patterns and make predictions without explicit programming, applying to a wide range of commodity prices [3], [4]. Generally, the price of food is directly related to crop production and the behavior of markets. Specifically, these factors are weather and climate behaviors, global trade of commodities, market trends and speculation, energy and phytosanitary prices, government policies, and even natural disasters or international conflicts. The impact of ML techniques for price forecasting in different types of food is widely represented in the literature [5], [6]. The increase in olive oil prices is attributed to a combination of complex factors. Adverse weather conditions and declining crop yields are primary causes. Added to this are high energy costs, market speculation, low stock levels and disruptions caused by the Russian-Ukrainian war.

In addition, there is a change in consumer behaviour, with consumers showing an increasing preference for healthier fats, strengthening the demand for Extra Virgin Olive Oil (EVOO), which is recognised for its beneficial properties. This trend suggests that consumers are willing to pay a premium price for a high quality product with functional benefits [7]. Olive oil price prediction has already been studied in the literature using soft computing techniques [8]. However, ML and deep learning techniques are currently the most widely used. Most of these methodologies use regression, the supervised learning technique used to understand the relationship between one dependent variable (olive oil price) and one or more independent variables (historical price series, weather, fuel prices, etc.).

This study proposes a ML approach to predict the price of EVOO, incorporating key variables identified in the literature. Time series of olive oil prices from Spanish and international markets are used, together with prices of other vegetable fats. Energy prices, especially fuels, and critical climatic factors such as drought are also included. The resulting dataset is processed with Oracle Data Mining, where various ML algorithms are evaluated. The objective is to approximate the function that relates the input variables to the price of EVOO. The study addresses the prediction of the price of EVOO in Jaén, highlighting in Section I its economic importance and complexity due to multiple factors, and proposing a ML approach. Section II, Methodology, describes the acquisition of historical data (2009-2023) of economic, climatic and production variables, and the application of several ML algorithms. The Results, Section III, show non-linear relationships and that Gradient Boosting and Random Forest are more accurate in cross-validation. The Conclusions, Section IV, confirm the success of the ML model and the effectiveness of non-linear models in capturing market complexity.

II. Methodology

A. Data acquisition

This initial phase focuses on obtaining quality data from official web sources. The relevant variables for the model, related to the factors that influence the price of EVOO, are precisely defined. In this case, extensive historical information is sought from 2009 to 2023. The variables considered include economic and agronomic factors:

- *Base price.* The base price of EVOO is obtained from the European Union's olive oil price website, specifically from the API which provides weekly data in JSON format by province, taking Jaén as a reference.This price represents the value of EVOO in the month prior to the calculation of the forecast [9].
- *Month.*Seasonality influences demand and supply. The values of all variables in each of the twelve months are considered.
- *Diesel prise.* The price of diesel and EVOO are interconnected by global economic factors and by the dependence on diesel in agricultural machinery for olive oil production, which implies that an increase in the price of diesel can increase the production costs of EVOO. Data on the average monthly price of diesel in the province of Jaén, obtained from the Spanish Ministry for Ecological Transition and the Demographic Challenge [10].
- *Accumulated rainfall.* The accumulated rainfall during the last 24 months is considered crucial for predicting the price of EVOO, as it directly influences the production, quality and costs of the oil, due to the biannual cycle of the olive tree. Data from the Andalusian Agroclimatic Information Network (RIA), which has more than twenty stations in Jaén [11].
- *Average level of reservoirs.* The level of reservoirs has a significant influence on the price of EVOO, as the availability of irrigation water directly affects the quantity and quality of olives. Historical data on Spanish reservoirs, available through the Ministry for Ecological Transition and the Demographic Challenge, allow this relationship to be analysed [12].
- *Consumer Price Index (CPI).* The Consumer Price Index, CPI, which reflects inflation and directly affects the price of EVOO, as increases in the CPI generate inflationary pressure in agriculture and alter consumer purchasing power, influencing demand. The CPI data, obtained from the National Statistics Institute (INE), allow this economic relationship to be analysed [13].
- *World olive oil production.* The price of EVOO in Spain is closely linked to world prices due to the globalisation of the market and Spain's dominant role as a producer and exporter. Fluctuations in global production, influenced by producing countries, are reflected in Spanish prices, as Spain competes in both local and export markets. World production data are obtained from the International Olive Oil Council (IOC).[14].
- *World production of other types of oil.* Data on the world production of other vegetable oils, obtained from FAOSTAT [15], are essential to understand the price dynamics of EVOO, as these oils are substitutes in the global market. Fluctuations in their prices directly impact the demand and competitiveness of EVOO, especially in key export markets. The price of sunflower oil, within vegetable oils, is crucial due to its strong substitution effect on EVOO, as consumers may opt for one or the other depending on its relative price. Moreover, the interconnectedness of the oil market implies that fluctuations in the price of sunflower oil affect the overall supply and demand dynamics, indirectly influencing EVOO.
- *Early prediction value of olive crop yield.* The olive crop yield is a crucial factor determining the supply of raw material for EVOO. High yields can lower prices due to abundance, while low yields raise prices due to scarcity. It also influences production costs and market strategies, with predictions based on climatic variables and satellite vegetation indices [16].
- *Early prediction value of olive oil production.* This variable provides an early estimate of the quantity of olive oil that will be available on the market, thus capturing the direct relationship between supply and price. This input value is obtained following the workflow described in the article Ramos et al. [16].
- *Price of fertilisers.* The price of fertilisers is a key variable in the prediction of EVOO prices due to its direct impact on production costs and crop yields. Fertiliser prices, obtained from the Ministry of Agriculture, Fisheries and Food (MAPA) and its Price and Market Information Service (SIPMA), influence the health and productivity of olive trees, as well as global economic trends affecting the olive oil sector.

Figure 1 shows the level of influence of the variables considered in the prediction of the EVOO price using a linear regression model. The most relevant variables include the base (historical) EVOO price, the olive crop yield prediction and

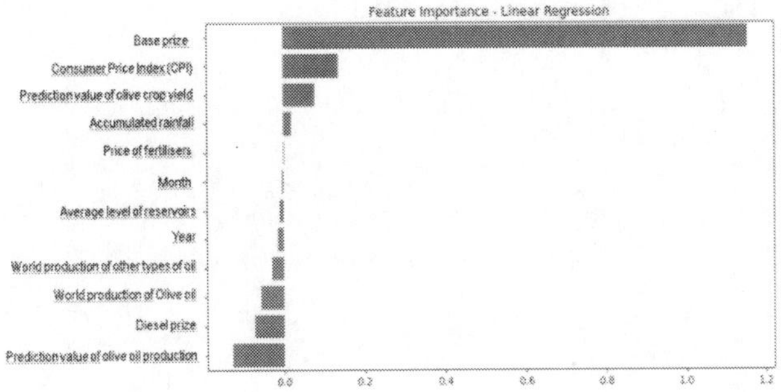

Figure 1. Feature Importance of variables in predicting EVOO price using Linear Regression.

the Consumer Price Index (CPI), which reflect the importance of price history, raw material supply and inflation. Overall, the figure highlights that the model considers both local factors (climate, costs) and global factors (world production, inflation), providing a comprehensive view of the dynamics affecting the price of EVOO.

B. Maching Learning algorithms

Data preparation for ML algorithms is essential to ensure compatibility, capture complex relationships and improve accuracy. This process includes transforming data into numerical, categorical or binary formats, handling outliers and missing values, and applying techniques such as temporal aggregation, spatial selection and seasonal categorisation.

Both linear and non-linear models have been selected in order to consider different types of relationships between attributes and target. As confirmed in the previous section, the variables considered have different influences on the target and even their seasonality is key in the predictive model. In this study, algorithms analysed are: Linear regression, Support Vector Machines, Neural Networks, Random Forest, Gradient Boosting and K-Nearest Neighbors.

III. RESULTS

The attributes considered in this study have different weights on the target attribute and the relationship between them does not follow a linear pattern. The level of accuracy of each of the algorithms used in this study can be analysed from the scatter plot, Figure 2. The figure displays six scatter plots, each evaluating a regression model by comparing actual (x-axis) and predicted (y-axis) values. A dashed red line $y=x$ represents perfect prediction. Closer points to this line indicate higher model accuracy, while deviations signify errors. The vertical distance from the line shows the absolute error. The dispersion of points reveals the model's fit (related to R^2, Systematic over or underestimation is visible by points clustering above or below the line. The models' handling of extreme values, like the point near 8, indicates their generalizability. These plots offer a robust visual method for model comparison, outlier identification, and prediction fidelity assessment.

The quality of each model is evaluated using the cross-validation method. This consists of generating a predictive model using data from all months of each year except the month to be tested. Then, the data for that excluded month (the last month of the set of all months of all years) is used to assess the accuracy of the model by comparing the prediction obtained with the actual price data for that month. This procedure is repeated for each month of the historical data set, excluding it from the training set and using it for validation. In this way, the model is tested against the actual value of several months independently. Finally, once the models have been evaluated, a final model is generated using all months of all years as training data. The accuracy of the algorithms varies significantly when predicting the price of EVOO. Linear Regression and Support Vector Machine (SVM) show lower accuracy due to their difficulty in modelling non-linear relationships. Random Forest, Gradient Boosting and K-Nearest Neighbors offer higher accuracy, with Gradient Boosting standing out for its accuracy. Gradient Boosting, when combining weak models and correcting errors, shows the best performance. The Neural Network is also accurate, but inferior to the ensemble models. If we analyse Figure 2 in detail, clearly the value of 8 reached in one of the months could be interpreted as an outlier. However, although it is an outlier, it is a real value which cannot be eliminated. As the volume of training data increases, the model will adjust to these oil price fluctuations.

IV. CONCLUSIONS AND FUTURE WORK

This study developed a ML model to predict the price of EVOO in Jaén, using a wide range of economic, climatic and cost variables. The Gradient Boosting and Random Forest models proved to be the most effective in capturing the complex and non-linear relationships in the market, suggesting that the EVOO market is influenced by multiple interconnected factors. The high accuracy of the models indicates that the input variables adequately reflect the market dynamics in Jaén and that the data sources and data processing were suitable for building predictive models.

REFERENCES

[1] T. Ulussever, H. M. Ertugrul, S. Kılıç Depren, M. T. Kartal, and O. Depren, "Estimation of Impacts of Global Factors on

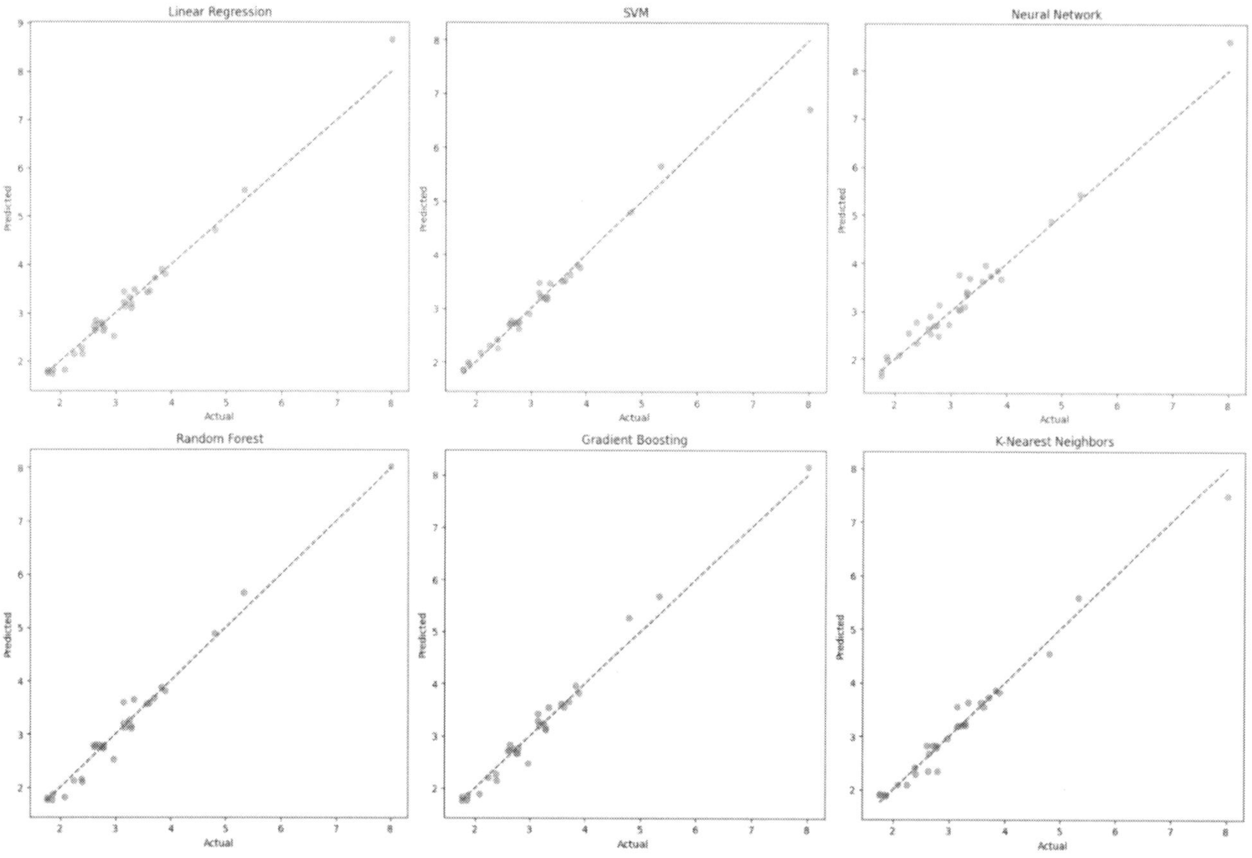

Figure 2. Scatterplots of Actual vs. Predicted Values per each algorithm.

World Food Prices: A Comparison of Machine Learning Algorithms and Time Series Econometric Models," *Foods*, vol. 12, no. 4, 2023, DOI: 10.3390/foods12040873.

[2] E. Breslin, A. Freedman, C. Huston, G. Marrero-Garcia, and T. Mossburg, "Ukraine Food Crisis: Understanding the Impacts of War on the Global Supply Chain and Applying to Future Events," in *2023 Systems and Information Engineering Design Symposium, SIEDS 2023*, Type: Conference paper, 2023, pp. 149–153. DOI: 10.1109/SIEDS58326.2023.10137902.

[3] X. Xu and Y. Zhang, "Price forecasts of ten steel products using Gaussian process regressions," *Engineering Applications of Artificial Intelligence*, vol. 126, p. 106 870, 2023, ISSN: 0952-1976. DOI: https://doi.org/10.1016/j.engappai.2023.106870.

[4] D. Ubilava, "A comparison of multistep commodity price forecasts using direct and iterated smooth transition autoregressive methods," *Agricultural Economics*, vol. 53, no. 5, pp. 687–701, Sep. 2022. DOI: 10.1111/agec.12707.

[5] P. Sharma, P. Dadheech, N. Aneja, and S. Aneja, "Predicting Agriculture Yields Based on Machine Learning Using Regression and Deep Learning," *IEEE Access*, vol. 11, pp. 111 255–111 264, 2023, DOI: 10.1109/ACCESS.2023.3321861.

[6] G. Murugesan and B. Radha, "An extrapolative model for price prediction of crops using hybrid ensemble learning techniques," *International Journal of Advanced Technology and Engineering Exploration*, vol. 10, no. 98, pp. 1–20, 2023, DOI: 10.19101/IJATEE.2021.876382.

[7] R. Zanchini *et al.*, "Eliciting consumers' health consciousness and price-related determinants for polyphenol-enriched olive oil.," *NJAS: Impact in Agricultural and Life Sciences*, vol. 94, no. 1, pp. 47–79, 2022, ISSN: 2768-5241.

[8] A. J. Rivera *et al.*, "A study on the medium-term forecasting using exogenous variable selection of the extra-virgin olive oil with soft computing methods," *Applied Intelligence*, vol. 34, no. 3, pp. 331–346, 2011, DOI: 10. 1007/s10489-011-0284-1.

[9] European Comission, *Olive oil prices*, https://agriculture.ec.europa.eu/data-and-analysis/markets/price-data/price-monitoring-sector/olive-oil_en. Accessed Feb. 2025.

[10] Ministry for the ecological transition and the memographic challenge https://www.miteco.gob.es/es/energia/servicios/consultas-de-carburantes.html. Accessed. Feb. 2025.

[11] *Department of Agriculture and Fisheries. Government of Spain*, https://www.mapa.gob.es/es/. Accessed Feb. 2025.

[12] Hydrographic Confederation. Spain https://www.chguadalquivir.es/inicio. Accessed Feb. 2025.

[13] Statistical National Institute. *Spain*, https://www.ine.es/ Accessed Feb. 2025.

[14] International Olive Council, *IOC-Olive Oil dashboard*, https://www.internationaloliveoil.org/. Accessed Feb. 2025.

[15] FAO. United Nations, *FAO*, https://www.fao.org/home/es. Accessed Feb. 2025.

[16] M. I. Ramos, J. J. Cubillas, R. M. Córdoba, and L. M. Ortega, "Improving early prediction of crop yield in Spanish olive groves using satellite imagery and machine learning," en, *PLOS ONE*, vol. 20, no. 1, e0311530, 2025, Publisher: Public Library of Science, ISSN: 1932-6203. DOI: 10.1371/journal.pone.0311530.

Individual Detection of Olive Trees Under Different Olive Planting Distributions

Pablo Latorre, Francisco García, David Jurado, Lidia Ortega, Juan M. Jurado
Department of Computer Engineering, University of Jaén
e-mail: phortela@ujaen.es, fcastill@ujaen.es, drodrigu@ujaen.es, lidia@ujaen.es, jjurado@ujaen.es

Abstract—**This work in progress addresses the challenge of individual detection of olive trees in different planting frames using advanced computer vision techniques and environmental analysis using point clouds. Accurate identification of individual trees is essential for efficient olive orchard management, especially in planting systems that vary in density, geometric layout and spacing between trees, aspects that strongly affect the way the field should be worked afterwards. Through the combination of image processing algorithms and geometric models, this study aims to develop a robust system that automates the identification of each tree, improving the monitoring of the crop and allowing for more accurate decision-making on the future treatment of each segmented entity in terms of health, maintenance, pruning. Preliminary results show the potential of these tools to optimize olive grove management in different planting configurations.**

Keywords-computer vision; plantation distribution; individual segmentation; point clouds.

I. INTRODUCTION

The digitization in agriculture is essential to improve the efficiency and sustainability of modern farming. In this context, image analysis using computer vision techniques and the application of algorithms based on spatial models plays an essential role in crop identification and monitoring, allowing applications such as disease detection, biomass calculation and optimization of agricultural resources once we are able to individualize each element of interest in the plantation.

In Spain, olive groves are one of the most representative crops. According to a 2019 report by the Undersecretariat of Agriculture, Fisheries and Food, the area occupied by olive groves in the Spanish territory amounts to 2,733,620 hectares, which represents 16.1% of the total cultivated area [1]. Moreover, Spain is the largest producer of olive oil in the world. Therefore, the possibility of individualizing the olive tree within a plantation is crucial for delimiting cultivated areas, making production estimates and improving soil and irrigation management.

Segmentation of olive groves from RGB (Red, Green, Blue) images presents several challenges. Factors such as variability in illumination, seasonal changes in vegetation, heterogeneity of terrain and its distribution, and the variability of ways to obtain the data make accurate tree identification difficult. Accurate detection and segmentation of olive trees are essential for monitoring crop health, optimizing resource allocation, and improving precision agriculture. Although traditional computer vision methods, such as segmentation algorithms in OpenCV, have been widely used, their effectiveness is often limited by environmental factors, such as variations in light, changes in foliage over the seasons, and terrain complexity. In contrast, deep learning-based methods, such as U-Net models and YOLO (You Only Look Once) architectures, have the ability to learn more robust features from large volumes of data, thus improving segmentation accuracy under changing conditions.

The purpose of this paper is to show the beginnings in addressing the challenge of individual olive tree identification in different planting distributions, using several advanced computer vision techniques as well as post-processing with spatial algorithms if necessary. Accurate identification of individual trees is crucial for efficient olive grove management, especially in planting systems that vary in density, geometric distribution, and spacing between trees. Through the combination of image processing algorithms and geometric models, this study seeks to develop a robust system that automates tree identification, improving crop monitoring and enabling more accurate decision making on the future treatment of each tree, in terms of health, maintenance, and pruning.

The remainder of the paper is organized as follows: Section II presents a review of existing related work, Section III describes the materials and methods used in the existing development to date, Section IV shows the results obtained, Section V discusses the results obtained, and finally, Section V provides conclusions and directions for future work.

II. RELATED WORK

The segmentation of vegetation in RGB imagery has been widely explored through both traditional computer vision techniques and more recent deep learning approaches [2][3]. Traditional methods have been extensively utilized due to their low computational cost and ease of implementation. However, with the rise of neural network-based models, these have become strong alternatives, offering superior performance under complex conditions [4] [5].

Among traditional approaches that do not require labeled datasets for training, the literature identifies three main strategies. The first strategy is based on color thresholds, where vegetation is segmented using predefined color value ranges, effectively differentiating vegetated areas from background elements. Another widely recognized methodology employs vegetation indices, which leverage combinations of spectral bands to enhance the detection of vegetation, such as the Normalized Difference Vegetation Index (NDVI) and other specialized indices [6]. The third strategy utilizes clustering methodologies, grouping pixels based on similar characteristics—such as color or intensity—to isolate regions corresponding to vegetation [7][8].

The advent of deep Convolutional Neural Networks (CNNs) has brought significant advances in segmentation tasks. These models are capable of learning complex hierarchical features from the images, achieving more robust and precise segmentations, particularly in heterogeneous environments [9].

In recent years, the integration of 3D modeling has further advanced vegetation segmentation, especially when combined with geometric and multisensor data. Unmanned Aerial Vehicle (UAV) platforms have proven highly effective for acquiring high-resolution spatial data, offering precise and real-time geometric information [10].

A particularly relevant development is the projection of RGB aerial imagery onto photogrammetric point clouds, enabling the alignment of 2D segmented regions with their corresponding 3D spatial structures. This projection process enhances the spatial understanding of vegetation and facilitates further geometric processing [11][12][13].

One of the main benefits of incorporating 3D analysis is the ability to filter out ground-level elements by applying relative height thresholds and techniques as voxelization [14] to split up the terrain or some algorithms based on regression [15] or Light Detection and Ranging (LiDAR) [16] techniques. This techniques are critical for isolating tree canopies from low vegetation and terrain noise, particularly in complex agricultural environments [17]. It is especially useful in olive groves, where understory vegetation can interfere with canopy-based measurements.

Additionally, the use of multisensor technologies—such as thermal, multispectral, and hyperspectral cameras—has enhanced the segmentation and mapping process [18][19] by providing a more comprehensive view of crop conditions. These sensors detect variations in reflectance that are not visible in the RGB spectrum, enabling differentiation between vegetation types and even revealing physiological traits that are useful for using traditional unsupervised algorithms for canopy segmentation [20]. The fusion of these multisensor datasets with advanced neural architectures (e.g., attention networks or 3D CNNs) [21] has helped overcome limitations of conventional methods by integrating spatial, spectral, and temporal information into more detailed and accurate segmentation outputs.

III. Materials and Methods

This study presents a comprehensive methodology for the individual identification of olive trees under different plantation distributions, including traditional, intensive, and super-intensive scenarios, the difference between these types of scenarios lies in the proximity of the trees, as well as the fact that in intensive or super-intensive, the trees are planted in well-defined rows. To thoroughly validate the proposed approach under realistic agricultural conditions, various representative scenarios characterized by significant differences in spatial distribution, density, and morphological structure were selected. Figure 1 illustrates visual examples of each plantation type considered in this research.

The input data for the proposed methodology consist primarily of high-resolution (0.25m) RGB imagery captured by Unmanned Aerial Vehicles (UAVs). These UAVs are equipped

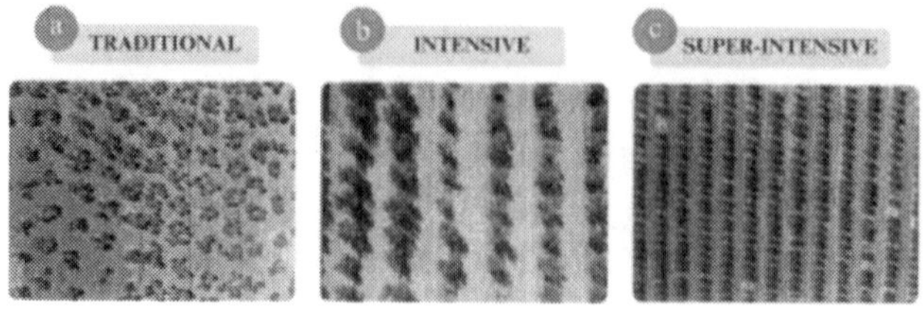

Figure 1. Comparison of olive orchard cultivation systems: (a) Traditional, (b) Intensive, and (c) Super-intensive.

with multiple sensor types, including multispectral, hyperspectral, and LiDAR sensors. The future integration of these multisensor data will enhance the comprehensive representation and characterization of the crops, significantly improving precision and reliability. Data acquisition was conducted through autonomous flight planning, achieving longitudinal and transversal overlaps exceeding 85%. Following data collection, precise three-dimensional models were reconstructed using Structure from Motion (SfM) photogrammetric techniques, resulting in detailed 3D point clouds with high spatial accuracy.

For the individual detection of olive trees within RGB images, a comparative study between previously trained neural networks and classical computer vision techniques was carried out (see Figure 2). It was observed that classical computer vision techniques offer greater efficiency and generalization across diverse plantation types, whereas neural networks required individual training tailored to each specific scenario. Therefore, classical computer vision techniques were ultimately selected for validating our proposal in the context of crop identification tasks.

Once individual trees are identified with the traditional image segmentation process within the RGB imagery, their labels are accurately projected into the three-dimensional point cloud space through a pinhole camera geometric model, represented mathematically by:

$$s\begin{bmatrix}u & v & 1\end{bmatrix} = K[R \quad t]\begin{bmatrix}X & Y & Z & 1\end{bmatrix} \tag{1}$$

where ***u,v*** represent image coordinates, ***X, Y and Z*** denote 3D spatial coordinates, ***K*** is the intrinsic camera calibration matrix, ***R and t*** represents the rotation and translation matrices for extrinsic parameters, and ***s*** is a scaling factor.

Subsequently, a filtering stage was performed to exclude ground points, utilizing relative height analysis by defining a minimum height threshold as follows:

$$P_{filt} = p \in P \mid z(p) > h_{min} \tag{2}$$

where ***P*** represents the original point cloud dataset, and ***z*** indicates the relative height of each point concerning the terrain.

The outcome of this process is a precisely labeled 3D point cloud, clearly depicting the individual geometric structure of each olive tree. Currently, the methodology is being expanded through the development of an advanced clustering stage, applying algorithms such as Density-Based Spatial Clustering of Applications with Noise (DBSCAN) and Mean Shift. These clustering methods aim to achieve fully automated segmentation of each individual tree. The DBSCAN algorithm applied can be expressed in the following general form:

$$DBSCAN(P, \epsilon, MinPts) = C_1, C_2, \ldots, C_n \quad (3)$$

where C denotes the resulting individual clusters, ϵ defines the neighborhood radius threshold, and ***MinPts*** specifies the minimum number of points required to constitute a valid cluster.

Implementing this integrated methodological framework will significantly enhance the robustness, accuracy, and automation capability required for intelligent agricultural management of olive plantations, making it suitable for diverse real-world and commercial scenarios.

IV. Results

This section presents the detailed results obtained from applying various methodologies for identifying vegetation and olive trees across different plantation frameworks, as thoroughly described in Section III. The analysis includes a comprehensive comparative assessment between the segmentation methods employed, carefully examining the strengths and limitations of traditional techniques versus more contemporary neural network-based approaches. This comparison provides a rationale for the selection of traditional methodologies, highlighting their advantages in terms of simplicity, efficiency, and interpretability.

A. Image segmentation

Image segmentation was approached following three main approaches: traditional computer vision techniques and two deep learning models, namely U-Net and YOLOv8-seg. Both models were trained with datasets generated from the available images, representative of different planting configurations.

Since a dataset with validated manual segmentation (ground truth) was not available, the evaluation of the results was carried out by visual validation by experts.

As can be seen in the results shown (see Figure 2), in scenarios with clearly defined and well separated trees, such as in traditional plantations, neural network-based models provide a more accurate segmentation of the crowns. However, when working with denser and more complex configurations, such as in intensive and super-intensive frameworks, these models show difficulties in clearly distinguishing each individual tree. This limitation is mainly due to the fact that the models are at an early stage of training and have been trained with poorly generalizable datasets.

In contrast, the traditional computer vision approach, although less accurate in ideal cases, has shown greater consistency and generalizability in all scenarios, especially the more complex ones. However, its main limitation lies in the fact that it segments all visible vegetation, including grass or other non-relevant elements, without specifically differentiating tree canopies.

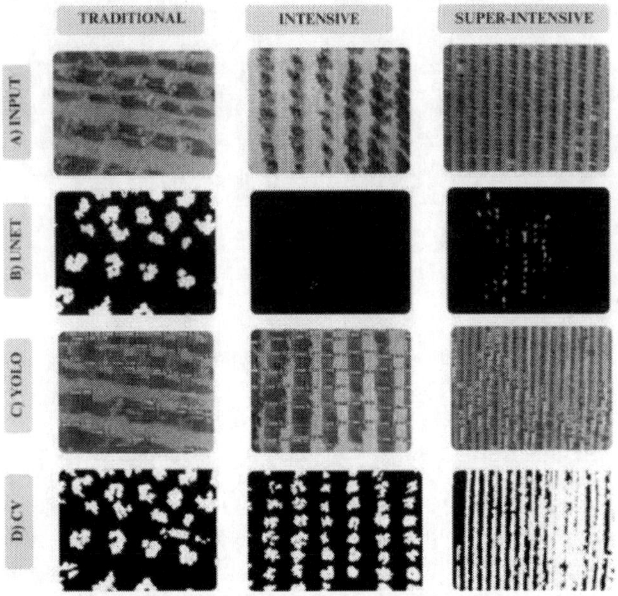

Figure 2. Olive tree segmentation process using the U-Net model(b), YOLOv8-seg architecture (c) and traditional computer visión techniques (d) on Input RGB aerial image (a).

In order to overcome this limitation, a post-processing based on three-dimensional terrain models is proposed, which allows discriminating low vegetation from tree canopy.

B. Geometrical post-processing

Once the most robust segmentation methodology had been selected, the binary masks generated on the RGB images were overlapped to obtain a clearer mask (Figure 3) and to be able to project onto the three-dimensional models of the environment, previously obtained by photogrammetry techniques like Structure from Motion (SfM) or by LiDAR scanning. This projection made it possible to visualize on the 3D model the initial result of the segmentation carried out on the RGB images.

Figure 3. Example of overlay masks with their corresponding RGB image for segmentation with traditional computer vision methods.

At this stage, it was observed that many of the points identified as vegetation actually corresponded to low vegetation

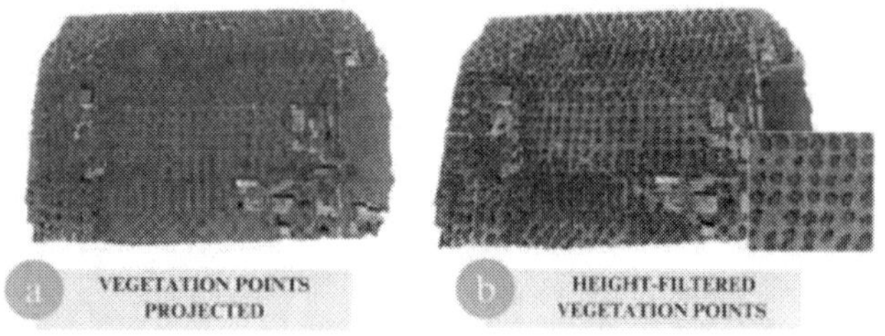

Figure 4. Comparison of point clouds: (a) vegetation points projected and (b) height-filtered vegetation points.

or ground elements, which generated noise in the representation of the tree canopy.

To solve this problem, geometric filtering was applied based on the relative height of the points, eliminating those whose elevation was below a defined minimum threshold with respect to the terrain. The result, shown in the Figure 4, shows a notable improvement in the cleanliness of the three-dimensional model, significantly reducing the number of unwanted points and retaining only those that represent the tops of the olive trees.

V. Conclusion and Future Work

This work presents the initial steps towards a robust methodology for individual olive tree identification across various planting designs. The aim is to spatially locate and monitor each tree entity using RGB drone imagery and 3D data representations.

A traditional image segmentation approach has proven to be effective and fast for isolating vegetation in various scenarios, demonstrating stability across all plantation types. Although preliminary experiments with neural networks such as U-Net and YOLOv8-seg show promising results, especially in simpler scenarios, their generalisability remains limited due to the early stage of training and the specificity of the datasets. Future refinement of these models is expected to improve their performance and potentially position them as the main segmentation tool for this project.

To complement image-based segmentation and to address problems such as interference from low vegetation, a 3D filtering methodology was applied. This process discards vegetation at ground level based on height thresholds, effectively isolating tree structures in the point cloud very quickly and successfully. However, current limitations include reduced robustness in terrain with significant topographic variation.

The current process allows us to segment vegetation with drones and isolate trees in 3D, laying the groundwork for clustering methods to identify individual olive trees. As future work, we plan to improve segmentation accuracy using advanced neural network models and develop a clustering mechanism capable of encapsulating individual trees with bounding boxes. This will allow the extraction of structural features and support precision agricultural applications such as tree health monitoring, pruning planning and yield estimation.

Acknowledgments

This project has been funded under the research projects with references PID2022-137938OA-I00, PID2021-126339OB-I00 and TED2021-132120BI00. These projects are co-financed by the Junta de Andalucía (Andalusian Regional Government), Ministerio de Ciencia e Innovación (Ministry of Science and Innovation) (Spain), and the European Union's ERDF funds.

References

[1] Ministerio de Agricultura, Pesca y Alimentación (Ministry of Agriculture, Fisheries and Food), "Analysis of Olive Plantations in Spain", Encuesta sobre Superficies y Rendimientos de Cultivos (Crop Area and Crop Yield Survey) (ESYRCE), Tech. Rep., 2019, Latest access: 25/02/2025.

[2] A. Abozeid, R. Alanazi, A. Elhadad, A. I. Taloba, and R. M. Abd El-Aziz, "A large-scale dataset and deep learning model for detecting and counting olive trees in satellite imagery", *Computational Intelligence and Neuroscience*, vol. 2022, no. 1, p. 1 549 842, 2022.

[3] C. Vasilakos and V. S. Verykios, "Burned olive trees identification with a deep learning approach in unmanned aerial vehicle images", *Remote Sensing*, vol. 16, no. 23, p. 4531, 2024.

[4] F. Sultana, A. Sufian, and P. Dutta, "Evolution of image segmentation using deep convolutional neural network: A survey", *Knowledge-Based Systems*, vol. 201, p. 106 062, 2020.

[5] N. O'Mahony *et al.*, "Deep learning vs. traditional computer vision", in *Advances in computer vision: proceedings of the 2019 computer vision conference (CVC), volume 1 1*, Springer, 2020, pp. 128–144.

[6] A. Casella *et al.*, "Segmentation of spot images from vegetation indices for the quantification of irrigated onion cultivation in the lower colorado river valley.", in *SELPER 2016: XVII Simposio Internacional en Percepción Remota y Sistemas de Información Geográfica (International Symposium on Remote Sensing and Geographic Information Systems)*, 2016, p. 387.

[7] S. H. Park, I. D. Yun, and S. U. Lee, "Color image segmentation based on 3-d clustering: Morphological approach", *Pattern Recognition*, vol. 31, no. 8, pp. 1061–1076, 1998.

[8] S. Marino and A. Alvino, "Vegetation indices data clustering for dynamic monitoring and classification of wheat yield crop traits", *Remote Sensing*, vol. 13, no. 4, p. 541, 2021.

[9] A. Safonova, E. Guirado, Y. Maglinets, D. Alcaraz-Segura, and S. Tabik, "Olive tree biovolume from uav multi-resolution image segmentation with mask r-cnn", *Sensors*, vol. 21, no. 5, p. 1617, 2021.

[10] Y. Liu *et al.*, "Study on individual tree segmentation of different tree species using different segmentation algorithms based on 3d uav data", *Forests*, vol. 14, no. 7, p. 1327, 2023.

[11] W. Zhang, F. Gao, N. Jiang, C. Zhang, and Y. Zhang, "High-temporal-resolution forest growth monitoring based on segmented 3d canopy surface from uav aerial photogrammetry", *Drones*, vol. 6, no. 7, p. 158, 2022.

[12] B. Chehreh, A. Moutinho, and C. Viegas, "Latest trends on tree classification and segmentation using uav data—a review of agroforestry applications", *Remote sensing*, vol. 15, no. 9, p. 2263, 2023.

[13] K. Zhang *et al.*, "Optimization of ground control point distribution for unmanned aerial vehicle photogrammetry for inaccessible fields", *Sustainability*, vol. 14, no. 15, p. 9505, 2022.

[14] L. Wang, Y. Xu, and Y. Li, "Aerial lidar point cloud voxelization with its 3d ground filtering application", *Photogrammetric engineering & remote sensing*, vol. 83, no. 2, pp. 95–107, 2017.

[15] K. Liu, W. Wang, R. Tharmarasa, J. Wang, and Y. Zuo, "Ground surface filtering of 3d point clouds based on hybrid regression technique", *Ieee Access*, vol. 7, pp. 23 270–23 284, 2019.
[16] G. Bailey *et al.*, "Comparison of ground point filtering algorithms for high-density point clouds collected by terrestrial lidar", *Remote Sensing*, vol. 14, no. 19, p. 4776, 2022.
[17] M. Zeybek and İ. Şanlıoğlu, "Point cloud filtering on uav based point cloud", *Measurement*, vol. 133, pp. 99–111, 2019.
[18] Y. Zhang *et al.*, "Fusion of multispectral aerial imagery and vegetation indices for machine learning-based ground classification", *Remote Sensing*, vol. 13, no. 8, p. 1411, 2021.
[19] F. Furukawa *et al.*, "Comparison of rgb and multispectral unmanned aerial vehicle for monitoring vegetation coverage changes on a landslide area", *Drones*, vol. 5, no. 3, p. 97, 2021.
[20] P. Cinat, S. F. Di Gennaro, A. Berton, and A. Matese, "Comparison of unsupervised algorithms for vineyard canopy segmentation from uav multispectral images", *Remote Sensing*, vol. 11, no. 9, p. 1023, 2019.
[21] I. Ulku, E. Akagündüz, and P. Ghamisi, "Deep semantic segmentation of trees using multispectral images", *IEEE Journal of Selected Topics in Applied Earth Observations and Remote Sensing*, vol. 15, pp. 7589–7604, 2022.

How Did Shared E-scooter Usage Change Before and After the Enforcement of Parking Regulations? Empirical Evidence from Stockholm, Sweden

Pengxiang Zhao [1,2], Aoyong Li [3], Ali Mansourian [1]
[1] GIS Centre, Department of Physical Geography and Ecosystem Science, Lund University, Lund, Sweden
[2] K2 — The Swedish Knowledge Centre for Collective Mobility, Lund, Sweden
[3] State Key Lab of Intelligent Transportation System, School of Transportation Science and Engineering, Beihang University, Beijing, China
e-mail: {pengxiang.zhao | ali.mansourian}@nateko.lu.se, liaoyong@buaa.edu.cn

Abstract—**Shared e-scooters have emerged as a popular mode of micro-mobility in urban areas, while their widespread adoption has also led to regulatory challenges, particularly concerning improper parking. Several governments and local authorities have established parking regulations to tackle the challenges. However, less is known about their effects on shared e-scooter usage patterns. This paper explores how shared e-scooter usage changed before and after the enforcement of parking regulations from statistical, spatial, and temporal perspectives by conducting a case study in Stockholm, Sweden. The results indicate that the parking regulations have a significant influence on shared e-scooter usage in terms of trip frequency, service area, and usage efficiency. This research is beneficial for urban planners and policy-makers to develop evidence-based parking regulations and practices for regulating shared micro-mobility.**

Keywords-Shared e-scooter usage; Micro-mobility; Parking regulations; Spatial and temporal patterns.

I. INTRODUCTION

The proliferation of shared micro-mobility services, especially shared e-scooters, has revolutionized urban transportation systems, and offered a sustainable and flexible alternative to traditional travel modes worldwide [1]. These services have rapidly gained popularity due to their potential to mitigate traffic congestion, reduce carbon emissions, and address the First-Mile-Last-Mile (FMLM) problems in urban areas [2], [3]. However, their rapid adoption has introduced a host of regulatory challenges, particularly related to public safety and parking management [4].

Parking rules and regulations for shared e-scooters are integral to their successful integration into urban transport systems. Poorly implemented or inadequately enforced parking policies often result in cluttered sidewalks, obstruction of pedestrian pathways, and hazards for individuals with disabilities [5]. Such outcomes can undermine the benefits of micro-mobility by creating friction between users, non-users, and city authorities. Conversely, well-designed parking strategies have the potential to improve service usability, reduce urban clutter, and foster a positive public perception of shared e-scooters, encouraging their wider adoption.

To combat the bad reputation of shared e-scooter services, a number of countries and local governments have implemented a range of strategies, including designated parking zones, geofencing, and financial penalties for non-compliance [6]. These regulations vary significantly across regions and cities, reflecting differing urban layouts, population densities, and governance priorities [7]. For instance, it is permitted to park e-scooters on the pavement in France as long as it does not obstruct pedestrians. However, parking on pavements is prohibited in Paris, and 49 Euros could be imposed. To tackle the parking and regulatory challenges, new parking rules regulating scooter traffic have also come into force in Sweden on 1 September 2022. Concretely, parking on pavements or cycle paths is prohibited, and e-scooters may only be parked in specially designated parking spaces.

In this context, it is important and necessary to understand the influence of parking rules on shared e-scooter usage for effective regulatory strategies and transportation management. Scholars have conducted a strand of studies on shared e-scooter usage patterns and influencing factors in different cities [8]–[10]. For instance, a comparison study is implemented to reveal the similarities and differences of shared e-scooter usage patterns in 30 European cities [9]. Despite the growing implementation of parking rules and studies on understanding shared e-scooter usage, limited research has systematically examined the impact of parking rules on shared e-scooter usage. To fill the above-mentioned research gap, this study aims to conduct an empirical study to explore how shared e-scooter usage patterns changed before and after the enforcement of parking regulations from a spatiotemporal perspective, with a case study dataset from Stockholm, Sweden.

The paper is structured as follows. Section II reviews the existing literature on regulations and usage patterns of shared e-scooters. Section III outlines the data and methods used to analyze the influence of parking rules on e-scooter usage patterns. Section IV presents and discusses the main results, highlighting the spatiotemporal variations of shared e-scooter usage patterns in the case study area. Finally, Section V concludes the paper with key findings and future research.

II. RELATED WORK

A. Shared micro-mobility regulations

Shared micro-mobility regulatory challenges and parking regulations have attracted notable attention in recent years. A number of studies have documented a high number of scooter-related injuries and accidents [11], which calls for more attention to the research on regulatory frameworks, policies, and regulations. Shaheen et al. [12] systematically discussed shared micro-mobility policies and practices for managing vehicles and operations, such as service area limitations, designated parking areas, maximum allowable operating speeds. Mehranfar and Jones [5] emphasized the need for comprehensive analysis of e-scooter incident data and targeted interventions to address safety risks (e.g., helmet use, speeding, and infrastructure adaptation), and highlighted the importance of tailored regulatory frameworks, rider education, and device design to enhance stability, reduce injury severity, and improve overall safety. Although these regulations and strategies have been indicated to be effective in mitigating shared micro-mobility regulatory challenges, they also present a significant influence on shared micro-mobility usage. Lo et al. [13] conducted an online survey to explore the relationship between potential scooter-share regulations and ridership in New Zealand, and indicated that the regulations governing user behavior negatively impact shared e-scooter usage. Wincent et al. [14] also developed a survey to examine the effects of parking regulations on shared e-scooter usage in Sweden. It is reported that the usage frequency, walking distance, and travel time for e-scooter trips have been affected in Stockholm and Malmö after the introduction of parking regulations. The usage in Gothenburg was affected to a less extent, which could be due to the delay in the introduction of parking regulations .

B. *Shared e-scooter usage patterns*

The increasing availability of vehicle availability data and empirical trip data from micro-mobility operators has led to a large amount of studies on understanding shared e-scooter usage patterns. For instance, Jiao and Bai [8] examined the spatial and temporal usage patterns of shared e-scooters in Austin by analyzing monthly trip counts, total vehicle miles traveled, average trip distance, and average operation time. McKenzie [15] explored the spatial and temporal differences in usage patterns between six shared micro-mobility services in Washington, D.C. Notable differences in spatial and temporal usage patterns were observed between the micro-mobility services. Heumann et al. [16] analyzed the spatial and temporal usage patterns of shared e-scooters in Berlin, and suggested that the usage patterns are influenced by points of interest characteristics. Foissaud et al. [17] examined the spatial and temporal patterns of e-scooter trips in 4 European cities, including Paris, Malaga, Bordeaux, and Hamburg. The results displayed similar usage patterns across the cities but also local characteristics in each city. In recent studies, scholars further investigated how shared e-scooters are used to improve the FMLM connectivity in public transport. For example, Guo et al. [18] explored the integration between shared e-scooters and public transport and how the integration was influenced by the urban built environment in Stockholm and Helsinki. Aarhaug et al. [19] analyzed the relationships between shared e-scooters and public transport in Oslo, and also demonstrated that shared e-scooters can both complement and compete with public transport. Li et al. [20] investigated how shared e-scooters are used as a feeder to complement public transport for solving the FMLM problem by conducting a comparison study in 124 European cities. The results showed that these cities can be divided into 4 clusters according to the temporal usage patterns.

III. METHODOLOGY

A. *Study area and data*

The data was collected in Stockholm, the largest city and capital of Sweden. The trip records of shared e-scooters were collected from two micro-mobility operators from September 1st to December 31st, in 2021 and 2022. The abnormal trips were filtered out first based on the criteria of duration (more than 1 minute and less than 1.5 hours) and distance (more than 100 m and less than 10 km) according to the previous study [21]. After the data preprocessing, the dataset contains 2,139,381 and 542,337 trips in the periods of 2021 and 2022. Each trip record consists of the fields of vehicle id, longitude, latitude, and timestamp of start and end points. Since the parking regulations came into force in Sweden on September 1, 2022, the dataset was divided into two parts based on the date, namely the Period Before Regulations (PBR) and the Period After Regulations (PAR). A summary of data description is displayed in Table I.

TABLE I
BASIC INFORMATION OF THE E-SCOOTER TRIP DATA DURING PBR AND PAR.

	The number of trips		The number of active vehicles	
Operator	PBR	PAR	PBR	PAR
Operator1	1,705,810	378,077	7,141	2,256
Operator2	433,571	164,260	6,983	1,715

In addition, Sweden's regional division data based on DeSOs (demographic statistical areas) as well as public transport stations in Stockholm were also collected.

B. *Indicators for shared e-scooter usage measurement*

According to the survey results in previous studies [13], [14], parking regulations presented negative effects on shared e-scooter usage. In this study, three indicators are calculated to model the shared e-scooter usage patterns before and after the introduction of parking regulations, including trip frequency, service area, and usage efficiency.

Trip frequency reflects the usage intensity of shared e-scooters, which have been commonly used in shared micro-mobility analysis. To examine the temporal variations of trip distribution before and after the enforcement of parking regulations, a trip frequency signature for each period is constructed to capture the temporal fluctuations of e-scooter trip frequency. Considering that the date ranges of the two periods are not completely consistent due to data gaps in the collection process, the temporal signature for each period is calculated by aggregating and averaging the trips based on the day of a week and the hour of a day, according to the method by Li et al. [9]. The signature can be denoted as a 1×168 vector that covers the average trip frequency on each hour from Monday to Sunday:

$$S = [F_{1,0}, ..., F_{i,j}, ..., F_{7,23}] \quad (1)$$

where S represents the temporal signature of trip frequency. i is from 1 to 7 to represent the day of a week from Monday to Sunday, j is from 0 to 23 to represent each hour of a day.

Service area describes the areas where shared e-scooters are active, which can be used to explore how parking regulations influence users' parking behavior. Since it is not publicly available from micro-mobility operators, we calculated the service areas before and after the introduction of parking regulations in a data-driven manner. Concretely, the Stockholm city was split into cells with a 0.001 longitude × 0.001 latitude size. The number of origins and destinations of trips is calculated within each cell. Only the cells that contain origins and destinations are used to calculate the service area.

The indicator Time to Booking (TtB) is calculated to measure the usage efficiency of shared e-scooters. Compared to traditional usage indicators such as cycling duration, usage frequency, and turnover rate, TtB provides a more accurate reflection of supply and demand in a specific area, making it a more effective measure of usage efficiency in that region [22]. It can be used to clearly indicate the change in usage efficiency of shared e-scooters after the enforcement of parking regulations in terms of idle time. Longer idle time implies lower usage efficiency.

C. Shared e-scooter usage in combination with public transport

We further investigate how shared e-scooter usage in combination with public transport changed before and after the introduction of parking regulations. In particular, the integration between shared e-scooters and public transport at the trip level is explored according to the spatial relationships between origins and destinations of e-scooter trips and public transport stations [18], [20]. Concretely, an e-scooter trip is classified as complementary if either its origin or destination falls within the catchment area of public transport stations, indicating that the trip involves people traveling to or from these stations (e.g., addressing the first/last mile problem). Conversely, if both the origin and destination are within the catchment areas, the trip is considered competitive, as it suggests that e-scooters are being used within the service range of public transport, potentially competing with it. If neither of the origin and destination is within a catchment area of a public transport station, the trip is classified as the category of 'others'.

IV. Results and Discussion

In the experiment, statistical, temporal, and spatial analyses were implemented to examine the changes in shared e-scooter usage patterns based on the above-mentioned three indicators.

A. Trip frequency

As displayed in Table I, there are 2,139,381 and 542,337 trips during PBR and PAR. It can be observed that the number of trips decreased dramatically, approximately 74.6% of the trips, after the introduction of parking regulations. The significant decrease could also be related to another issued policy, which reports that a maximum of 12,000 e-scooters were legally registered in 2022.

Next, the temporal variations of trip frequency on an hourly basis before and after the parking regulations were explored. As described in the method section, a temporal signature of trip frequency in terms of a 1 × 168 vector was calculated for each period. As shown in Figure 1, the temporal distribution of trip frequency from Monday to Sunday displayed similar patterns between the two periods. First, the usage of e-scooters on weekdays showed three obvious peaks during morning (i.e., 8:00–9:00), noon (12:00-13:00), and evening (i.e., 17:00–18:00), corresponding to the two commuting peaks and lunchtime. The findings are consistent with the e-scooter usage patterns in Zurich [21]. By comparison, the temporal distribution of trip frequency also presented similar patterns on weekends during the two periods, while the peak was shifted to the afternoon on weekends. Although the temporal distribution of trip frequency showed similar patterns, the average hourly trip frequency decreased during PAR.

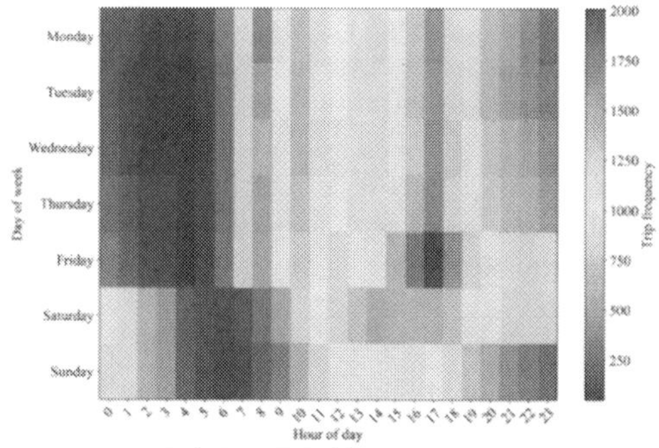

(a) PBR

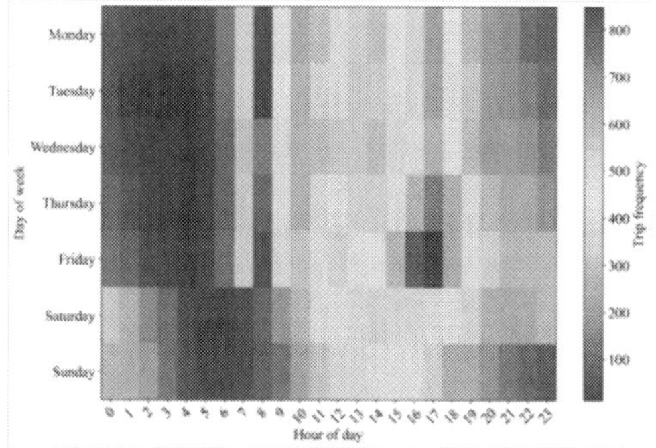

(b) PAR

Figure 1. Temporal distribution of trip frequency on an hourly basis during (a) PBR and (b) PAR.

B. Service area

In this subsection, the service areas during PBR and PAR were calculated, respectively, as shown in Figure 2. It can be observed that the service area during PAR shrank in the peripheral area of Stockholm. In addition, the trip frequencies at the cell level in terms of the number of origins and destinations were visualized during the two periods, which were classified into five classes with the natural breaks (Jenks) method. The red cells represent the areas with high trip frequency, which were mainly concentrated in the central area of Stockholm. We also calculated the global Moran's I based on the spatial distribution of trip frequency, which are 0.57 and 0.38, respectively, during the two periods. The high Moran's I values also indicated the clustering characteristics of trip frequency. By comparing the two periods, it can also be seen that the number of red cells decreased during PAR. These results demonstrated the lower popularity of shared e-scooter usage after the introduction of parking regulations.

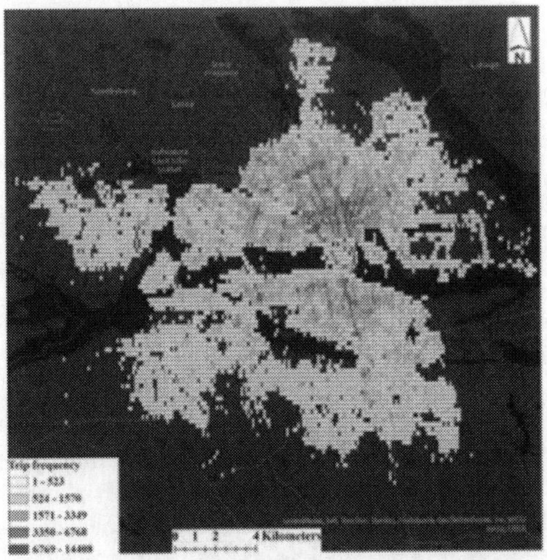

(a) PBR

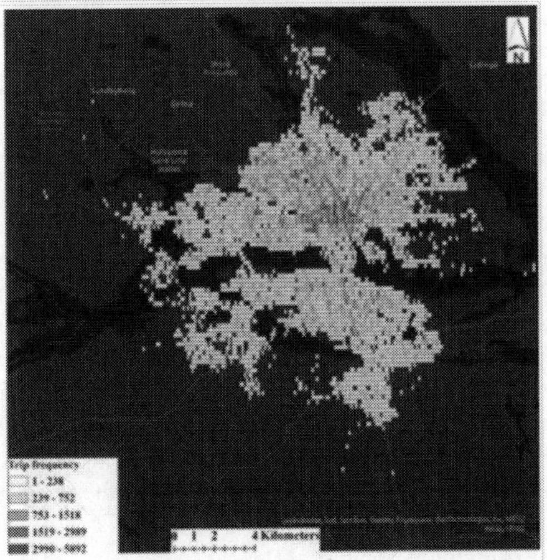

(b) PBR

Figure 2. Service areas and spatial distribution of trip frequency during (a) PBR and (b) PAR.

C. Usage efficiency

In this subsection, the time to booking values at the trip level were calculated based on the trips during the two periods. Figure 3 displays the statistical distribution of time to booking on a monthly basis in terms of a boxplot during PBR and PAR, respectively. The numbers in each boxplot represent the median of Ttb in the specific month during the two periods. It can be seen that the median values of Ttb decreased in each month accordingly after the introduction of parking regulations, indicating the improvement of usage efficiency of shared e-scooters.

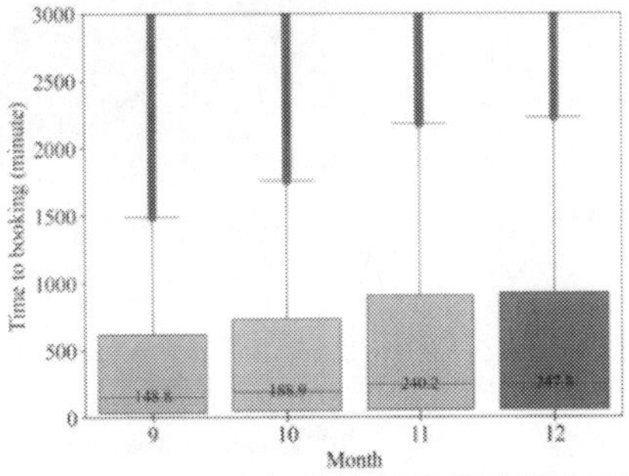

(a) PBR

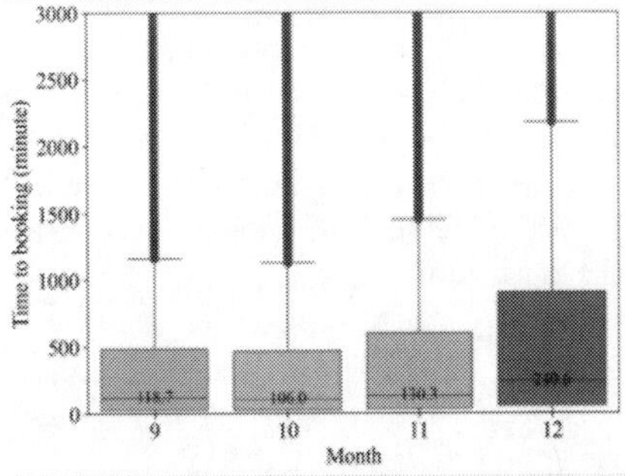

(b) PAR

Figure 3. Statistical distribution of time to booking on a monthly basis during (a) PBR and (b) PAR.

Figure 4 presents the spatial distributions of Ttb medians at the DeSO level during PBR and PAR. The Ttb medians were categorized into five classes with the natural breaks method. Since the Ttb medians are visualized with the same classification scheme, the two maps are comparable to each other. In the maps, the yellowish DeSOs represent the areas with low Ttb values and high usage efficiency of shared e-scooters. It can be observed that the number of yellowish DeSOs increased dramatically during PAR. It may conclude that the usage efficiency of shared e-scooters is lower, even if the number of e-scooter trips is higher than that after the introduction of parking regulations. It could be due to the oversupply of shared e-scooters before the introduction of parking regulations.

D. Integration between shared e-scooter and public transport

According to the method described in subsection III-C, the e-scooters were classified into complementary, competitive, and other categories. The complementary trips were further divided into the ones for the first-mile and last-mile connection. The proportions of complementary trips during PBR and PAR are very close, which are 32.0% and 32.2% respectively.

Figure 4. Spatial distribution of time to booking during (a) PBR and (b) PAR.

Likewise, we also aggregated and averaged the proportions of the first-mile and last-mile trips on an hourly basis during PBR and PAR. Figure 5 displays the temporal variations of the proportions during the two periods. It can be observed that the patterns of the integration between shared e-scooters and public transport are similar before and after the enforcement of parking regulations. The first mile trips occupied a major portion in the morning on weekday and weekend compared with the last mile trips, and then the last mile trip became dominant in the evening. The findings are consistent with the study by Li et al. [20].

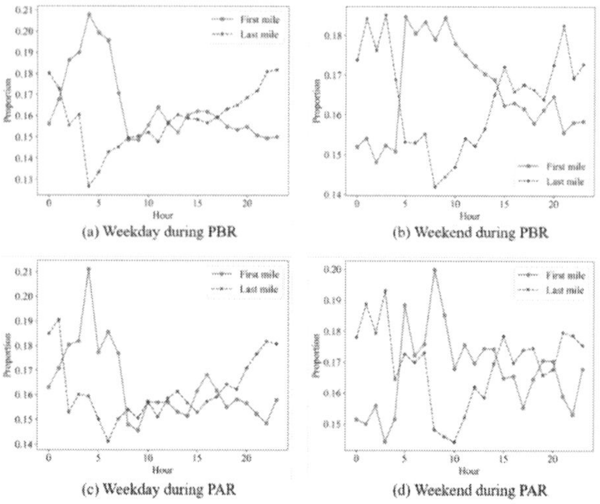

Figure 5. Temporal distribution of proportions of first mile and last mile trips on an hourly basis during (a) PBR and (b) PAR.

V. Conclusion and Future Work

Shared e-scooters offer a sustainable and flexible alternative to traditional transport modes. Considering the regulatory challenges caused by their widespread adoption, parking regulations have been introduced to tackle them in many cities worldwide. However, less is known about how the parking regulations influence shared e-scooter usage in urban areas. In this paper, we explore how shared e-scooter usage changed before and after the enforcement of parking regulations in terms of three usage indicators and their integration with public transport by conducting a case study in Stockholm, Sweden. The main findings of this study are summarized as follows.

First, the trip frequency decreased dramatically after the introduction of parking regulations. This could also be due to the permit constraint on the number of shared e-scooters in urban areas, in addition to the parking regulations. However, the temporal usage patterns were similar before and after the parking regulations. Second, the service areas of shared e-scooters shrank after the introduction of parking regulations, which were mainly concentrated in the peripheral areas of Stockholm. The areas with high trip frequency were still focused on central Stockholm. Third, the usage efficiency of shared e-scooters in terms of time to booking displays improvement after the introduction of parking regulations. Lastly, the changes in the integration between shared e-scooters and public transport in terms of the proportions of the first mile and last mile trips are tiny before and after the introduction of parking regulations.

Overall, the research findings are beneficial for urban planners and policy-makers to develop evidence-based parking regulations and practices for regulating shared micro-mobility. The following aspects deserve to be studied in future work. First, more analyses will be implemented to investigate how the parking regulations influence the integration between shared e-scooters and public transport from the perspectives of accessibility and equity, especially in the context of multiple cities. Second, it is also interesting to see whether the parking regulations affect the relationships between the integration patterns and influence factors, such as the urban built environment and socio-demographics.

Acknowledgments

This research has been supported by the Young Scientists Fund of the National Natural Science Foundation of China (52202389), and a grant administered through K2 - The Swedish Knowledge Centre for Collective Mobility (grant number 2023001).

References

[1] A. Li, P. Zhao, H. Haitao, A. Mansourian, and K. W. Axhausen, "How did micro-mobility change in response to covid-19 pandemic? a case study based on spatial-temporal-semantic analytics", *Computers, environment and urban systems*, vol. 90, p. 101 703, 2021.

[2] S. Gössling, "Integrating e-scooters in urban transportation: Problems, policies, and the prospect of system change", *Transportation Research Part D: Transport and Environment*, vol. 79, p. 102 230, 2020.

[3] R. L. Abduljabbar, S. Liyanage, and H. Dia, "The role of micro-mobility in shaping sustainable cities: A systematic literature review", *Transportation research part D: transport and environment*, vol. 92, p. 102 734, 2021.

[4] L. Avetisyan *et al.*, "Design a sustainable micro-mobility future: Trends and challenges in the us and eu", *Journal of Engineering Design*, vol. 33, no. 8-9, pp. 587–606, 2022.

[5] V. Mehranfar and C. Jones, "Exploring implications and current practices in e-scooter safety: A systematic review", *Transportation Research Part F: Traffic Psychology and Behaviour*, vol. 107, pp. 321–382, 2024.

[6] P. Hurlet, O. Manout, and A. O. Diallo, "Policy implications of shared e-scooter parking regulation: An agent-based approach", in *The 15th International Conference on Ambient Systems, Networks and Technologies (ANT)*, vol. 238, 2024, pp. 444–451.

[7] "Parking challenges and recommendations", Micromobility for Europe, 2023, [Online]. Available: https : / / micromobilityforeurope . eu / parking - challenges - recommendations/.

[8] J. Jiao and S. Bai, "Understanding the shared e-scooter travels in austin, tx", *ISPRS International Journal of Geo-Information*, vol. 9, no. 2, p. 135, 2020.

[9] A. Li *et al.*, "Comprehensive comparison of e-scooter sharing mobility: Evidence from 30 european cities", *Transportation Research Part D: Transport and Environment*, vol. 105, p. 103 229, 2022.

[10] H. Badia and E. Jenelius, "Shared e-scooter micromobility: Review of use patterns, perceptions and environmental impacts", *Transport reviews*, vol. 43, no. 5, pp. 811–837, 2023.

[11] H. Stigson, I. Malakuti, and M. Klingegård, "Electric scooters accidents: Analyses of two swedish accident data sets", *Accident Analysis & Prevention*, vol. 163, p. 106 466, 2021.

[12] S. Shaheen, A. Cohen, and J. Broader, "What's the'big'deal with shared micromobility? evolution, curb policy, and potential developments in north america", *Built Environment*, vol. 47, no. 4, pp. 499–514, 2021.

[13] D. Lo, C. Mintrom, K. Robinson, and R. Thomas, "Shared micromobility: The influence of regulation on travel mode choice", *New Zealand Geographer*, vol. 76, no. 2, pp. 135–146, 2020.

[14] B. B. Wincent, E. Jenelius, and W. Burghout, "Parking of electric scooters: Survey of effects and opinions regarding the parking ban in stockholm, gothenburg and malmö", *KTH Arkitektur och samhällsbyggnad Avdelningen för transportplanering*, 2023.

[15] G. McKenzie, "Urban mobility in the sharing economy: A spatiotemporal comparison of shared mobility services", *Computers, Environment and Urban Systems*, vol. 79, p. 101 418, 2020.

[16] M. Heumann, T. Kraschewski, T. Brauner, L. Tilch, and M. H. Breitner, "A spatiotemporal study and location-specific trip pattern categorization of shared e-scooter usage", *Sustainability*, vol. 13, no. 22, p. 12 527, 2021.

[17] N. Foissaud, C. Gioldasis, S. Tamura, Z. Christoforou, and N. Farhi, "Free-floating e-scooter usage in urban areas: A spatiotemporal analysis", *Journal of transport geography*, vol. 100, p. 103 335, 2022.

[18] Z. Guo, J. Liu, P. Zhao, A. Li, and X. Liu, "Spatiotemporal heterogeneity of the shared e-scooter–public transport relationships in stockholm and helsinki", *Transportation research part D: transport and environment*, vol. 122, p. 103 880, 2023.

[19] J. Aarhaug, N. Fearnley, and E. Johnsson, "E-scooters and public transport–complement or competition?", *Research in transportation economics*, vol. 98, p. 101 279, 2023.

[20] A. Li, K. Gao, P. Zhao, and K. W. Axhausen, "Integrating shared e-scooters as the feeder to public transit: A comparative analysis of 124 european cities", *Transportation research part C: emerging technologies*, vol. 160, p. 104 496, 2024.

[21] P. Zhao, H. Haitao, A. Li, and A. Mansourian, "Impact of data processing on deriving micro-mobility patterns from vehicle availability data", *Transportation Research Part D: Transport and Environment*, vol. 97, p. 102 913, 2021.

[22] A. Li, P. Zhao, Y. Huang, K. Gao, and K. W. Axhausen, "An empirical analysis of dockless bike-sharing utilization and its explanatory factors: Case study from shanghai, china", *Journal of Transport Geography*, vol. 88, p. 102 828, 2020.

Spatio-Temporal Big Data Standards: Status and Progress

Peter Baumann
Computer Science & Electrical Engineering
Constructor University
Bremen, Germany
email: pbaumann@constructor.university

Abstract–**In standardization, the term *coverage* captures the digital representation of space/time-varying phenomena. Coverages are supported by a mature set of standards, maintained in a continuous cooperation of the International Organization for Standardization (ISO) and Open Geospatial Consortium (OGC), with manifold uptake and implementation. At its heart is the OGC/ISO Coverage Implementation Schema (CIS) data standard. We give a condensed overview of the CIS standard and its current progress, looking at the ISO 19123-1 concepts and their realization with ISO 19123-2. We do this in our capacity as primary editor of the standards discussed.**

Keywords- coverages, datacubes, standards, ISO, OGC, rasdaman.

I. INTRODUCTION

Phenomena observed on, in, or above Earth often represent *fields* as defined in physics (e.g., quantum field theory [8]): some quantity that has a value for each point in space and time within some region. In other words: the quantity varies in space and time. Examples include the Earth's magnetic field, surface wind maps, and river water temperature at some location; Figure 1 shows a kaleidoscope of data from various geo application domains.

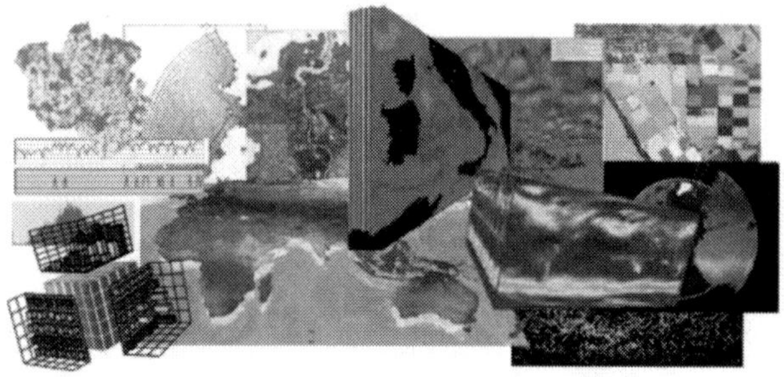

Figure 1. Basic building blocks of a coverage.

Such fields are multi-dimensional by nature – in the above examples we find 4-D (four-dimensional) x/y/z/t for the magnetic field, 3-D x/y/t for the wind map, and 1-D for the water temperature timeseries. Obviously, the dimension axes can be spatial or temporal; however, they even can have further dimensions, such as a spectral dimension for wave frequencies occurring; a second time axis, as used in weather forecasting; a species axis for measuring habitat changes in a region over time.

Mathematically, such a field can be seen as a function which assigns a value (from its range) to every point in the region where the function is defined (its domain). In standardization, the term *coverage* subsumes digital representations of such space/time varying phenomena. Technically, coverages encompass regular and irregular grids, point clouds, and general meshes. Most notably, they serve to represent raster data and spatio-temporal datacubes. To cite common phrases, such data typically constitute "Big Data", which are "too big to transport", so that processing requires to "ship code to the data".

The central standard is the Open Geospatial Consortium (OGC) *Coverage Implementation Schema* (CIS) [27] and the parallel International Organization for Standardization (ISO) 19123-2 [11], likewise nicknamed CIS. They are embedded in a larger ecosystem of data and service standards. In this contribution, we only look at the coverage data standards. Table 1 shows the correspondence of ISO and OGC coverage standards; see also the overview in [33].

Recently, these standards have undergone a revision and now are better structured (cf. Table I):

- *conceptual level*: ISO 19123-1 / OGC Abstract Topic (AT) 6.1 defines the information concepts, together with the pertaining terminology;
- *logical level*: ISO 19123-2 Clauses 5 to 10 / OGC CIS defines concrete data structures as object classes;
- *physical level*: ISO 19123-2 Clause 11 and 12 / OGC CIS plus further separate encoding standards define the mapping of logical-level data to byte streams such as XML, JSON, GeoTIFF, NetCDF, JPEG2000, etc.

ISO 19123-1 [10], which defines coverage concepts and terms, was adopted in 2023 replacing outdated 19123:2005. Several reasons prompted this evolution: difficult to understand; errors and omissions, such as excluding 1-D; definitions not state of the art, such as rasters defined as "corresponding to the display on a cathode ray tube"; mixed conceptual, logical, and physical levels making comprehension difficult.

TABLE I. CORRESPONDENCE OF OGC AND ISO COVERAGE STANDARDS.

ISO	OGC	contents
19123-1 [10]	Abstract Topic 6.1 [28]	Coverage data model: concepts & terminology
19123-2 [11]	CIS [27]	Coverage Implementation Schema
19123-3 [12]	Abstract Topic 6.3 [29]	Coverage processing model: concepts & terminology, based on OGC WCPS [26]

Consequently, 19123:2005 got split and replaced by two parts: 19123-1 [10] establishes the conceptual model using interfaces describing the high-level observable behavior of a coverage object, leaving implementation details open. Such detail is provided by 19123-2 [11] which contains the logical model and – clearly separated – the physical-level encoding. The standard is organized into packages resembling self-contained units where each one establishes a particular coverage concept.

The author is active OGC contributor since 2004 and in this capacity main editor of the currently 23 coverage / datacube / Web Coverage Service (WCS) standards [26]-[29][31], OGC delegate to ISO, ISO project lead / editor of the 19123-1/2/3 family of coverage standards [10]-[12], and German delegate and WCS drafting team member for EU INSPIRE, the European legal framework for a common spatial data infrastructure. Further, he is initiator and co-editor of ISO SQL/MDA (Multi-Dimensional Arrays) [9][19].

The remainder of this paper is organized as follows. In Section II, we present the concepts and terminology of coverages, followed by the concrete, implementation-oriented coverage structures in Section III. A brief lookout on a data language tailored to coverage analytics is given in Section IV. Related coverage standards are discussed in Section V. Section VI provides a summary.

II. Coverage Conceptual Model

The notion of a field as a function C: $D \rightarrow V$ suggests a rather simple definition of a coverage, plus an access method: just evaluate the function at any position $p \in D$, yielding $C(p) = v \in V$. As per ISO 19107 [14], this is called the *evaluate function*, commonly denoted as

$$evaluate_C: D \rightarrow V,\ evaluate_C(p) = v$$

While this is conceptually elegant, it is normally highly inefficient to ask for single coordinates, so this is not the kind of functionality specifically supported in coverage services; rather, extraction and processing of larger regions is common, e.g., in WCS [31] and Web Coverage Processing Service (WCPS) [3][26].

Actually, the above function definition needs an extension to allow multiple values for a location:

$$evaluate_C: D \rightarrow P(V),\ evaluate_C(p) = \bigcup_{f \in C} f.contains(p)$$

where $P(V)$ denotes the power set of V, i.e., the set of all sub-multisets (a multiset is an unordered set where elements can repeat). The *contains*() predicate, likewise defined in ISO 19107, indicates whether a point coordinate lies inside a geometric object. For example, a point cloud may contain more than one value for a given point; the evaluation function will return the multiset of these values for that point. The same holds for curves, surfaces, and solids which all may overlap.

A. Coordinates and Coordinate Reference Systems

The n-D region which a coverage domain spans (we avoid the mathematical term "space" because coverage axes can span more than physical space) is built from n>0 axes. Consequently, point coordinates form an n-tuple where the ith component is taken from the ith axis a_i. The ordered list of axes defines the function domain, described through a Coordinate Reference System (CRS).

Handling of coordinates is normatively established in the ISO 19111:2019 standard [13] whose use is also mandated by 19123-1. Conveniently, beyond geodetic CRSs 19111:2019 also opens the door for further axes and CRSs, as well as combining CRSs. One example for this is image timeseries where a horizontal CRS (contributing two axes) is combined with a 1-D CRS (adding one further axis) into a 3-D CRS. With the OGC CRS shorthand notation the World Geodetic System 1984 (WGS84) CRS [*EPSG:4326*] and datetime CRS [*OGC:AnsiDate*] get combined as ordered list [*EPSG:4326*],[*OGC:AnsiDate*].

More details about CRS syntax and handling are specified in the concretization standard 19123-2.

B. Coverage Structures

ISO 19123-1 defines the basic coverage components domain set, range set, and range type:

- *Domain set*: "where are values available?" Points for which values are stored are called *direct positions*.
- *Range set*: "what is the value at a particular position?" Such values consist of records with one or more components (atomic, such as in grayscale images, or composite structures such as color images).
- *Range type*: "what do these values mean?" This describes the semantics for each range value record component (also known as bands / channels / variables).
- *Metadata*: "what else do we know about this coverage?" This item is a black box which literally can be anything, not understood by the coverage but duly transported.

19123-1 does not hardwire the above structure. Rather, several organization schemes are provided:

- by domain and range, plus a mapping between them;
- as a set of direct position / value pairs;
- partitioning of the coverage into sub-coverages.

We discuss each alternative in turn.

The domain/range separation follows directly from the structuring in Figure 2. The advantage is that the domain representation can be chosen independently, which is very important particularly with grid coverages where a detailed structure with several variants is required. On the other hand, the connection between direct positions and values is lost and needs to be established separately. Typically, such a mapping is done through sequence rules inside the coverage function structure defining the correspondences between (implicitly) enumerated direct positions and the simple sequence of values in the range set are established.

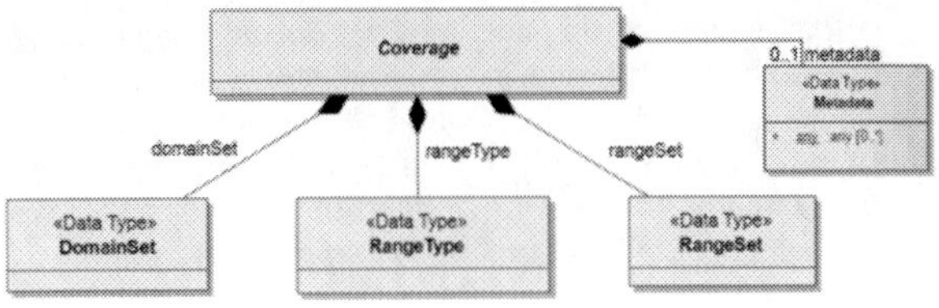

Figure 2. Basic building blocks of a coverage.

The position/value pair approach is attractive whenever the geometry and its associated value are used in conjunction. This is often the case, for example with point clouds. On gridded data, on the other hand, many algorithms work without reference to the geographic coordinates of the pixels, and hence can very efficiently iterate over the values only, disregarding the domain set.

Partitioning can be seen as a generalization of the position / value pair approach where not single pairs, but sets of such pairs are built. Every partition forms a complete, self-contained coverage, and all partitions together must be non-overlapping and contiguous without "holes". Partitioning schemes are common for splitting large coverages (i.e., "Big Data" files) into smaller "tiles" or "chunks". In [2], a method for user-invisible flexible partitioning of datacubes is introduced.

C. *Coverage Function*

Historically, in the coverage definition of the Geography Markup Language (GML) [15], an alternative was foreseen for defining the coverage function analytically. This has never been detailed, GML only vaguely mentions that the Mathematics Markup Language (MathML) might be used. Today, the coverage function is mostly used for describing the internal range set array sequencing through its *sequence rule* subitem.

D. *Domain Set*

The coverage domain describes for which positions in the coverage's multi-dimensional space values are available, in other words: where evaluation of the coverage function is defined. Within this multi-dimensional space defined by the domain's CRS and the bounding box extent, the coverage domain contains a set of geometric objects which together determine the direct positions, i.e., the locations in this space where the coverage offers a value. This description can be given through direct enumeration of the direct positions (example: point clouds) or through containment descriptions (example: areas and volumes), or some other mechanism (example: Ground Control Points in sensor models). The coverage's "extent" gives a bounding box – i.e., lower and upper bounds along every coordinate axis – within which all its direct positions are located. A quick overview on the footprint of the coverage can be obtained through the coverage envelope.

Coverage coordinates are defined through a single CRS which defines all axes, using ISO 19111:2019. Each axis is described by an axis name, a Boolean axis direction (*true* for positive direction along the axis, *false* for inverse direction), a unit of measure, and a (possibly empty) set of interpolation methods applicable along this axis. As discussed, axes can be of spatial, temporal, or abstract (in ISO 19111:2019: "parametric") nature.

Note again that this does not yet define a concrete data structure; many different incarnations are possible ultimately carrying the same information. For example, a concrete implementation schema may choose to not define interpolation methods always per axis, but may group several axes – such as Lat and Lon – into a single description.

E. *Envelope*

A typical first step when shaking hands with a coverage is to ask about its region covered, i.e., its axes and extent along each axis. This information is available in the domain set: By determining the minimum and maximum of point coordinates for each component, the overall extent of the region along each axis is determined. These boundaries determine an axis-parallel minimum bounding box, or *bbox*.

While it is possible to obtain this information from the coverage domain set, it is not straightforward: the n-dimensional domain is described through n axes, possibly of different types, and in some without explicit indication of the lower and upper bounds. Additionally, the domain might employ a CRS different from the desired one. For example, the European Terrestrial Reference System 1989 (ETRS89) system used in Europe consists of 60 different Universal Transverse Mercator (UTM) zones whereas a US GIS may want to see all data in the single WGS84.

The envelope concept provides a shortcut to such information. It contains the bbox of the coverage in a CRS which, for the users' convenience, can be different from the domain set CRS (as long as a conversion exists between envelope and domain CRS). There is no need for the envelope to be minimal, although it should get as close as possible to the coverage footprint.

F. *Range Set and Range Type*

Range values listed must adhere to the definition given in the coverage's range type, following a dynamic typing approach. The range values can be scalar or a record. For simplicity, more involved structures – such as variable-length lists, arrays, graphs, etc. – are not supported in order to keep implementations simple in this respect.

For example, a coverage might assign to each direct position in a county the temperature, pressure, humidity, and wind velocity components *u* and *v*, at a specific time, at that point. The coverage then maps every direct position in the county to a record of these components. The coverage range type, therefore, is a record of these components, each of its individual type.

Type information goes beyond the mere data type as in programming languages. Essential extra information is provided, in particular: Data type; unit of measure; null values, if any. For example, RGB images might have as their range type a record consisting of three components *red*, *green*, and *blue* (in that order), each of them of type unsigned 8-bit integer with unit Watt per square meter – in Unified Code for Units of Measure (UCUM) syntax: *W.m-2* – and no null values. The 19123-2 concretization of ISO 19123-1 adds further details.

G. *Interpolation*

Having space and time axes, a coverage is a finite, discretized representation of some typically infinite, continuous phenomenon. Digital representations of such fields, therefore, must find appropriate data structures to represent the infinity of points by a finite data volume. Obviously, it is desirable that even positions can be queried for which no value is stored – typically, between direct positions. The general approach is to store a finite number of "representative" points with their values alongside with rules how to derive values at further points.

Under certain conditions, such values can be derived algorithmically through interpolation. Hence, direct positions plus interpolation can emulate the continuous nature of the original phenomenon. Many interpolation methods are known for such purposes, obviously the technically appropriate method has to be chosen carefully to remain sufficiently close to the original.

The interpolation applicable is co-determined by the range type. For example, radiometry data, such as hyperspectral satellite imagery, is normally amenable to linear, quadratic, and cubic interpolation due to the continuous nature of the radiation measured. Categorial data like land use, on the other hand, allow only nearest-neighbour interpolation – the average of street and building does not make sense. Further particularities can have an impact, like the lack of direct positions; kriging is a family of special interpolations used in particular in geophysics.

In summary, interpolation is determined by both domain and range of the coverage function:

- The coverage axis. For example, atmospheric linear interpolation may be fine in Latitude and Longitude, but not vertically when measured in pressure levels. Also, time axis behavior may need to be considered separately. Index axes, finally, with their integer coordinates, do not even allow for addressing fractional coordinates. Within one and the same coverage, different interpolations may apply along different axes.
- The range type (possibly individually for each record element). For example, categorial data (like land use) only allow nearest-neighbour interpolation whereas radiometry etc. also allow linear interpolation.

The coverage standard guides application of interpolation, but does not itself define interpolation methods; these are rather taken from ISO 19107. Only for the reader's convenience, ISO 19123-1 Annex B addresses interpolation in a non-normative way.

Notably, the abstract coverage concept allows only one interpolation. The reason is that interpolation is a consequential of the physical field structure emulated by the coverage, and different interpolation yields different in between values so represent different fields. For practical reasons – to avoid duplicating Big Data – in 19123-2 CIS a set of "allowed interpolation methods" is foreseen.

A further complication may be the applicability of interpolation around a direct position. Naively, any position between two adjacent direct positions can be queried, and interpolation (if any) will yield a range value. However, being "too far away" from any direct positions, when the neighboring direct positions happen to be far apart from each other, might be to "unsafe" and so interpolation may be forbidden. The concept of a *region of validity* around direct positions captures this, as first introduced for the time axis [5] and implemented in the rasdaman datacube engine. See [6] for future-directed concepts.

Based on these concepts, the original distinction of 19123:2005 into discrete and continuous coverages can be grasped exactly: An axis is called *discrete* if every possible interval with finite bounds describes a finite set of values, otherwise (when interpolation is enabled) such an axis is called *continuous*. A coverage is called *discrete* if its axis list contains only discrete axes. A coverage is called *continuous* if its axis list contains at least one continuous axis. Technically, a continuous coverage is a discrete coverage which can be interpolated.

H. *Coverage Classification*

The coverage concept in ISO 19123-1:2023 defines a series of different approaches to establish digital structures for spatio-temporally varying phenomena. The idea is to exploit additional knowledge that may exist about the phenomenon. For example, if point values measured sit on a grid (aka grid or raster coverage) rather than arbitrarily in space (aka point clouds) then Computer Science knows specific, very efficient methods to exploit this knowledge.

Following this line, the standard classifies coverage regions into features – points, curves, surfaces, or solids – with potentially additional conditions imposed such as a grid lineup. To keep coverage handling tractable in implementation, only one kind of feature is allowed in any given coverage. This gives a natural classification of coverage, sorted along the topological dimensions of its elements: 0-D point, 1-D line, 2-D surface, and 3-D solid coverages. This is mirrored by the coverage types in Clause 6 onwards in ISO 19123-1:2019 in multi-point, multi-curve, multi-surface, and multi-solid coverage.

A *multi-point* coverage is a coverage consisting of a collection of 0-D points. As points may coincide, there can be more than one value correspond to a given direct position, therefore the evaluation returns a multi-set of values with possibly more than one value.

A *multi-curve* coverage resembles a set of geometric objects of the ISO 19107 type *CurveData*. Curves defined there encompass a wide range, from polygon strings to splines. AIS worldwide ship tracking system trajectories represent an example of multi-curve coverages. Trajectories may intersect, hence *evaluate*() may deliver more than one trajectories as values.

A *multi-surface* coverage is a coverage consisting of a collection of surfaces. The feature type used is given by the ISO 19107 geometric object type *SurfaceData*. Such surfaces are described through bounding curves which in turn are delimited by start and end points. A typical example for a multi-surface coverage is an iso-surface set.

A *multi-solid* coverage consists of a collection of solids, modeled through ISO 19107 *SolidData* which adopts a Boundary Representation where solids are bounded by surfaces delimited by curves delimited by points.

I. *Grid Coverages*

A grid coverage is a special case of multi-point coverage: all direct positions must sit on a grid. As the grid structure is of prime practical importance, we unfold it separately.

Mathematically, an n-D grid is the cross product over the admissible coordinates of each contributing axis. For some n>0 let $A = (a_1, \ldots, a_n)$ be a finite ordered set of axes where each axis $a_i = \{v_{i,1},..., v_{i,mi}\}$ is an ordered set of $m_i>0$ values inducing a grid $G = a_1\times...\times a_n$. G can be interpreted as a set of coordinates yielding the direct positions, $G = \{ (x_1, ..., x_n) \mid x_i \in a_i \text{ for } 1 \leq i \leq n \}$.

Such a grid consists of points only. These points are aligned in a special way, and we often like to draw lines between neighboring points so that the alignment becomes easier to see. However, these lines are artifacts and not part of the coverage grid. Notably, the gridded nature does not affect the CRS in any way – the grid is just about constraints on the coordinates.

Geometrically, grids generally can be constructed based on triangles, rectangles, or hexagons (meaning: the grid points can be aligned so that, *would* they be connected, we *would* see such geometric shapes). In the context of ISO 19123-1, rectangular grids are modeled through grid coverages, hexagonal grids can be mapped to grid coverages, and triangular grids are modeled through meshes, i.e., multi-surface or multi-solid coverages. In the sequel, for simplicity the term "grid" is understood as a rectangular grid.

Intuitively speaking, in a coverage grid, every direct position (except at the rim) has exactly one immediate neighbor with a lower coordinate and exactly one immediate neighbor with a higher coordinate along each axis (Figure 3. This neighborhood establishes the grid topology; the grid geometry is determined by the concrete coordinates, which in turn are described by the axis types.

The grid alignment constraint also has a further consequence: As it is not possible any longer that two points coincide, there will be always one range value per direct position, and we can simplify the *evaluate*() function from a value set to a single value:

$evaluate_C: D \rightarrow V, evaluate_C(p) = v$

J. *Regular and Non-Regular Grids*

In general, rectangular grids do not need to have an equidistant spacing between the direct positions. Figure 4 and Figure 5, taken from the standard document, illustrate some cases of regular and irregular grids. A grid can be regular along some axes but irregular along others, as Figure 5 shows. In particular, when grid connections are drawn as curved lines, this should not be interpreted as reality.

The grid concept can be generalized to the situation that n-D grids can be embedded in some $(n+m)$-D space for some $m > 0$. Actually, Figure 5 (c) models such a situation where a 2D grid is warped in 3D space.

K. *Grid Axis Types*

ISO 19123-1 categorizes the coverage grid domain by its individual axes, allowing free combinations such as regular spatial with irregular temporal axes. Notably, this axis *classification* establishes several ways to describe the coordinates of the direct positions, not the grid CRS which contains the axis *definitions*.

Every axis has one of the following axis types: index, regular, irregular, warped, and (sensor) model.

An *index axis* is a 1D unit-less axis (in ISO 19111:2019 named "Cartesian axes"); there is no georeference, and admissible coordinates are at discrete, integer positions only. The corresponding CRS is *Index1D* for a single axis, and *Index2D* etc. for a multi-axis setup. For two lower and upper bounds *lo* and *hi* with $lo, hi \in \mathbf{Z}$ and $lo \leq hi$, the direct positions are taken from the closed interval $S = \{ x \in \mathbf{Z} \mid lo \leq x \leq hi \}$.The bounds, at the same time, constitute the bbox along this axis.

A *regular axis* has an equi-distant spacing like an index axis, but is continuous and not constrained to integer positions and distances. It can be georeferenced, i.e., it can have a spatial or temporal (or other) semantics attached, given by its CRS. It can be described conveniently by lower and upper bound plus resolution.

An *irregular axis* lists (possibly georeferenced) positions $P = \{p_1,..., p_n\} \subseteq C$ explicitly where C denotes the coordinate value set defined for this axis in the CRS. Direct positions exist for every coordinate tuple where the coordinate value of the irregular axis is from P.

A *displacement axis nest* (or *warped nest*) is a set of possibly georeferenced axes forming a subset of the CRS's axes. Direct positions have maximum freedom of location, the only rule being that coordinates along each participating axis remain ordered and no duplicate coordinates appear. Direct positions are given by the coordinate tuples where the coordinate of each axis participating in the displacement axis nest is in the coordinate value set of this axis.

By combining all the above axis types freely, any type of grid shape can be modeled. The list of possible axis types in the standard is not exhaustive, some standard or application may define their own additional axis types.

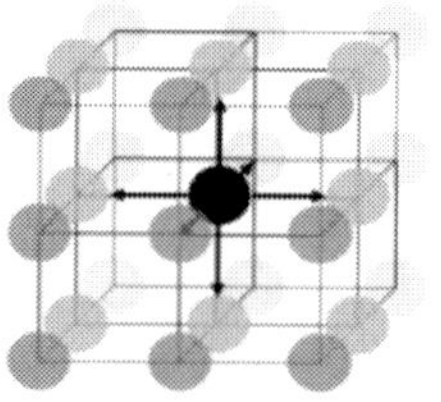

Figure 3. Multi-dimensional neighbourhood in a grid [10].

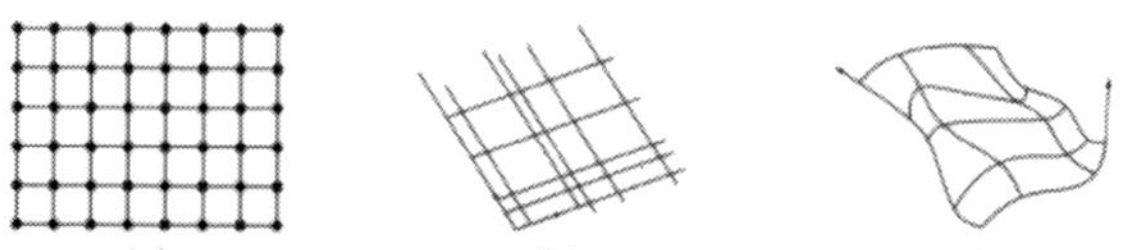

(a) (b) (c)

Figure 4. Sample regular 2-D grid (a), 2-D irregular grid (b), 2-D warped nest grid (c) [10].

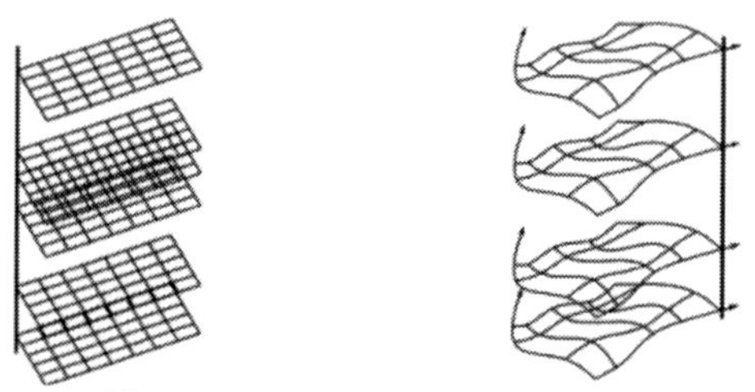

(a) (b)

Figure 5. Sample 3-D x/y/t grid representing the combination of regular Lat/Long with irregular time (a) and warped nest with irregular time (b), time axis running vertically [10].

Obsoleted ISO 19123:2005 differentiates on grid level distinguishing only rectified and referenceable grid coverage. Based on the above grid construction mechanisms, these terms can be defined precisely:

- A *rectified grid coverage* is a grid coverage where every axis is either an index axis or a regular axis;
- A *referenceable grid coverage* is a grid coverage where at least one axis is neither index nor regular axis.

L. Grid Cells

Inspired by the Computer Science term of "array cells" – storage locations in memory for the values, lined up in sequence – geo informatics also has a common notion of "grid cells", however with different understanding. In a grid cell view, the imaginary lines suggest to be boundaries of an area which suddenly becomes the first-class citizen. Consequently, questions arise like "is the real cell location at the direct position or rather between the direct positions, in the center of the cell?" and "is the cell extent still a point like the direct position, or is it an area now?"

This is captured by the commonly used, yet not clearly defined distinctions *pixel-in-corner* versus *pixel-in-center* on the one hand and *pixel-is-point* versus *pixel-is-area* on the other hand.

These questions will be addressed in a forthcoming paper, aiming at a comprehensive conceptual treatment.

III. Coverage Implementation Schema

We next address the coverage concretization standard, ISO 19123-2 [11], known as Coverage Implementation Schema (CIS). CIS is a compliant standardization target of ISO 19123-1:2023, meaning: it relies on the concepts, terms, definitions, and interfaces of the abstract data model to establish a logical schema expressed in the Unified Modeling Language (UML) implementing the interfaces defined there. Additionally, this document defines several format encodings for the single logical schema.

Current ISO 19123-2:2018 was adopted from OGC CIS 1.0; integration of OGC CIS 1.1 [27] is under work as a version update. In the sequel, we introduce the latest, yet unpublished draft (named CIS for short), thereby providing the most up-to-date information to the public while work is still in progress.

OGC CIS 1.1 does not supersede, but extend OGC CIS 1.0. When integrating both into a self-contained ISO 19123-2 a specific structure had to be found for the combined document because both differ in places due to historical reasons. With a similar approach as in 19123-1, the CIS 1.1 coverage classes have been put into the specification body while isolating the legacy – consisting of the rectified and referenceable grid coverages – in a separate annex.

One important reason for fencing CIS 1.0 and 1.1 is due to the GML legacy. The GML 3.2.1 coverage structure [15] is both overly complicated and too restrictive. The complication comes from a particular modeling style of GML which might be academically justified but in practice almost duplicates the number of structuring elements in the GML encoding. The most important of the restrictions is due to the coordinate types which normatively are fixed to numbers in GML. However, in today's timeseries and datacube world temporal axes require date and time stamps, such as "2025-01-25" – nobody wants to count seconds since January 1st 1970. All communities made clear that support for convenient calendar and time syntax is an absolute must. Still, despite manifold requests and discussion the GML working group was not willing to extend GML with strings. Therefore, CIS 1.1 carefully deviates from GML to allow any type of coordinates.

Additionally, the domain set description in the CIS 1.1 *GeneralGridCoverage* has been made more straightforward.

In a nutshell, the main changes of CIS over its predecessor version ISO 19123-2:2018 are as follows:

- CIS has been adjusted to ISO 19123-1 in terminology and concept use, with a clear focus and separation into logical level (UML structures) and physical level.
- All CIS 1.1 coverage classes are adopted unchanged. Legacy grid coverage classes *RectifiedGridCoverage* and *ReferenceableGridCoverage* (the latter from a separately adopted OGC standard [35]) have been retained, but moved into a separate (normative) Annex B. These two types are legacy and will be deprecated in the next version – anyway, *GeneralGridCoverage* can model these cases while simpler in structure.
  Technically, gridded coverages still consist of an n-D matrix (mathematically: tensor), ornamented with extra information realizing the spatio-temporal semantics.
- The JSON encoding of CIS 1.1 has been reworked to comply with modern JSON Schema.
- Due to resource reasons, the Resource Data Framework (RDF) encoding present in CIS 1.1 has not been included at this time and is left for future work.

Realizing the structuring opportunities of 19123-1:2023 CIS likewise offers several structuring variants: a separation of domain and range, partitioning into sub-coverages, and direct enumeration of position/value pairs (sometimes also called "geometry / value pairs" or "interleaved representation"). In this overview, we limit ourselves to the very common domain/range representation.

B. Coordinates and Coordinate Reference Systems

Direct positions are expressed as coordinate tuples, as laid down in ISO 19123-1. Coordinate values are of data type *string* as they must accommodate data types as diverse as numbers (such as 1.23 degrees or 500 nm), dates and times (such as "2016-03-08T11:23Z"), categorial values (such as "orange", "apple"), and possibly more.

Similarly, resolution specifications are of type string as they have to accommodate, e.g., "1.23" for degrees or meters and "PT2h" for a 2-hour duration. As per ISO 19111:2019, any coordinate representation scheme must convey some total ordering so that expressions like "lowerBound ≤ upperBound" are valid for any axis.

We briefly focus on date and time coordinates as these convey a more involved syntax. The ISO 19108:2002 standard [16] applies here which defines the date and time syntax used, such as "2023-01-01T10:15:22.345Z" and "2023-01-01T00:00:00.000CET". Note the time zone identifiers, "Z" (for Zulu time aka UTC) and "CET". Such timestamps are called "fully qualified"; shorter time strings with different temporal resolution are possible, such as "2023-01-01" and "2023". The basis for date and time is one basic time CRS counting in seconds. On top of this, calendar CRSs are built such as *GregorianDateTime* (following the syntax sketched above), *UnixTime*, and *ChronometricGeologicTime*.

Several vertical CRSs are available in the OGC registry. What still has to be added are proxies such as pressure altitude (measured in *hPa* or *psi*) for altitude in the atmosphere. Their description likely is possible through parametric CRSs foreseen in ISO 19111:2019.

Such coverage axes are defined by the coverage CRS as laid down in ISO 19111:2019 [13]. Any combination of spatial, temporal, and "abstract" (i.e., non-spatio / temporal) axes is possible. This coverage CRS – its so-called *native CRS*, in which data are stored in the coverage – is a single *n*-D CRS for the *n*-D coverage. (This is an important difference to other spatio-temporal data standards in OGC which split CRS components over several places, an approach which is not only more difficult to oversee but also comes with significant conceptual restrictions.)

OGC several years back has resolved that CRSs are to be expressed through URLs, such as the following for WGS84, which has EPSG [36] code 4326:

https://www.opengis.net/def/crs/EPSG/0/4326

In the *crs-compose/* branch, component CRSs can be added constituting a concatenation as per ISO 19111:2019. For example, a 3-D t/x/y CRS can be built from ETRS89 LAEA and date/time by concatenating two CRS URLs:

https://www.opengis.net/def/crs-compound?
 1=https://www.opengis.net/def/crs/OGC/0/AnsiDate&
 2=https://www.opengis.net/def/crs/EPSG/0/3035

Such URLs can be "resolved" using the OGC CRS Resolver service [32] which returns the XML-encoded definition of the CRS.

These long, hard-to-read URLs mostly are geared towards machine consumption – nevertheless, they were felt unwieldy, and so the rasdaman team at some time suggested a bracket notation as shorthand. Meanwhile these shortcuts are adopted by the OGC Naming Authority and permitted as alternatives to the CRS URLs. Rules are simple:

- A non-composite CRS URL of pattern
  https://www.opengis.net/def/crs/{*authority*}/{*version*}/{*id*}
  is identical to the shorthand
  [{*authority*}:{*id*}]
  Version number is 0 by definition, interpreted as "latest available". For example, [*EPSG:4326*] expands to
  https://www.opengis.net/def/crs/EPSG/0/4326
- A composite CRS URL is translated into a comma-separated sequence of the component CRSs, each of which is transcribed individually as per the rule above. For example, [*EPSG:4326*],[*OGC:AnsiDate*] is equivalent to the long version
  https://www.opengis.net/def/crs-compound?
   1=https://www.opengis.net/def/crs/OGC/0/AnsiDate&
   2=https://www.opengis.net/def/crs/EPSG/0/4326

Such CRS shorthand can be used, e.g., in the *srsName* attribute of a coverage domain set (see below), like:

srsname="[EPSG:4326],[OGC:AnsiDate]"

Note, however, that not all coverage implementations necessarily implement this feature; notably, the rasdaman WCS reference implementation does support it.

Based on this CRS infrastructure, we can define *n*-tuple coordinates for direct positions in coverages. Thanks to the generalization of CIS 1.1 and the liberation from GML restrictions, coordinates can be numeric and non-numeric alike.

C. *Coverage Domain Set*

The coverage domain set specializes into specific structures for multi-point, grid, multi-curve, multi-surface, and multi-solid domain set specifications as discussed earlier. All have in common, though, the *srsName* attribute holding the CRS of the coverage using either URL or bracket notation. In attribute *axisLabels*, the list of axis names in the CRS is provided in proper order, whitespace separated. These axis names are used inside the coverage for axis identification in the domain set's axis list. In attribute *uomLabels* the unit of measure is indicated for each axis in a whitespace-separated list in proper axis order. Best practice is to use UCUM notation [38] such as "m", "ft", "yr", etc.

In grid coverages, the *GeneralGrid* structure inside the *DomainSet* serves to span the *n*-D raster grid. For each axis its type is defined which mirrors the 19123-1 definitions.

An *IndexAxis* constitutes the simplest axis type, with only integer coordinates allowed. No resolution and no unit of measure are required.

A *regular axis* employs as coordinates any totally ordered value set, such as numbers and date/time strings. Additionally, the unit of measure – recommended: UCUM – plus the (constant) resolution need to be kept.

An *irregular axis* is like a regular one in that it can use any totally ordered value set for coordinates, with the unit of measure to be indicated. The coordinates contributing the direct positions are enumerated explicitly.

We omit the further axes types – irregular correlated grid axes (also called *displacement axis nest* or *warped nest*) and *transformation model* – to avoid undue complexity in this overview paper.

D. *Coverage Range Set and Range Type*

The range set usually forms the by far largest part of the coverage in terms of its storage footprint. Therefore, this part is designed as compact as ever possible, with no redundancy – the structure simply resembles an ordered list of values. It is essential, therefore, to have a linearization rule establishing a clear correlation between the multi-dimensional direct positions and the 1-D value sequence. The default row major / left-to-right sequencing rule can be overridden in the *sequenceRule* part of *CoverageFunction*.

The range type adds technical metadata required for a program to interpret the coverage range values correctly. CIS makes use of the OGC Sensor Web Enablement (SWE) Common [25] *DataRecord*. This ensures that the semantics from upstream sensor acquisitions into downstream services (like WCS) is carried over losslessly. Each range value can be a record characterized by component field name, unit of measure, and a characterization into Quantity, Count, or

Category. Further optional parts include nil (null) value list, definition (a URL pointing to a human-readable definition), and further more.

Besides *DataRecord*, there is an optional list of interpolation methods applicable. Common interpolation methods include *nearest-neighbor, linear, quadratic, cubic, barycentric*, and more. Interpolation is tightly connected with the region-of-validity concept, something to be reflected in subsequent standardization progress once there are conclusive results from the ongoing research [5][6].

E. Metadata

The metadata slot is as defined abstractly before: some byte string without further semantics known to the coverage. Use of this slot is manifold: To enhance the coverage information; to provide further domain-specific information; to create profiles, such as EU INSPIRE metadata [20].

F. Coverage Encodings

Many encoding formats are in active use for coverages in practice. Several of those are already standardized, such as GeoTIFF, NetCDF, GRIB2, and JPEG2000 – see the list at [31]. XML and JSON encodings are already contained in OGC CIS 1.1 [27] as separate conformance classes.

The XML encoding has a strong legacy from GML [10] to which it was aligned at the heydays of XML use. GML coverages came with several constraints (such as numerical coordinates only), and so a cautious liberation of GML was started with OGC CIS 1.1 allowing date / time strings and simplifying the structure.

Further, OGC CIS 1.1 added a conformance class for JSON. While reworking this into the new version of 19123-2 this was reshaped to match with current technology, in particular: JSON Schema [21].

The ASCII formats XML and JSON are "informationally complete" by containing all of the coverage information defined, but they not efficient in particular for voluminous data. Efficient binary formats, on the other hand, tend to grasp only part of the coverage information. For an encoding which is both informationally complete and storage efficient the multi-part conformance class was added. It defines a container which, as first item, contains an overall coverage description in some well-known complete format like XML or JSON. Instead of the storage-heavy parts – typically the range set – a reference is provided to one or more files also stored in the container. These further parts can be in any well-known format, typically in a compact binary encoding.

IV. Coverage Wrangling Standards

While this paper focuses on the coverage data structure, we still discuss briefly the corresponding service standards. The direct companion service standard to the coverage data standards is the OGC *Web Coverage Service* (WCS) which offers versatile extraction, conversion, analysis, and fusion on general multi-dimensional datasets [31]. Part of the modular WCS suite is the *Web Coverage Processing Service* (WCPS) [3][26], a geo datacube analytics language built for server-side evaluation. WCS is supported by manifold implementations [30], such as Oracle, Hexagon, GeoServer, ESRI, and rasdaman.

For map visualization, OGC Web Map Service (WMS) and Web Map Tiling Service (WMTS) are available. As opposed to WCS, these are specialized on 2D map rendering of datasets with two horizontal axes. WMS returns color pixels (like hill shading), a WCS delivers the original data (like height in feet) in a way that allows further processing.

For WCS and WMTS, rasdaman is official OGC Reference Implementation.

Given that coverages are "Big Data", they typically are "too big to download", hence processing requires "shipping code to data". From a service provider perspective, unguarded acceptance of programming language code is unsafe; from a user perspective, coding requires extra skills making exploitation infeasible for non-experts and time-consuming for experts. Therefore, OGC, ISO, and INSPIRE have adopted the dedicated datacube analytics language Web Coverage Processing Service (WCPS) [3][12]. This language defines expressions on coverages which evaluate to ordered lists of either coverages or scalars (whereby "scalar" here is used as a summary term of all data structures that are not coverages). Like the SQL data analytics language, WCPS is "safe in evaluation": every query is guaranteed to terminate in finite time, as opposed to programming languages like Python where such a guarantee is not possible.

We present WCPS through some examples illustrating basic mechanisms; see also the WCPS tutorial on EarthServer [22] and the ChatCUBE WCPS query assistant [23]. A forthcoming paper, updating the original WCPS 1.0 overview [3], will address WCPS 1.1 in detail.

- "Retrieve coverages A, B, and C in GeoTIFF":
```
for $c in ( A, B, C )
return encode( $c, "image/tiff" )
```
- "Apply mask M to coverage A, B, and C" (fusion):
```
for $s  in ( A, B, C ), $m in ( M )
return encode( $s * $m, "image/tiff" )
```
- "Create 3D x/y/t coverage from input stream $1":
```
for $t in ( TemperatureCube )
return encode(
  coverage MySatelliteDatacube
  domain
    crs "EPSG:4326+OGC:unixTime" with
    Lat regular (10:30) resolution 0.5
      interpolation linear,
    Lon regular (10:30) resolution 0.5
      interpolation linear,
    Date irregular ( "2017-01-01", "2017-02-01",
                     "2017-07-01", "2017-11-01" )
  range type panchromatic: integer
  range decode( $1 ),
  "netcdf"
)
```
- "Timeseries of temperature average over Berlin":
```
for $t in ( TemperatureCube )
return encode(
   avg( $t[ Lat(52.51: 52.53), Lon(13:39:13.41) ] ),
   "json"
)
```

- "Absolute of wind speed":
```
for $w in ( WindCube )
return encode(
   sqrt( $w.u * $w.u + $w.v * $w.v ),
   "netcdf"
)
```
- "Logarithm of intergalactic matter temperature ":
```
for $c in ( UniverseTemperature )
return encode(
   switch
      case $temp > 0 return log( $temp )
      default        return 0,
   "netcdf"
)
```

The syntax of WCPS tentatively is aligned with XQuery – a majority of geo metadata are stored in XML, so naturally queried with XPath / XQuery. This allows for an integration of the two languages into a seamless data / metadata continuum. Furthermore, XQuery is also suited for querying JSON structures, so future oriented.

V. Related Standards

The coverage standards, aligned between ISO and OGC, are generally accepted and widely implemented. In this section we inspect related standards.

With SQL Part 15 (*Multi-Dimensional Arrays, MDA*) [9], ISO has added multi-dimensional arrays to the relational model. MDA defines how attribute values can be arrays of arbitrary extent and number of dimensions, including operational support in the SQL query language. These arrays are domain-agnostic and not aware of spatial nor temporal semantics. The OGC/ISO *Web Coverage Processing Service* (WCPS) language [3][12] is different in that (i) it adopts an XQuery syntax flavor to be better aligned with the many geo metadata stored worldwide and (ii) is aware of space and time, knowing, e.g., about regular and irregular grids. However, the operational semantics is the same as SQL/MDA, except that WCPS is space/time semantics aware. This is exploited, for example, in the rasdaman array database system where WCPS queries internally get translated, with the help of geo-specific metadata, into SQL/MDA style queries which ultimately are executed in the federated engine [9].

CoverageJSON [34] is an OGC community standard for datacubes. Despite its name it is not the JSON encoding of coverages, but an incompatible variant – a "hijacking" of the normatively defined name "coverage".

W3C QB4ST [1] establishes a datacube ontology, expressed in Resource Data Framework (RDF) syntax and queryable through the RDF query language, SPARQL. QB4ST only addresses datacube metadata, but not the "payload" itself. While an interesting approach in itself, with a potential to bridge into the Semantic Web world, QB4ST likewise is not aligned with the coverage standards.

While focus here is on the coverage data model we briefly address service APIs. The first and foremost coverage service standard is the *Web Coverage Service* (WCS). In its core, it offers only subset extraction and format encoding so as to keep the implementation hurdle as low as possible. A series of optional extensions adds further functionality. Particularly noteworthy is WCPS, a high-level geo datacube query language.

Further relevant standards include *Web Map Service* (WMS) for map visualization. WMS and WCS differ in that WMS focuses on map visualization, hence returns colors (such as color shading for elevation levels) whereas WCS delivers the true data (such as elevation), suitable for further processing and analytics by tools.

Some further standards, such as *Environmental Data Retrieval* (EDR) [24], use (incompatible) CoverageJSON.

OAPI-Coverages offer access to coverages based on OpenAPI technology and http. Functionality is mostly parallel to WCS. The specification is draft since about 2018, but still incomplete, with random changes, without a comprehensive example set nor a test suite, and altogether not suspected to become OGC standard in the near future.

Another recent OGC activity has started work on a *GeoDataCube* API which itself consists of two incompatible API definitions, openEO and OAPI-Processes. It is likewise an early-stage draft under discussion.

The European legal framework for a common spatial data infrastructure, *INSPIRE*, relies on the OGC coverage standards, including WCS and WCPS [20].

VI. Conclusion

Standardization not only fosters interoperability, but also offers guidance to implementers, thereby accelerating development cycles. Conversely, scientific and technological progress in the understanding of generation, management, and use of coverage structures nurtures the standards continuously. Coverages have matured in concepts and implementation, culminating in CIS 1.1. The integration of both is to become the next version of ISO 19123-2.

This paper provides a lookout on this new standard synoptically on three levels of abstraction: the concepts and terminology of ISO 19123-1, the logical-level coverage data model of ISO 19123-2 which currently is under adoption vote, and the physical (encoding) level of ISO 19123-2 providing XML and (revised) JSON support, in addition to the existing binary coverage formats. The first ISO vote ("ballot") was finished with only minor comments. These have been worked in, making the specification ready for the next stage ballot (Draft International Standard, DIS). From DIS status onwards only editorial changes will be allowed. Altogether, the document can be considered quite stable.

Coverage data and service standards have an immense impact on Big Geo Data, in particular datacubes – examples include 1-D sensor timeseries; 2-D satellite, airborne drone and underwater data, on Earth or on planetary bodies; 3-D x/y/t image timeseries over all these; 3-D x/y/z geophysical data, such as with oil, gas, and water exploration; 4-D x/y/z/t atmospheric and ocean data; and general n-D statistical datacubes. These few examples may illustrate the importance of coverages for geo data in science and industry.

The contribution, therefore, aims at spreading information about coverages in general and datacubes in particular, and conversely solicits feedback by the community into standardization.

ACKNOWLEDGEMENT

The rasdaman team is doing brilliant work in shaping a datacube engine implementing the standards comprehensively. The author is grateful for the many intense discussions in OGC. Work in part was supported by NATO SPS Cube4EnvSec, EU FAIRiCUBE and EU EFRE FAIRgeo.

REFERENCES

[1] R. Atkinson, *"QB4ST: RDF Data Cube extensions for spatio-temporal components"*. W3C Working Group Note / OGC Document, pp. 16-142, 2017, https://www.w3.org/TR/qb4st, [retrieved: 04, 2025].

[2] P. Baumann, S. Feyzabadi, C. Jucovschi, *"Putting Pixels in Place: A Storage Language for Scientific Data"*. Proc. IEEE ICDM Workshop on Spatial and Spatiotemporal Data Mining (SSTDM'10), December 14, 2010, Sydney, Australia, pp. 194 – 2012010.

[3] P. Baumann, *"The OGC Web Coverage Processing Service (WCPS) Standard"*. Geoinformatica, 14(4)2010, pp. 447-479.

[4] P. Baumann, *"A Database Array Algebra for Spatio-Temporal Data and Beyond"*. Intl. Workshop on Next Generation Information Technologies and Systems (NGITS), July 5-7, 1999, Zikhron Yaakov, Israel, LNCS 1649, pp. 173-189

[5] P. Baumann, *"Enhanced Calendar Support for Temporal Datacube Queries"*. Transactions in GIS, 28, pp. 2089-2112, DOI: 10.1111/TGIS.13215.

[6] P. Baumann, *"On the Analysis-Readiness of Spatio-Temporal Earth Data and Suggestions for its Enhancement"*. Environmental Modelling and Software, Volume 176, 2024, DOI: 10.1016/j.envsoft.2024.106017.

[7] A. Dumitru, V. Merticariu, P. Baumann, *"Exploring cloud opportunities from an array database perspective"*. ACM SIGMOD DanaC, 2014, pp. 10:1-10:4.

[8] R. Haag, *"Local Quantum Physics: Fields, Particles, Algebras"*. Springer, 1996.

[9] ISO, *"Information technology - Database languages - SQL - Part 15: Multi-Dimensional Arrays"*, ISO 9075-15:2019.

[10] ISO, *"Geographic information - Schema for coverage geometry and functions - Part 1: Coverage implementation schema"*. IS 19123-1:2023, https://www.iso.org/standard/70743.html, [retrieved: 04, 2025].

[11] ISO, *"Geographic information - Schema for coverage geometry and functions - Part 2: Coverage implementation schema"*. IS 19123-2:2018, https://www.iso.org/obp/ui/#iso:std:iso:19123:-2:ed-1:v1:en, [retrieved: 04, 2025].

[12] ISO, *"Geographic information - Schema for coverage geometry and functions - Part 3: Processing fundamentals"*. ISO 19123-3, https://committee.iso.org/sites/tc211/home/projects/projects---complete-list/iso-19123-3.html, [retrieved: 04, 2025].

[13] ISO, *"Geographic information – Referencing by coordinates"*. IS 19111:2019, https://www.iso.org/standard/74039.html, [retrieved: 04, 2025].

[14] ISO, *"Geographic information - Spatial schema"*. ISO 19107:2019, https://committee.iso.org/sites/tc211/home/projects/projects---complete-list/iso-19107.html, [retrieved: 04, 2025].

[15] ISO, *"Geographic information - Geography Markup Language (GML) Part 2, "Extended schemas and encoding rules"*, ISO 19136-2:2015.

[16] ISO, *"Geographic information - Temporal schema"*. ISO 19108:2002, https://www.iso.org/standard/26013.html, [retrieved: 04, 2025].

[17] C. Jucovschi, P. Baumann, S. Stancu-Mara, *"Speeding up Array Query Processing by Just-In-Time Compilation"*. IEEE Intl. Workshop on Spatial and Spatiotemporal Data Mining (SSTDM), Pisa, Italy, 2008, pp. 408 – 413.

[18] V. Merticariu and P. Baumann, *"Massively Distributed Datacube Processing"*. IEEE Geoscience and Remote Sensing Society (IGARSS), Yokohama, Japan, 2019.

[19] D. Misev and P. Baumann, *"Enhancing Science Support in SQL"*. IEEE Big Data Workshop on Data and Computational Science Technologies for Earth Science Research, Santa Clara, USA, 2015, pp. 2201 – 2204.

[20] N.n., *"INSPIRE Coverages Demystified"*. https://inspire-wcs.eu, [retrieved: 04, 2025].

[21] N.n., *"JSON Schema"*. https://json-schema.org, [retrieved: 04, 2025].

[22] N.n., *"EarthServer Datacube Federation"*. https://earthserver.world, [retrieved: 04, 2025].

[23] N.n., *"Say Hello to Datacubes*. https://ai-cu.be/chatcube, [retrieved: 04, 2025].

[24] OGC, *"OGC API - Environmental Data Retrieval Standard*. Document 19-086r6, http://www.opengis.net/doc/IS/ogcapi-edr-1/1.1, [retrieved: 04, 2025].

[25] OGC, *"SWE Common Data Model Encoding Standard 2.0*. Document 08-094r1, https://portal.ogc.org/files/?artifact_id=41157, [retrieved: 04, 2025].

[26] OGC, *"Web Coverage Processing Service (WCPS) Language Interface Standard*. Version 1.1, OGC Document 08-068r3, https://docs.ogc.org/is/08-068r3/08-068r3.html, [retrieved: 04, 2025].

[27] OGC, *"Coverage Implementation Schema"*, version 1.1.1. OGC 09-146r8, http://docs.opengeospatial.org/is/09-146r8/09-146r8.html, [retrieved: 04, 2025].

[28] OGC, *"Abstract Specification Topic 6.1 – Schema for Coverage Geometry and Functions – Part 1: Fundamentals"*. OGC Document 07-011r2, https://docs.ogc.org/as/07-011r2/07-011r2.pdf , [retrieved: 04, 2025].

[29] OGC, *"Abstract Specification Topic 6.3 – Schema for Coverage Geometry and Functions – Part 3: Processing Fundamentals"*. OGC Document 21-060r2, https://docs.ogc.org/as/21-060r2/21-060r2.pdf, [retrieved: 04, 2025].

[30] OGC, *"Registered WCS Implementations"*. https://portal.ogc.org/public_ogc/compliance/implementing.php?&specid=533, [retrieved: 04, 2025].

[31] OGC, *"Web Coverage Service (WCS)"*. https://www.ogc.org/publications/standard/wcs, [retrieved: 04, 2025].

[32] OGC, *"CRS Definition Resolver"*. https://external.ogc.org/twiki_public/CRSdefinitionResolver/WebHome, [retrieved: 04, 2025].

[33] N.n., *"OGC Spatio-Temporal Coverage / Datacube Standards"*. https://myogc.org/go/coveragesDWG, [retrieved: 04, 2025].

[34] OGC, *"OGC CoverageJSON Community Standard"*. OGC 21-069r2, https://docs.ogc.org/cs/21-069r2/21-069r2.html, [retrieved: 04, 2025].

[35] OGC, *"Coverage Implementation Schema – ReferenceableGridCoverage Extension with Corrigendum"*. OGC 16-083r3, http://docs.opengeospatial.org/is/16-083r3/16-083r3.html, [retrieved: 04, 2025].

[36] OGP, *"EPSG Geodetic Parameter Dataset"*. https://epsg.org

[37] rasdaman team, *"rasdaman"*. https://rasdaman.org, DOI: https://doi.org/10.5281/zenodo.1040170, [retrieved: 04, 2025]

[38] Regenstrief Institute, *"UCUM"*. https://ucum.org, [retrieved: 04, 2025].

Coordinates Are Just Features: Rethinking Spatial Dependence in Geospatial Modeling

Yameng Guo
Department of Business Informatics and Operations Management
Ghent University
Gent, Belgium
Seppe vanden Broucke
Department of Business Informatics and Operations Management
Ghent University
Gent, Belgium
Research Centre for Information Systems Engineering
KU Leuven
Leuven, Belgium
e-mail: {yameng.guo | seppe.vandenbroucke}@ugent.be

***Abstract*—Geospatial inference is crucial for various spatial prediction tasks, where the choice of modeling approach significantly impacts both inference performance and computational efficiency. Traditional geospatial statistical models, such as Geographically Weighted Regression (GWR) and Kriging, explicitly account for spatial dependence, but often come with high computational costs. In this study, we argue that treating coordinates as standard input features can yield competitive inference performance while significantly reducing computational costs when selecting a predictive model with an appropriate level of complexity. To support this, we compare geospatial statistical models with various machine learning approaches, including linear methods, tree ensemble methods, hybrid kernel-based methods that incorporate explicit geospatial learning, and a recent state-of-the-art tabular deep learning model—TabPFN—to assess their effectiveness in spatial prediction tasks (to the best of our knowledge, this is the first study to investigate the performance of TabPFN in the geospatial domain using explicit coordinate inputs). Our results demonstrate that when coordinates are sufficiently informative, tree-based ensemble models and tabular deep learning can implicitly capture spatial dependence without requiring explicit geospatial modeling, achieving superior performance whilst maintaining a reasonable computational cost.**

***Keywords-geospatial regression*; *ensembles modeling*; *spatial statistics*; *comparative performance*.**

I. Introduction

Spatial inference plays an increasingly critical role across various industries, including environmental science [1][2], urban planning [3], and disaster management [4][5], where predicting unobserved values at specific locations is essential.

Over the years, researchers have developed two primary approaches towards modeling spatial inference. *Explicit* approaches rely on the principle that geographically closer observations tend to be more similar. Traditional methods, such as Kriging [6][7] and Geographically Weighted Regression (GWR) [8], incorporate this principle through variograms or distance-decay weighting, offering both interpretability and predictive power which have been widely adopted for spatial interpolation and regression tasks.

Alternatively, Machine Learning (ML) models have emerged as powerful tools for handling large and complex datasets. These models treat coordinates as standard input features, allowing them to capture spatial dependence *implicitly*. Among them, tree-based ensembles—such as random forests and gradient boosting machines—excel at modeling nonlinear relationships and variable interactions. By incorporating spatial features into their predictive framework, they achieve competitive performance without the need for explicit geospatial modeling.

A hybrid approach has also gained traction, combining the interpretability of spatial models with the predictive power of machine learning. Techniques that integrate Kriging with ML-based kernels have demonstrated promising results by leveraging both domains' strengths [9][10].

The advancement of Tabular Deep Learning (TDL) further expands spatial inference possibilities. Whilst typically confronted with challenges, such as the need for extensive hyperparameter tuning and risk of overfitting, especially on small datasets, pre-trained models have appeared which aim to offer a robust alternative. For instance, the recently developed Prior-Data Fitted Network (PFN) Transformer [11], designed for tabular data, is pre-trained offline, enabling supervised learning on small datasets without additional hyperparameters tuning.

While traditional geospatial statistical models provide a rigorous framework for modeling geospatial dependence, they often struggle to balance predictive performance and computational efficiency, particularly with large datasets or nonlinear relationships. Conversely, TDL and ML—especially tree-based ensemble models—offer strong predictive performance with reasonable training and tuning costs as these models avoid constructing the geospatial distance function explicitly in a large scale.

Therefore, in this study, we reflect on the way traditional geospatial statistics leverage the distance matrix to model geospatial dependence and argue for the efficiency of considering the coordinates as just standard input features for spatial inference tasks. We do so by presenting a comprehensive comparison of geospatial statistical models (e.g., Kriging and GWR), machine learning models (with a focus on tree ensembles), hybrid kernel-based models, and a state-of-the-art tabular deep learning model, i.e., TabPFN. Summarized, this work presents the following key contributions:

- We conduct a comparative experiment across statistical, ML, hybrid and TDL methods, with an emphasis on tree ensembles and TabPFN, to assess predictive performance and training efficiency;
- We analyze the practical considerations of training and tuning these models in real-world geospatial applications;
- We reflect on risks of putting a large emphasis on explicit spatial dependence usage, especially when coordinate information is sufficiently informative or strong ML models are available;
- The source code and datasets used in our work are publicly available on our GitHub page [12].

This paper is structured as follows: Section II provides a detailed explanation of related methodologies used in the field of geospatial reference. Section III introduces the experimental setup, covering the datasets, models, hyperparameter grids, and evaluation metrics used in the comparison. Section IV presents the results and discusses the effectiveness of all methods. The conclusion and future work are provided in Section V.

II. Methodology Review

This section clarifies the mechanisms underlying geospatial statistical models, ML, hybrid models and TabPFN, i.e., the techniques we will compare in this work, as well as their distinct ways to incorporate spatial dependence principles. By examining the mechanisms of these approaches, we aim to establish a foundation for comparing their performance and applicability in geospatial inference tasks.

A. Spatial Dependence-Based Models

Kriging and GWR are the most representative models in this group. Although they both rely heavily on the principle of spatial dependence, where observations close to each other are more similar than those farther apart, the emphasis of spatial relationships modeling of these two models are slightly varied.

1) Kriging: The main goal of Kriging is to quantify **spatial autocorrelation** to model and estimate the target values by using a variogram based on the assumption of jointly Gaussian distribution of the data, and then computes optimal weights for predictions by solving a system of linear equations, ensuring that predictions are best linear unbiased estimates.

The Kriging [13] predictor can be defined as:

$$\hat{Z}(\mathbf{s}_0) = \sum_{i=1}^{n} \lambda_i Z(\mathbf{s}_i),$$

where:

- $Z(\mathbf{s}_i)$: Observed value at location $\mathbf{s}_i$,
- λ_i: Weight assigned to $Z(\mathbf{s}_i)$, determined by spatial correlation.
- n: Number of observed locations.

The spatial correlation between locations is modeled using a **variogram** [14] which is defined as:

$$\gamma(h) = \frac{1}{2}\text{Var}[Z(\mathbf{s}) - Z(\mathbf{s} + \mathbf{h})],$$

where:

- h: Distance between two locations,
- $\gamma(h)$: Semi-variance at lag h.

By using the variogram, we can calculate the covariance matrix to solve the Kriging system,

$$C(\mathbf{s}_i, \mathbf{s}_j)\Lambda = C(\mathbf{s}_i, \mathbf{s}_0)$$

where Λ indicates the weight assigned to known nodes for the interpolation of an unknown node $\mathbf{s}_0$.

Based on the definition above, Kriging provides an estimate of prediction uncertainty that is defined as:

$$\sigma^2_{\text{Kriging}}(\mathbf{s}_0) = C(\mathbf{s}_0, \mathbf{s}_0) - \sum_{i=1}^{n} \lambda_i C(\mathbf{s}_i, \mathbf{s}_0) - \mu.$$

2) GWR: Compared with Kriging focusing on spatial autocorrelation and estimating the proximity similarity, GWR [15] is more based on the assumption of spatial heterogeneity. Though GWR also utilizes the distance matrix as weights to model the spatial variation, it fits a separate regression model locally at each location, weighting observations based on their proximity using a kernel function (e.g., Gaussian or bisquare), which allows for spatial variation in relationships between dependent and independent variables.

Essentially, the GWR can be defined as a linear combination:

$$y_i = \beta_0(\mathbf{s}_i) + \sum_{k=1}^{p} \beta_k(\mathbf{s}_i) x_{ki} + \epsilon_i,$$

where:

- y_i: Dependent variable at location $\mathbf{s}_i$,
- $\beta_0(\mathbf{s}_i)$ and $\beta_k(\mathbf{s}_i)$: Intercept and coefficient (for the k-th independent variable) at location $\mathbf{s}_i$,
- x_{ki}: Independent variable at location $\mathbf{s}_i$,
- ϵ_i: Random error term at location $\mathbf{s}_i$,
- p: Number of independent variables.

The regression coefficients $\boldsymbol{\beta}(\mathbf{s}_i)$ are estimated by solving the weighted least squares problem, which is expressed as

$$\boldsymbol{\beta}(\mathbf{s}_i) = \left(\mathbf{X}^\top \mathbf{W}(\mathbf{s}_i)\mathbf{X}\right)^{-1} \mathbf{X}^\top \mathbf{W}(\mathbf{s}_i)\mathbf{y},$$

where $\mathbf{W}(\mathbf{s}_i)$ represents the diagonal weight matrix of the weights assigned to the location which is close to the point of interest.

To estimate the weight matrix, two kernel functions are commonly used, including:

- Gaussian kernel:

$$w_{ij} = \exp\left(-\frac{d_{ij}^2}{2b^2}\right),$$

- Bisquare kernel:

$$w_{ij} = \begin{cases} \left(1 - \left(\frac{d_{ij}}{b}\right)^2\right)^2 & \text{if } d_{ij} \leq b, \\ 0 & \text{if } d_{ij} > b, \end{cases}$$

where:

- d_{ij}: Distance between locations $\mathbf{s}_i$ and $\mathbf{s}_j$,
- b: Bandwidth parameter controlling the spatial extent of the weights.

Classical GWR models the local geospatial variation under the assumption of the same spatial scale, while a modification of GWR, namely Multiscale Geographically Weighted Regression (MGWR) [16], provides a more flexible and scalable framework by allowing different processes to operate at different spatial scales.

Although Kriging and GWR are widely used for spatial inference tasks, the application scenarios are slightly different. Kriging is more applied in spatial interpolation, such as estimating soil properties [17], pollutant concentrations [18][19], or precipitation levels [20], while GWR is more commonly applied in spatial regression scenarios, such as modeling house prices [21], socioeconomic factors [22], or environmental influences [23], where relationships vary spatially.

B. Machine Learning Models

Machine learning methods provide a data-driven approach to modeling, focusing on capturing patterns and relationships within the data without explicit assumptions about spatial dependence.

Typically, given a dataset $\{X, Y\}$ consisting of instances $\{x_i, y_i\}$ from a certain distribution $P(Y|X)$, the goal is to learn a function f that maps input features $\mathbf{x} \in \mathbb{R}^d$ to an output $y \in \mathbb{R}$. The general objective is:

$$\hat{f} = \arg\min_{f} \frac{1}{n} \sum_{i=1}^{n} \ell(y_i, f(\mathbf{x}_i)),$$

where:

- $\ell(y_i, f(\mathbf{x}_i))$: Loss function measuring the error between predicted $f(\mathbf{x}_i)$ and actual y_i,
- n: Number of training instances.

To minimize the loss function (e.g., mean squared error for regression or cross-entropy for classification), a wide range of optimization algorithms, such as gradient descent and tree-based heuristics are developed to capture complex linear or nonlinear relationships between features. Specifically, tree ensemble models often outperform simpler models on structured data by building a series of decision trees and updating iteratively to minimize the loss,

$$f_m(\mathbf{x}) = f_{m-1}(\mathbf{x}) + \gamma_m h_m(\mathbf{x}),$$

where:

- $f_m(\mathbf{x})$: Prediction at iteration m,
- $h_m(\mathbf{x})$: Weak learner (e.g., a shallow decision tree),
- γ_m: Step size for the weak learner.

Unlike the spatial dependence-based models which integrate the geospatial information explicitly, machine learning models theoretically are available for all kinds of tabular data inference tasks, but can be applied to the geospatial field easily by engineering the geographical features (e.g., raw coordinates, distance to landmarks, elevation, or land use types) and including location information (i.e., coordinates in most cases).

C. Hybrid Kernel-Based Models

Recent advances have sought to explore hybrid approaches to boost the strengths of handling of spatial dependence.

The most straightforward trail is to consider Kriging as an extension of GWR, but train these two components separately. Following this basic hybrid idea, Geographically Weighted Regression Kriging (GWRK) [24] was developed and its efficiency proven on datasets from different domains [25][26].

Another possible combination is merging Kriging with ML models. By using Kriging as the base model and ML models as either internal learners for residuals [27] or as a super learner [9], this hybrid approach helps mitigate the limitations of both model types, allowing effectively incorporating spatial relationships while enhancing predictive performance.

Moreover, the variogram function in Kriging or a local linear function are not the only choices to model geospatial dependence. E.g., Gaussian Processes (GPs) can also model spatial dependencies explicitly through kernel functions and by weighting proximal observations spatially. The Gaussian kernel is defined as:

$$k(\mathbf{s}_i, \mathbf{s}_j) = \exp\left(-\frac{\|\mathbf{s}_i - \mathbf{s}_j\|^2}{2\ell^2}\right),$$

where:

- $k(\mathbf{s}_i, \mathbf{s}_j)$: Covariance between points $\mathbf{s}_i$ and $\mathbf{s}_j$,
- ℓ: Length scale parameter, determining how quickly the correlation decays with distance,
- $\|\mathbf{s}_i - \mathbf{s}_j\|$: Euclidean distance between points $\mathbf{s}_i$ and $\mathbf{s}_j$.

In theory, by embedding spatial correlation into machine learning workflows, these kernel-based methods enhance predictive performance while retaining the capacity to model non-linearities and complex interactions.

D. TabPFN

TabPFN is a single Transformer pre-trained to approximate probabilistic inference using a designed prior based on Bayesian Neural Networks. It is built on Prior-Data Fitted Networks (PFNs) [28], which can directly sample from and approximate the Posterior Predictive Distribution (PPD). Unlike conventional neural networks and tree ensembles that rely on fixed structures, such as neural layers or constrained tree depth, TabPFN [11] incorporates not only a Bayesian Neural Network-based prior [29][30] but also Structural Causal Models [31][32] to capture complex feature dependencies and analyze underlying causal mechanisms, particularly in tabular data. It has demonstrated superior inference performance across various datasets spanning different domains. As a pre-trained Transformer, TabPFN embeds all input features as tokens and processes them through a feed-forward mechanism, treating coordinates as standard input features alongside others.

In summary, these three types of models leverage geospatial dependence in two distinct ways: either by directly integrating geographic information as a distance matrix to model interactions between the target point and its proximal neighbors or by engineering proximity as hard features, incorporating location information as standard features while ignoring autocorrelation among points. Although a vast body of literature applies these methods to tackle various real-world challenges, researchers rarely discuss the advantages and efficiency of explicitly using spatial dependence. Models like Kriging and GWR often entail high computational costs and are susceptible to singular distance matrices, which can render the Kriging system or covariance matrix unsolvable.

In contrast, ML and TDL models mitigate computational cost and solvability concerns, as they do not require solving linear systems based on distance matrices. Instead, they directly model the mapping function from tabular features and approximate the prior distribution of the given dataset, which is particularly efficient with larger datasets.

To uncover the most efficient approach for different geospatial inference tasks, we conducted an extensive experiment evaluating various models in terms of predictive performance and computational cost. We hope this study provides new insights into modeling geospatial variables and selecting practical models for real-world applications, especially under the presence of stronger ML models, as well as very recent TDL approaches.

III. Experimental Setup

In this section, we describe an exhaustive experiment to compare a wide range of ML models with other well-known geospatial predictive modeling techniques, covering a collection of real-life datasets.

A. Datasets

There are two primary types of public datasets used in this work to evaluate the performance of geospatial statistical models and machine learning models, i.e., **property datasets** obtained from Kaggle and biology related datasets from the **R package Spatstat.data**.

All these datasets contain at least coordinates (either geographical or geometric coordinates), but not all of them have additional features, such as hedonic features of property data. To validate the capability of various models on capturing geospatial information and the utility of geospatial dependence, we divide the dataset further into two categories that consist of coordinates-only and full-feature datasets. Each dataset was cleaned to remove duplicate values and was re-scaled so features fall in a range of 0 to 1. We partitioned each dataset into a training set (70%), a validation set (10%) and a test set (20%). Note that when a timestamp was available (such as for real estate datasets), we perform the train-validation-test split in a temporal manner (i.e., chronologically).

Moreover, we carefully process the coordinates to ensure reliable geospatial inference. First, all coordinates are converted into a Cartesian coordinate system according to the dataset's geographical location, ensuring unified features to each model, and avoiding potential spherical distortions on statistic models which are based on distance matrices. Specifically, for GWR and Kriging, we keep the Cartesian coordinates unscaled to maintain consistent Euclidean distance calculations. For ML and TDL models, we scale the coordinates similarly to the other input features.

B. Models

As shown in Table I, we select a diverse set of models that cover different methodological categories to comprehensively evaluate the effectiveness of geospatial statistical models, ML and TDL approaches. The selected models are categorized into machine learning, TDL, kernel-based methods, and geospatial statistical models.

Machine learning models include Linear Regression with Ridge regularization [33], Support Vector Machine (SVM) [34][35][36]) and tree ensemble methods (Random Forest (RMF) [37], XGBoost [38], LightGBM (LGBM) [39], and CatBoost [40]). Strictly speaking, the kernel-based models covering Gaussian Processes [41], Tweedie Regression [42], and the hybrid Kriging-LGBM approach could also be placed under the ML group. But since they combine machine learning and geospatial statistics, we categorize them separately. The hybrid model—Kriging-LGBM [27], is the most representative in this group. It uses a LightGBM regressor as an internal kernel and then gathers and processes geospatial information with Kriging on target residuals. Moreover, a recent state-of-the-art tabular deep learning model—TabPFN—is also included in this experiment. To the best of our knowledge, this is the first study to investigate the performance of TabPFN in the geospatial domain using explicit coordinate inputs. Finally, we include the most classical geospatial statistical models, i.e., GWR [15], and Regression Kriging [43][44][45].

Each model's hyperparameters are tuned according to the grid values listed in the table, to ensure a fair and comprehensive evaluation across different modeling approaches. Hyperparameters for all models were systematically tuned on the validation set using root mean square error (RMSE). The best parameter combination was then used to test on the completely unseen test set to report the evaluation results. All models share the same data partitions. Note that TabPFN claims to be able to reach competitive results without any hyperparameter tuning, so for this pre-trained model, no tuning was performed.

C. Comparative Setup

To clarify the extent of importance of coordinates in various inference tasks and assess the efficiency of different models in terms of leveraging spatial locations, we evaluate the model performance under two main dataset configurations: one using only spatial coordinates, and the other one incorporating both coordinates and additional features when available.

TABLE I
OVERVIEW OF MODELS AND THEIR HYPERPARAMETERS USED IN THE COMPARISON.

Category	Type	Model	Hyperparameters
Machine Learning	Linear	Ridge LR	α: [0.1, 0.2, ..., 0.9]
		SVM	C: [1, 11, ..., 101]
			ϵ: [0.1, 0.2, ..., 0.9]
	Tree Ensemble	RandomForest	min_samples_split: [2, 3, 5]
			min_samples_leaf: [3, 5, 10]
		XGBoost	learning_rate: [0.1, 0.01, 0.005]
			reg_alpha: [0.0, 0.1, ..., 1.0]
			reg_lambda: [0.0, 0.1, ..., 1.0]
		LGBM	learning_rate: [0.1, 0.01, 0.005]
			reg_alpha: [0.0, 0.1, ..., 1.0]
			reg_lambda: [0.0, 0.1, ..., 1.0]
		CatBoost	iterations: [100, 200]
			learning_rate: [0.001, 0.005, 0.01, 0.05, 0.1]
			l2_leaf_reg: [0.1, 0.5, 1, 5]
Kernel Based	Gaussian	Gaussian Process	kernel: C(1.0) * RBF(length_scale_bounds=(1e-2, 1e2))
			alpha: [0.1, 0.2, ..., 0.9]
	Power	Tweedie	power: [0, 1, 1.2, 1.5, 1.8, 2, 3]
			alpha: [0.0, 0.1, ..., 0.9] + [2, 5, 8, 10]
	ML Kernel	Kriging LGBM	Kriging params: nlags = [30, 60, 90, 120]
			variogram_model: ["gaussian", "linear"]
			Lightgbm params: reg_alpha: [0.0, 0.5, 1.0]
			reg_lambda: [0.0, 0.5, 1.0]
			learning_rate: [0.1, 0.01, 0.005]
Geospatial Statistics	Geospatial Heterogeneity	GWR	best bandwidth for kernel
	Geospatial Autocorrelation	Kriging	nlags: [30, 60, 90, 120]
			variogram_model: ["gaussian", "linear"]
Deep Learning	Tabular DL	TabPFN	—

The primary evaluation metric to quantify the predictive performance of each model is the Root Mean Squared Error (RMSE). Additionally, we assess the computational efficiency by measuring the training time per model per run during the hyperparameter tuning. This dual assessment allows us to analyze the trade-offs between model performance and computational cost, providing insights into the practicality of each approach in geospatial prediction tasks.

The experiment is conducted on an Intel Core i9-13900 (13th Gen) CPU with 64 GB of RAM and an NVIDIA RTX A5000 GPU.

IV. DISCUSSION

All the results are shown in Table II and Table III. Since Regression Kriging only accepts coordinates as input, its predictive results remain the same for both datasets, with and without hedonic features.

Interestingly, we find that TabPFN consistently achieves the lowest RMSE across both datasets with hedonic features and without (coordinates only). In particular, on datasets with hedonic features, TabPFN outperforms all other models virtually all cases, which serves as one of the first illustrations of the competitive power of this recent approach in the domain of geospatial inference.

Tree ensemble models, especially LightGBM, XGBoost, and CatBoost, rank second. Although they do not surpass TabPFN, their performance is still clearly better than geospatial statistical models. In contrast, linear models, including Ridge Regression and SVM, consistently yield the worst predictions among all models, indicating that ML models can sufficiently capturing geospatial dependencies without having to deal with coordinates in a specific manner, as long as the chosen ML model is strong enough.

Notably, Gaussian Processes, Kriging, and the Kriging LGBM Regressor, which explicitly utilize geospatial information, also demonstrate strong performance on a few datasets where only coordinates were included. However, they do

TABLE II
COMPARISON OF MODEL PERFORMANCE (RMSE) ACROSS DIFFERENT DATASETS WITH **ONLY COORDINATE FEATURES**.

Data	Ridge LR	SVM	GWR	Kriging	Kriging LGBM	Gaussian P	Tweedie	RMF	LGBM	XGBoost	CatBoost	TabPFN
anemones	0.1756	0.1870	0.1841	0.1826	0.1826	0.1804	0.1755	0.1753	**0.1747**	0.1779	0.1766	0.1810
beijing	0.1833	0.1342	0.1390	0.1284	0.1284	0.1380	0.1833	0.1296	0.1279	0.1279	0.1273	**0.1272**
bronzefilter	0.1736	0.2364	0.2133	0.1835	0.1835	0.1754	0.1622	0.1553	0.1623	0.1615	0.1795	**0.1535**
dubai	0.1941	0.1584	0.1668	**0.1373**	**0.1373**	0.1539	0.1911	0.1384	0.1448	0.1413	0.1404	0.1391
london	0.0885	0.0717	0.0676	**0.0641**	**0.0641**	0.0704	0.0885	0.0643	0.0650	0.0652	0.0667	0.0653
longleaf	0.3114	0.2978	0.2546	0.2750	0.2750	0.2923	0.2531	0.2641	0.2798	0.2639	0.3037	**0.2451**
melbourne	0.0944	0.0708	0.0751	0.0603	0.0602	0.0652	0.0922	0.0608	0.0610	0.0599	0.0599	**0.0588**
newyork	0.1104	0.1018	0.0955	0.0964	0.0964	0.0981	0.1104	0.0928	0.0931	0.0930	0.0939	**0.0925**
paris	0.0216	0.0615	0.0208	0.0213	0.0213	0.0217	0.0216	0.0205	0.0203	0.0203	0.0203	**0.0202**
perth	0.0555	0.0444	0.0350	0.0348	0.0348	0.0384	0.0548	**0.0339**	0.0340	0.0341	0.0344	0.0340
seattle	0.1448	0.1181	0.1147	0.1101	0.1101	0.1154	0.1448	**0.1092**	0.1096	0.1095	0.1103	0.1100
spruces	0.2038	0.2361	0.1984	0.2284	0.2284	**0.1889**	0.1942	0.2204	**0.1889**	0.2004	0.1911	0.1928
waka	0.1240	0.1398	0.1237	0.1295	0.1295	0.1233	0.1235	0.1293	0.1235	0.1234	0.1232	**0.1230**

TABLE III
COMPARISON OF MODEL PERFORMANCE (RMSE) ACROSS DIFFERENT DATASETS WITH **COORDINATE AND ADDITIONAL FEATURES**.

Data	Ridge LR	SVM	GWR	Kriging	Kriging LGBM	Gaussian P	Tweedie	RMF	LGBM	XGBoost	CatBoost	TabPFN
beijing	0.1718	0.1378	0.1329	0.1284	0.1285	0.1608	0.1693	0.1031	**0.1003**	0.1045	0.1036	0.1008
dubai	0.1801	0.1982	0.1852	0.1373	0.1303	0.1982	0.1905	0.1194	0.1202	0.1201	0.1122	**0.1038**
london	0.0846	0.0757	0.0859	0.0641	0.0628	0.0776	0.0846	0.0589	0.0586	0.0588	0.0602	**0.0562**
melbourne	0.0803	0.0702	0.0673	0.0603	0.0389	0.0687	0.0581	0.0326	0.0296	0.0313	0.0291	**0.0263**
newyork	0.0863	0.0759	0.0721	0.0822	0.0726	0.0751	0.1002	0.0565	0.0562	0.0560	0.0561	**0.0532**
paris	0.0213	0.0246	0.0206	0.0213	0.0213	0.0217	0.0214	0.0202	0.0202	**0.0201**	**0.0201**	**0.0201**
perth	0.0494	0.0460	0.0355	0.0348	0.0324	0.0375	0.0489	**0.0270**	0.0277	0.0274	0.0282	0.0275
seattle	0.1252	0.1100	0.0966	0.1101	0.0981	0.1134	0.1253	0.0838	0.0820	0.0836	0.0831	**0.0790**

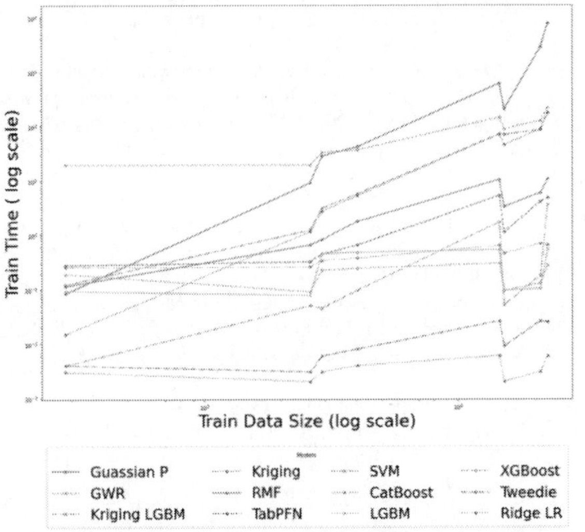

Figure 1. All features: visualizations of training time (s) per hyperparameter run across different models in log scale.

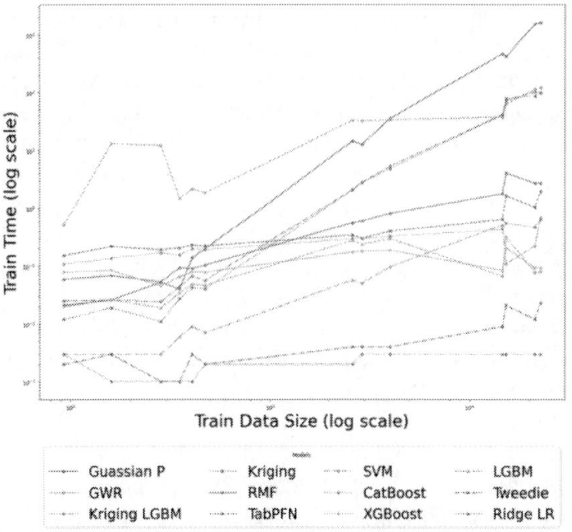

Figure 2. Coordinates features: visualizations of average training time (s) per hyperparameter run across different models in log scale.

encounter challenges in terms of incorporating additional features, limiting their effectiveness in such cases.

Figure 1 and Figure 2 evaluate model performance from a more practical perspective. Due to computational constraints, models that require less time for training and tuning are more advantageous for real-world applications. It is evident that models which are heavily reliant on spatial dependence (i.e., Gaussian Processes, Kriging, and GWR) experience exponentially increasing training and tuning times as the dataset size grows.

TabPFN, on the other hand, requires significantly less time due to its pre-trained nature. Given its superior predictive performance, TabPFN offers a balance between predictive power and efficiency. Similarly, tree ensemble models incur lower computational costs compared to statistical models, thanks to their optimized tree structures, which enable faster training while maintaining competitive predictive performance.

Our experimental results highlight the utility of geospatial dependence in predictive modeling. Tabular deep learning, i.e., TabPFN and tree ensemble methods demonstrate strong predictive performance using only coordinates, as well as when additional features are included, in many cases outperforming traditional geospatial statistical models like GWR and Kriging. This suggests that explicit spatial modeling is not always necessary, especially when models are strong enough to implicitly capture spatial dependencies from coordinate features. Moreover, by treating coordinates as standard input features rather than relying on computationally intensive geospatial models, we can significantly reduce training and inference costs while maintaining competitive regression performance, which is particularly valuable for large-scale geospatial applications.

V. Conclusions

The primary goal of this work was to explore the balance between expressiveness, efficiency, and predictive power among different modeling approaches, including geospatial statistical models, machine learning models, kernel-based models, and tabular deep learning. Traditionally, geospatial inference research explicitly models spatial dependence by leveraging distance matrices. However, we argue that overemphasizing explicit spatial learning is not always necessary, as it neither guarantees superior predictive performance nor ensures computational efficiency compared to more effective approaches, such as tabular deep learning and tree ensemble models.

To further support our argument, we conducted a comparative experiment evaluating the predictive capabilities and computational costs of geospatial statistical models, machine learning models, kernel-based models, and tabular deep learning on datasets containing only coordinates, as well as datasets with additional features. The results demonstrate that TabPFN achieves an optimal balance between expressiveness, efficiency, and predictive power, making it the most effective choice for geospatial regression tasks in this study. These findings prompt a reconsideration of the learning paradigm in geospatial inference. Instead of relying on variograms or local functions based on distance metrics—which impose a heavy computational burden—incorporating coordinates as standard features in tabular deep learning or tree ensemble models may provide a more efficient and predictive alternative.

Although we have included several publicly available datasets, certain limitations should be acknowledged. A more exhaustive study should incorporate a wider range of datasets and modeling techniques from diverse fields beyond real estate, while also considering regions with varying population densities rather than focusing solely on highly urbanized areas. This would provide a broader and more generalizable evaluation. Additionally, future research could explore additional hybrid models, such as MGWR and GWRK, as well as expand the hyperparameter tuning grid to further optimize on performance.

References

[1] P. K. Rai, V. N. Mishra, and P. Singh, *Geospatial technology for landscape and environmental management: sustainable assessment and planning*. Springer, 2022.

[2] J. K. Thakur, S. K. Singh, A. Ramanathan, M. B. K. Prasad, and W. Gossel, *Geospatial techniques for managing environmental resources*. Springer Science & Business Media, 2012.

[3] B. Jiang and X. Yao, *Geospatial analysis and modelling of urban structure and dynamics*. Springer Science & Business Media, 2010, vol. 99.

[4] L. A. Manfré *et al.*, "An analysis of geospatial technologies for risk and natural disaster management", *ISPRS International Journal of Geo-Information*, vol. 1, no. 2, pp. 166–185, 2012.

[5] N. N. Kussul *et al.*, "Disaster risk assessment based on heterogeneous geospatial information", *Journal of Automation and Information Sciences*, vol. 42, no. 12, 2010.

[6] D. G. Krige, "A statistical approach to some basic mine valuation problems on the witwatersrand", *Journal of the Southern African Institute of Mining and Metallurgy*, vol. 52, no. 6, pp. 119–139, 1951.

[7] G. Matheron, "Principles of geostatistics", *Economic geology*, vol. 58, no. 8, pp. 1246–1266, 1963.

[8] C. Bitter, G. F. Mulligan, and S. Dall'erba, "Incorporating spatial variation in housing attribute prices: A comparison of geographically weighted regression and the spatial expansion method", en, *Journal of Geographical Systems*, vol. 9, no. 1, pp. 7–27, Apr. 2007, ISSN: 1435-5949.

[9] G. Erdogan Erten, M. Yavuz, and C. V. Deutsch, "Combination of machine learning and kriging for spatial estimation of geological attributes", *Natural Resources Research*, vol. 31, no. 1, pp. 191–213, 2022.

[10] Z.-Y. Chen, R. Zhang, T.-H. Zhang, C.-Q. Ou, and Y. Guo, "A kriging-calibrated machine learning method for estimating daily ground-level no2 in mainland china", *Science of The Total Environment*, vol. 690, pp. 556–564, 2019.

[11] N. Hollmann, S. Müller, K. Eggensperger, and F. Hutter, "Tabpfn: A transformer that solves small tabular classification problems in a second", *arXiv preprint arXiv:2207.01848*, 2022.

[12] ArmonGo, *Github: Geocoordsfeats*, Accessed: March 31, 2025.

[13] M. A. Oliver and R. Webster, "Basic steps in geostatistics: The variogram and kriging", Springer, Tech. Rep., 2015.

[14] M. Oliver and R. Webster, "A tutorial guide to geostatistics: Computing and modelling variograms and kriging", *Catena*, vol. 113, pp. 56–69, 2014.

[15] C. Brunsdon, S. Fotheringham, and M. Charlton, "Geographically weighted regression", *Journal of the Royal Statistical Society: Series D (The Statistician)*, vol. 47, no. 3, pp. 431–443, 1998.

[16] A. S. Fotheringham, W. Yang, and W. Kang, "Multiscale geographically weighted regression (mgwr)", *Annals of the American Association of Geographers*, vol. 107, no. 6, pp. 1247–1265, 2017.

[17] Q. Zhu and H. Lin, "Comparing ordinary kriging and regression kriging for soil properties in contrasting landscapes", *Pedosphere*, vol. 20, no. 5, pp. 594–606, 2010.

[18] V. Van Zoest, F. B. Osei, G. Hoek, and A. Stein, "Spatio-temporal regression kriging for modelling urban no2 concentrations", *International journal of geographical information science*, vol. 34, no. 5, pp. 851–865, 2020.

[19] S. Araki, K. Yamamoto, and A. Kondo, "Application of regression kriging to air pollutant concentrations in japan with high spatial resolution", *Aerosol and Air Quality Research*, vol. 15, no. 1, pp. 234–241, 2015.

[20] M. P. Lucas *et al.*, "Optimizing automated kriging to improve spatial interpolation of monthly rainfall over complex terrain",

Journal of Hydrometeorology, vol. 23, no. 4, pp. 561–572, 2022.

[21] B. Huang, B. Wu, and M. Barry, "Geographically and temporally weighted regression for modeling spatio-temporal variation in house prices", *International journal of geographical information science*, vol. 24, no. 3, pp. 383–401, 2010.

[22] Z. Zhu, B. Li, Y. Zhao, Z. Zhao, and L. Chen, "Socio-economic impact mechanism of ecosystem services value, a pca-gwr approach", *Polish Journal of Environmental Studies*, vol. 30, no. 1, pp. 977–986, 2020.

[23] S. Li, Z. Zhao, X. Miaomiao, and Y. Wang, "Investigating spatial non-stationary and scale-dependent relationships between urban surface temperature and environmental factors using geographically weighted regression", *Environmental Modelling & Software*, vol. 25, no. 12, pp. 1789–1800, 2010.

[24] P. Harris, A. Fotheringham, R. Crespo, and M. Charlton, "The use of geographically weighted regression for spatial prediction: An evaluation of models using simulated data sets", *Mathematical Geosciences*, vol. 42, pp. 657–680, 2010.

[25] S. Kumar, R. Lal, and D. Liu, "A geographically weighted regression kriging approach for mapping soil organic carbon stock", *Geoderma*, vol. 189, pp. 627–634, 2012.

[26] M. Imran, A. Stein, and R. Zurita-Milla, "Using geographically weighted regression kriging for crop yield mapping in west africa", *International Journal of Geographical Information Science*, vol. 29, no. 2, pp. 234–257, 2015.

[27] B. S. Murphy, "Pykrige: Development of a kriging toolkit for python", in *AGU fall meeting abstracts*, vol. 2014, 2014, H51K–0753.

[28] S. Müller, N. Hollmann, S. P. Arango, J. Grabocka, and F. Hutter, "Transformers can do bayesian inference", *arXiv preprint arXiv:2112.10510*, 2021.

[29] R. M. Neal, *Bayesian learning for neural networks*. Springer Science & Business Media, 2012, vol. 118.

[30] Y. Gal and Z. Ghahramani, "Dropout as a bayesian approximation: Representing model uncertainty in deep learning", in *Proceedings of the 33nd International Conference on Machine Learning, ICML 2016, New York City, NY, USA, June 19-24, 2016*, ser. JMLR Workshop and Conference Proceedings, vol. 48, JMLR.org, 2016, pp. 1050–1059.

[31] J. Pearl, *Causality*. Cambridge university press, 2009.

[32] J. Peters, D. Janzing, and B. Schölkopf, *Elements of causal inference: foundations and learning algorithms*. The MIT Press, 2017.

[33] A. E. Hoerl and R. W. Kennard, "Ridge Regression: Biased Estimation for Nonorthogonal Problems", *Technometrics*, vol. 12, no. 1, pp. 55–67, 1970, ISSN: 0040-1706.

[34] B. E. Boser, I. M. Guyon, and V. N. Vapnik, "A training algorithm for optimal margin classifiers", in *Proceedings of the fifth annual workshop on Computational learning theory*, ser. COLT '92, New York, NY, USA: Association for Computing Machinery, Jul. 1992, pp. 144–152, ISBN: 978-0-89791-497-0.

[35] M. Hearst, S. Dumais, E. Osuna, J. Platt, and B. Scholkopf, "Support vector machines", *IEEE Intelligent Systems and their Applications*, vol. 13, no. 4, pp. 18–28, Jul. 1998, ISSN: 2374-9423.

[36] N. Cristianini and J. Shawe-Taylor, *An Introduction to Support Vector Machines and Other Kernel-based Learning Methods*. Cambridge: Cambridge University Press, 2000, ISBN: 978-0-521-78019-3.

[37] L. Breiman, "Random forests", English, *Machine Learning*, vol. 45, no. 1, pp. 5–32, 2001, ISSN: 0885-6125.

[38] T. Chen and C. Guestrin, "Xgboost: A scalable tree boosting system", in *Proceedings of the 22nd acm sigkdd international conference on knowledge discovery and data mining*, 2016, pp. 785–794.

[39] G. Ke *et al.*, "Lightgbm: A highly efficient gradient boosting decision tree", in *Advances in Neural Information Processing Systems*, I. Guyon *et al.*, Eds., vol. 30, Curran Associates, Inc., 2017.

[40] L. Prokhorenkova, G. Gusev, A. Vorobev, A. V. Dorogush, and A. Gulin, "Catboost: Unbiased boosting with categorical features", *Advances in neural information processing systems*, vol. 31, 2018.

[41] C. K. Williams and C. E. Rasmussen, *Gaussian processes for machine learning*. MIT press Cambridge, MA, 2006, vol. 2.

[42] P. McCullagh, *Generalized linear models*. Routledge, 2019.

[43] I. O. Odeh, A. McBratney, and D. Chittleborough, "Further results on prediction of soil properties from terrain attributes: Heterotopic cokriging and regression-kriging", *Geoderma*, vol. 67, no. 3-4, pp. 215–226, 1995.

[44] T. Hengl, G. B. Heuvelink, and A. Stein, "A generic framework for spatial prediction of soil variables based on regression-kriging", *Geoderma*, vol. 120, no. 1-2, pp. 75–93, 2004.

[45] T. Hengl, G. B. Heuvelink, and D. G. Rossiter, "About regression-kriging: From equations to case studies", *Computers & geosciences*, vol. 33, no. 10, pp. 1301–1315, 2007.

A Workflow for Map Creation in Autonomous Vehicle Simulations

Zubair Islam, Ahmaad Ansari, George Daoud, and Mohamed El-Darieby
Faculty of Engineering and Applied Science
Ontario Tech University
Oshawa, Canada
e-mail: {zubair.islam | ahmaad.ansari | george.daoud | Mohamed.El-Darieby}@ontariotechu.net

***Abstract*—The fast development of technology and artificial intelligence has significantly advanced Autonomous Vehicle (AV) research, emphasizing the need for extensive simulation testing. Accurate and adaptable maps are critical in AV development, serving as the foundation for localization, path planning, and scenario testing. However, creating simulation-ready maps is often difficult and resource-intensive, especially with simulators like CARLA (CAR Learning to Act). Many existing workflows require significant computational resources or rely on specific simulators, limiting flexibility for developers. This paper presents a custom workflow to streamline map creation for AV development, demonstrated through the generation of a 3D map of a parking lot at Ontario Tech University. Future work will focus on incorporating SLAM technologies, optimizing the workflow for broader simulator compatibility, and exploring more flexible handling of latitude and longitude values to enhance map generation accuracy.**

Keywords-Autonomous Valet Parking (AVP); Simulation Testing; Autoware; Point Cloud Data (PCD); Lanelet2

I. Introduction

With rapid technological advancement, the design and development of Autonomous Vehicles (AVs) has become increasingly common. AVs provide many benefits, such as increased safety, reduced traffic congestion, improved fuel efficiency, and enhanced mobility for individuals who are unable to drive. However, there are many challenges, such as high development costs, lack of detailed regulations, and ethical concerns for decision-making procedures. To address these challenges, research must be conducted on all aspects of an AV, such as path planning, object detection, object avoidance, localization, simulation testing, sensor fusion, and machine learning. Autoware [1], an open-source software stack for AVs, provides these functionalities out of the box. For this study, it was selected as the primary software platform due to its widespread adoption in AV research and its robust support for localization and simulation testing. Autoware simplifies development and facilitates integration with simulation platforms. This area of research is especially important for simulation testing due to the accessibility and safety of digitally simulated AVs, allowing for the validation and verification of autonomous systems in a controlled environment without the risks and costs of real-world testing.

To enable the use of AVs in real-life scenarios, they must first be tested extensively in a simulated environment. A key component of these simulations is high-definition (HD) maps, which provide detailed, centimeter-level accuracy for road layouts, lane markings, and traffic infrastructure. HD maps are essential for localization, perception, and planning, as they allow AVs to understand their position and navigate accurately. The simulated environment can be run in an existing 3D simulation engine, built to support the development and integration of these simulations. Current 3D game engines such as Unity, Unreal Engine, and Godot allow for the creation of highly detailed and interactive virtual environments, which are important for testing the behaviors of AVs. These game engines are utilized to simulate the real world, such as the physics, traffic, pedestrians, and the AV along with its hardware and functionalities. In addition, the maps created for simulation are not only used for virtual testing but also serve as a foundation for real-world deployment. By ensuring accuracy in simulation maps, developers can generate HD maps that are later used by AVs to navigate real-life roads, allowing a seamless transition from testing to deployment.

Currently, there are a few simulators that utilize these game engines. These include Godot, which uses the Godot Engine, AWSIM [2], which uses the Unity Engine, and CARLA, [3] which uses the Unreal Engine. These simulators are built to support user interaction for testing scenarios between AVs and the real world. They are packaged and distributed as easy-to-setup and ready-to-use software designed to aid developers. While these simulators offer customization options to test user-defined environments, the process of developing and integrating new features can be challenging, potentially requiring significant effort to understand and adapt to the tools and workflows specific to each platform. Among these options, AWSIM was selected for this project due to its user-friendly interface and native compatibility with Autoware [4], enabling efficient testing and development of AV algorithms. AWSIM supports the project's objectives by enabling detailed testing of localization and vehicle interactions in a controlled and customizable environment.

In this paper, a custom workflow is presented that simplifies the creation of maps that are compatible with AWSIM. Section 2 provides the motivation behind the study. Section 3 reviews related work in HD map generation and simulation-based AV testing. Section 4 details the methodology, describing the tools used, their functionalities, and their integration into the proposed workflow. Section 5 presents the results of implementing the workflow. Section 6 discusses the performance, limitations, and practical advantages of the approach. Finally, Section 7 concludes the paper and outlines directions for future work. While this workflow is tailored for AWSIM, it has the flexibility to be adapted for other simulators, although this potential is not explored in this paper.

II. MOTIVATION

At the time of development, AWSIM and Autoware offered only a single simulation map, which represented a large city environment. However, this map lacked an important feature, which was a parking lot. Parking lots are essential for testing real-world AV deployment in low-speed, complex environments where interactions with nearby vehicles are common.

This limitation highlighted the need for a custom parking lot environment. Although documentation existed for creating custom environments in AWSIM, it was difficult to interpret and follow. Through this process, one key requirement was clear, which was that creating a custom environment requires a Lanelet2 OSM file, a PCD (Point Cloud Data) file, and a 3D mesh file. Due to the complexity of the existing documentation, an alternative solution was needed to streamline the map creation process.

Through extensive research and troubleshooting, a custom workflow was developed that utilized multiple tools with different functionalities to generate the required files. By using an OpenStreetMap (OSM) [5] file and following a series of steps in the workflow, the required files can be exported from the workflow. This allows for the use of a custom environment inside Autoware and AWSIM, enabling simulation testing for any outdoor area available on OSM. OSM was selected as a starting point because it is open-source and has very wide geographic coverage of maps across the globe.

III. RELATED WORK

During the development of the workflow, a literature review revealed no prior research specifically addressing map creation using AWSIM. As a result, the workflow was constructed incrementally through extensive Google searches and iterative problem-solving. Each step built upon the previous one, beginning with the extraction of an OSM file, followed by generating a 3D mesh, converting the mesh into a point cloud, and continuing through the necessary processing steps. To emphasize the significance of this workflow and its practical applications, several related studies are discussed below.

In researching methods for creating simulation environments for Autoware and AWSIM, literature was found describing workflows based on different simulation platforms, primarily CARLA and LGSVL. These works often used earlier versions of Autoware or relied on a deprecated simulator, such as LGSVL, making them less applicable to modern systems such as AWSIM.

Feng, Ye, and Angeloudis [6] proposed a pipeline for Autoware that transforms OSM data into maps compatible with both CARLA and LGSVL. Their workflow begins by converting an OSM file from OpenStreetMap into a 3D model using Blender, a 3D graphics software. This model is then exported in FBX format. Simultaneously, the OSM file is converted into OpenDRIVE format, resulting in both an OpenDRIVE file and a FBX file required by both simulators. Next, a PCD file is generated using CARLA's PCD recording function, which simulates an AV equipped with a LiDAR sensor that navigates through the environment and captures the PCD data. Finally, the OpenDRIVE file is used to generate a Lanelet2 vector map, enabling integration with Autoware.

Santonato [7] presents a similar pipeline, though focused solely on CARLA. The process begins by generating an OSM file and converting it into OpenDRIVE format. A plugin called StreetMap for Unreal Engine is then used to render the streets and buildings and to generate the 3D environment. The OpenDRIVE and 3D files are then imported into CARLA to create the simulation map. Lastly, they generate the PCD and Lanelet2 vector map files to be used for Autoware. As in the work by Feng, Ye, and Angeloudis, CARLA is used to record and generate the PCD file, while the OpenDRIVE file is used to create a Lanelet2 vector map.

Both Feng, Ye, and Angeloudis, and Santonato developed workflows capable of creating 3D maps from OSM files. However, their approaches rely on CARLA to generate PCD files. Feng, Ye, and Angeloudis used LGSVL as their primary simulator, which is now deprecated, but depended on CARLA for generating compatible files. Santonato on the other hand, used CARLA as their main simulator, which streamlined the process by keeping all file generation within a single platform. In contrast, the workflow presented in this paper is independent of any specific simulator for file generation. Instead, it utilizes lightweight, open-source tools that are easy to install and do not require running a simulator to produce the necessary files. This flexibility reduces computational overhead and simplifies deployment, particularly for researchers working outside the CARLA ecosystem.

Beyond simulator-based workflows, recent research has explored high-definition (HD) map generation using real-world sensor data. Li et al. [8] introduced HDMapNet, a deep learning-based framework for generating semantic HD maps online using inputs from cameras and/or LiDAR. Jeong et al. [9] presented a detailed tutorial for HD map generation using physical vehicles equipped with LiDAR, GNSS, and cameras, involving manual annotation, sensor calibration, and integration with a now-deprecated version of Autoware based on the ROS 1 framework. While both approaches produce high-accuracy maps suitable for deployment, they require significant hardware, real-world data collection, and complex processing pipelines. In contrast, the workflow proposed in this paper is designed specifically for simulation use. It operates entirely offline using publicly available OpenStreetMap data and a set of lightweight, open-source tools to generate Autoware-compatible maps. This makes it especially valuable for early-stage development, academic research, and rapid prototyping within simulation environments like AWSIM, where real-world precision is not critical and accessibility is a key concern.

IV. METHODOLOGY

The workflow is made up of four steps and is shown in Figure 1. The process goes from manually selecting the desired location and inputting that file into an Automated Mapping Docker Container [10], shown in Figure 2, which builds the location file into a 3D mesh and extracts the simulated pointcloud.

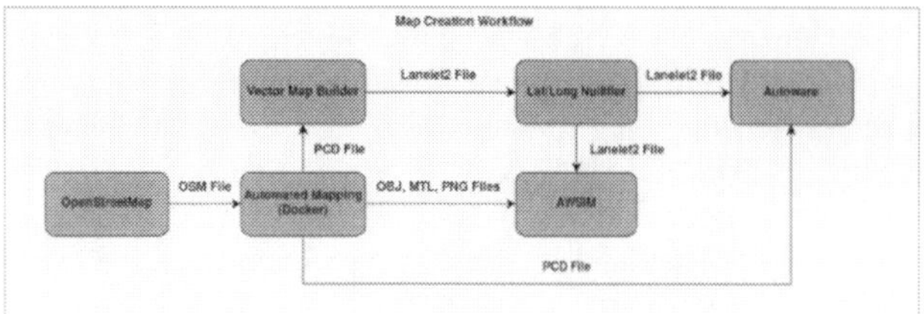

Figure 1. Workflow of map creation.

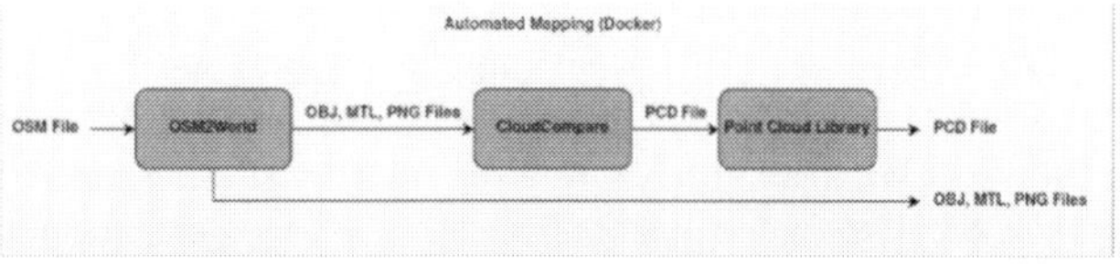

Figure 2. Workflow of automated mapping Docker container.

After the Automated Mapping Pipeline, the lanes of traffic or parking lots must be manually defined. After this, all the necessary files are generated and can be used for integration with Autoware and AWSIM. Each step requires different tools, each providing different functionalities. The tools will be discussed below and how they were used to develop a map environment for Ontario Tech University's SIRC parking lot.

A. Functionalities and Usage

1) **OpenStreetMap (OSM) Selection**
OpenStreetMap [5] is a resource for getting geospatial data of the world. It allows users to select a certain location to create an environment for. Using this tool, the desired location can be extracted as an OSM file (.osm). This OSM file contains many elements that define the geography and features of the selected location, such as nodes, ways, relations, and tags.
This tool is provided as a website. Using this website, the campus location can be found using its address, providing an aerial view. Using the select tool, the SIRC parking lot can be selected as shown in Figure 3, and exported as an OSM file, containing the geospatial information of this location.
2) **Automated Mapping Pipeline Docker Container**
This Docker container uses OSM2World [11] to first generate the 3D model of the map. Next, it uses CloudCompare to generate the Point Cloud Data file, and lastly uses the Point Cloud Library to further process the Point Cloud Data file.
   a) **OSM2World Conversion**
   OSM2World is a conversion tool that generates a 3D mesh based on the provided OSM file. It creates a three-dimensional model that closely represents the actual location. The model consists of three different file formats:

Figure 3. Exporting an OSM file from OpenStreetMap.

      i) **OBJ File (.obj)**: This file contains information about the geometry of 3D objects. Each object is defined by polygon faces, normals, curves, texture maps, and surfaces.
      ii) **Material Library File (.mtl)**: This file defines each of the materials in the 3D model, including their color, texture, and reflection properties.
      iii) **Portable Network Graphic Files (.png)**: Multiple PNG files are generated to store texture images for the 3D models. These files work with the MTL files to generate textures for the 3D surfaces.

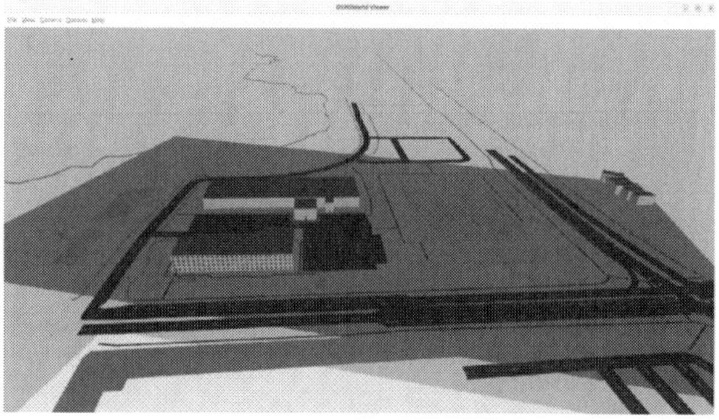

Figure 4. 3D model created in the OSM2World GUI.

   OSM2World comes preinstalled in the container and generates a 3D model shown in Figure 4, using the OSM file created earlier through its command line interface. The files are generated as one OBJ file, one MTL file, and a folder of multiple PNG files, containing pictures of the building texture, stop signs, grass, and roads.
   b) **CloudCompare Point Cloud Extraction**
   CloudCompare [12] is a 3D point cloud and triangular mesh processing software. This software is used in the container to import the 3D mesh, and export the point cloud (.pcd). This is done by first importing the 3D mesh and using the sample points feature, which calculates various

dense points based on the surfaces of the mesh to generate a point cloud. This point cloud contains the set of data points in a 3D coordinate system that represent the shape of the 3D mesh.

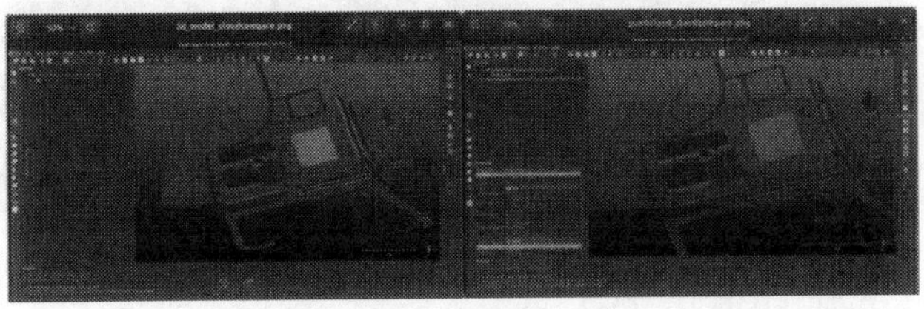

Figure 5. 3D model and point cloud shown in the CloudCompare GUI.

This software comes preinstalled inside the Docker container, and is then used through its CLI interface to import the 3D mesh obj file generated from OSM2World and generate a point cloud of the mesh. The 3D mesh file and point cloud are shown on the left and right of Figure 5 respectively. This point cloud is a single file, represented as a PCD file.

c) **Point Cloud Library (PCL) Processing**
Point Cloud Library (PCL) [13] is an open source project used for point cloud processing. This library contains various features on processing point clouds, such as viewing it in a 3D space, removing outliers, connecting point clouds, creating surfaces, and many more. In this pipeline, PCL is used to fix the orientation of the point cloud from a frontal view to a top-down aerial view. It then converts the point cloud file from ASCII format to binary format. This concludes the processing of the point cloud file, making it ready for use with Autoware. This file must then be renamed to `pointcloud_map.pcd`, due to Autoware naming conventions.

Figure 6. Orientations of point cloud before and after processing.

This library is used inside the Docker container, which already has the library installed. The library contains three useful functions. The first is `pcl_viewer`, which helps to view the point cloud and its initial orientation. Upon viewing it, the orientation will be seen as an initial frontal view. This must be changed so that the initial view is a top-down view. Therefore, the next command used is `pcl_transform_point_cloud` to transform the view to a top-down view. The initial view and transformed view are shown on the left and right in Figure 6 respectively. After this step, the last thing to do is to uncompress the file to binary format, using the command `pcl_convert_pcd_ascii_binary`. With these steps, the PCD file processing is completed.

3) **Vector Map Builder**
Vector Map Builder [14] is a tool provided by Tier IV, which is used for creating a Lanelet2 vector map, a specialized format for AV simulations. Although the resulting file uses the .osm extension, it is distinct from typical OpenStreetMap data. Lanelet2 files define road networks, lanes, and other road features essential for AV simulations. This Lanelet2 OSM file allows Autoware to run simulations on the predefined lanes. The tool has a feature to import a point cloud file, which can then be used to manually define lanes, parking lots, and parking spaces. These features can be customized as needed, but they are generally designed to conform with real-world features. After defining these features, the resulting Lanelet2 map can be exported as an OSM file.

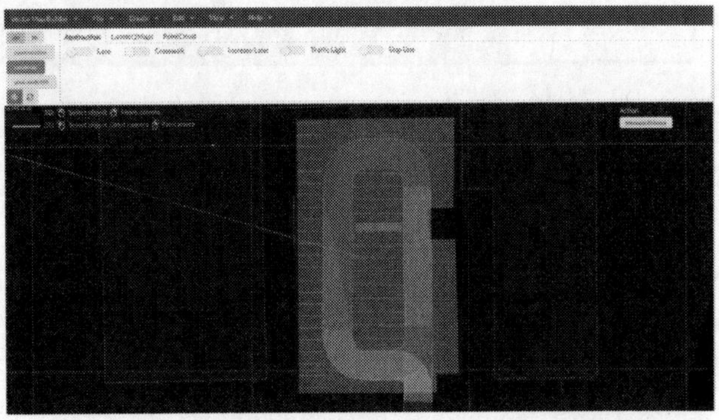

Figure 7. Lanelets and parking spaces created in VectorMapBuilder.

The tool can be accessed through the website, and can be used to import the point cloud file. After the import, features such as lanes and parking spots can be drawn. In the case of the SIRC parking lot, the lanes and parking spots were drawn as accurately as possible, shown in Figure 7. After completion, a `lanelet2_map.osm` file can be exported.

4) **Python Script for OSM Manipulation** A python script, `remove_lat_lon.py`, provided in [8], was created to nullify all latitude and longitude fields from the Lanelet2 OSM file. This is necessary for functionality with the Autoware software. If the lat/long coordinates are not NULL, the lanes will malfunction and stretch into infinity in Autoware.
This script is used in the Linux terminal, by invoking its command and giving it the `lanelet2_map.osm` file

as input. The script then sets all lat/long fields to NULL and outputs the updated Lanelet2 OSM file.

B. Integration

The workflow generates three essential files: a Lanelet2 OSM file, a PCD file, and 3D mesh files (OBJ, MTL, and PNG). To ensure compatibility with Autoware, the Lanelet2 OSM file must be named `lanelet2_map.osm`, and the PCD file should be named `pointcloud_map.pcd`. These files can then be imported into Autoware and AWSIM, as detailed below:

1) **Autoware**
   Autoware requires the Lanelet2 OSM file, and the PCD file. It is then launched with a specific ROS2 launch command with the map path argument pointing to the two files.

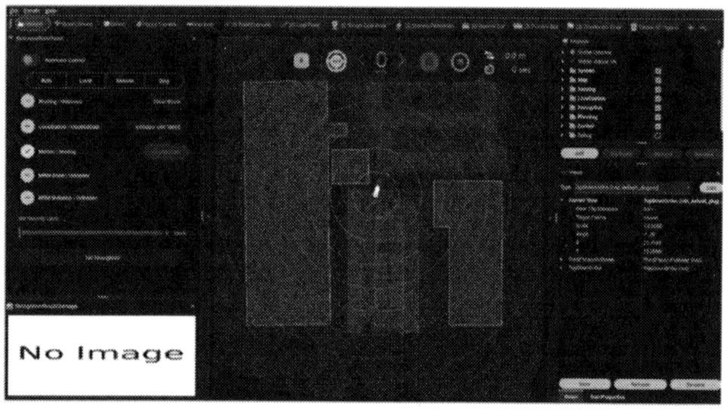

Figure 8. Lanelet2 map and point cloud imported into Autoware.

   Figure 8 shows the correct loading of the two files.
2) **AWSIM**
   AWSIM requires the 3D mesh and Lanelet2 OSM file to be imported in. The 3D mesh then needs some additional steps done to start working. Some scripts have to be added which define the 3D mesh as Mesh Colliders, so that they can be interacted with in the simulation. The 3D mesh file also has to have the read/write field enabled. Lastly, the Lanelet2 OSM file is loaded and aligned with the simulation environment to synchronize with Autoware. Figure 9 shows the correct loading of the 3D files and the Lanelet2 map.

Figure 9. Lanelet2 map and 3D model imported into AWSIM.

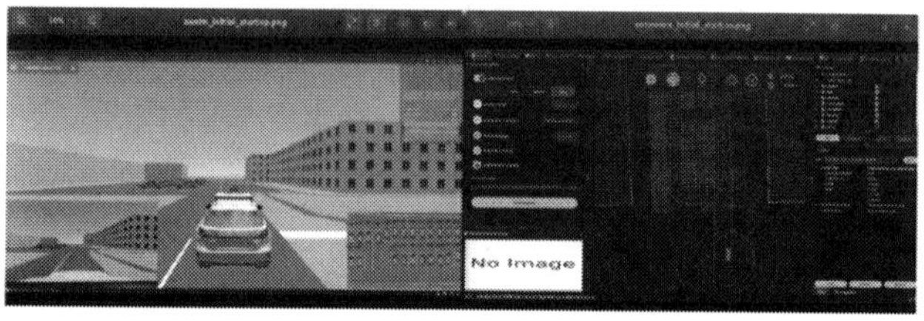

Figure 10. Initial startup of AWSIM and Autoware.

V. Results

After importing all the files of the newly created map, both Autoware and AWSIM are able to load the SIRC parking lot environment. To get both synced, AWSIM is run first, and then Autoware afterwards. In AWSIM, the ego vehicle is correctly spawned and activated inside the environment, with all its sensors functioning correctly. In Autoware, the ego vehicle is correctly localized to the position of the ego vehicle by receiving the location from AWSIM. The initialization of AWSIM and Autoware are shown in Figure 10.

After setting a goal pose inside a parking spot for the vehicle, which is shown in Figure 11, and activating the autonomous mode, both vehicles in AWSIM and Autoware accurately mimic each other and reach the destination correctly, which are shown in Figure 12.

The successful completion of route planning and parking demonstrates the map's effective integration into both simulation platforms, highlighting its accuracy and the ego vehicle's proper localization and navigation in AWSIM and Autoware. These results show the workflow's capability to support real-world applications and test AVP systems in simulation environments.

VI. Discussion

With this workflow, testing can be done in any outdoor environment that is available on OpenStreetMap. AWSIM has the ability to generate pedestrians and traffic, and also relays all this information back to Autoware. In any scenario, whether it is simple driving, or parking, Autoware can be used to test them. In order to deploy Autoware in real life, an alternative must be used for generating the PCD and Lanelet2 maps. This is because the 3D model generated by OSM2World is not perfect. The buildings are not true to reality. For example, the SIRC parking lot contains a soccer dome, and in OSM2World, this dome is represented as a simple rectangular building. However, in the case of real-life deployment, SLAM technologies can be used to generate the perfect and accurate point cloud.

Although the 3D models generated by OSM2World have limitations in geometric accuracy, the workflow remains highly practical compared to other HD map generation methods such as HDMapNet or CARLA-based pipelines. Unlike those approaches, which rely on real-world sensor data and manual annotation, this workflow generates all required map com-

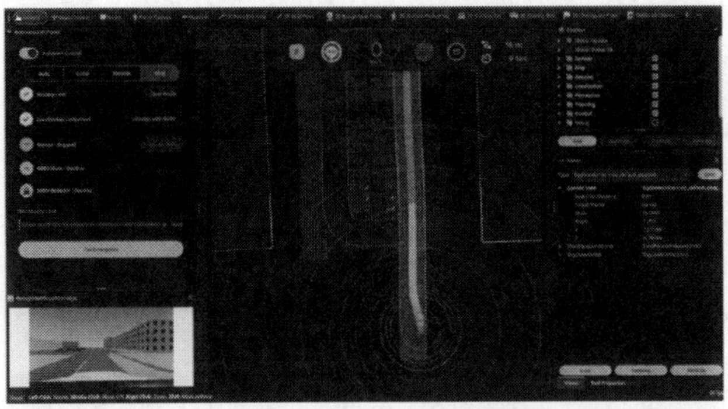

Figure 11. Goal pose selected and route calculated.

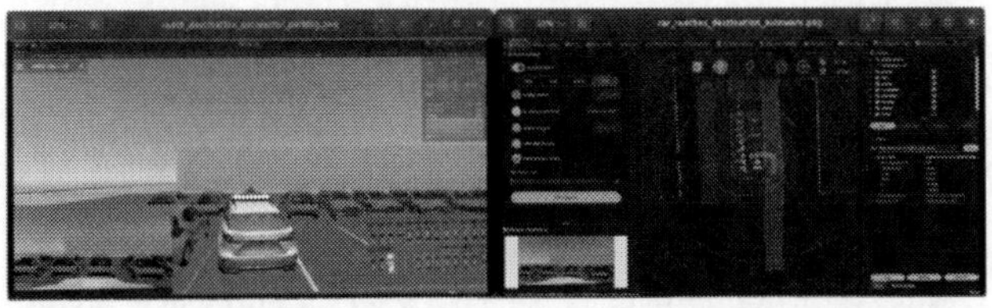

Figure 12. Car reaches the destination in AWSIM and Autoware.

ponents offline using only open-source tools and OSM data. This makes it especially suitable for simulation use, offering accessibility and ease of deployment in low-resource environments. Although formal evaluation metrics such as runtime or accuracy comparisons are not presented, the workflow's successful integration with AWSIM and Autoware demonstrates its effectiveness for early-stage research and prototyping.

VII. CONCLUSION

In this paper, a custom workflow was presented, which was designed to simplify the creation of maps for use with AWSIM. While primarily developed by AWSIM, this workflow can potentially be adapted for use with other simulators, though this aspect was not explored in detail. The workflow was developed within the context of an AVP project using Autoware, addressing a critical gap in the availability of simulation-ready environments for testing AV technologies.

Accurate and adaptable maps are essential for AV development. However, creating such maps can often be difficult and resource-intensive. Many existing workflows rely on significant computational resources or are tied to specific simulators, limiting their flexibility for developers. Moreover, documentation for creating custom maps can often be difficult to follow, complicating the process of integrating real-world locations into simulations. This workflow addresses these challenges by using lightweight tools to generate 3D mesh files, point cloud data files, and Lanelet2 files from OSM data, making it applicable to any location available on OSM.

HD maps are vital for testing AVs in simulated environments before real world deployment. These maps offer centimeter-level accuracy for road layouts, lane markings, and traffic infrastructure, supporting localization, perception, and planning tasks. The workflow demonstrated in this paper enables the creation of HD maps for use in 3D simulation engines, including AWSIM, which is compatible with Autoware. The simulated maps are not only valuable for virtual testing but also serve as the foundation for real-world deployment, ensuring a seamless transition from simulation to real-world navigation.

The methodology outlined in this paper, ranging from extracting data from OpenStreetMap to processing it through Docker containers for map generation, was used to create a functional 3D map of Ontario Tech University's SIRC parking lot. This map was successfully tested in both Autoware and AWSIM simulations, demonstrating the workflow's potential for use in a variety of real-world environments available on OpenStreetMap. Future work will focus on improving model accuracy, incorporating SLAM technologies, and optimizing the workflow for broader simulator compatibility. Additionally, exploring more flexible handling of latitude and longitude values could allow for better control over the nullification process and further enhance map generation accuracy.

ACKNOWLEDGMENT

We would like to extend our gratitude to our friends and team members, Waddah Saleh and Abdullah Waseem, for their encouragement and support throughout the project. Additionally, we would like to thank our research group for their continuous guidance and valuable insights during the course of this work.

REFERENCES

[1] tier4, "Tier4/AWSIM: Open source simulator for self-driving vehicles," GitHub, https://github.com/tier4/AWSIM (accessed 2025-02-15).
[2] C. Team, "Carla," CARLA Simulator, https://carla.org/ (accessed 2025-02-15).
[3] "Home Page," Autoware, https://autoware.org/ (accessed 2025-02-15).
[4] "CombinationWithAutoware," CombinationWithAutoware - AWSIM document, https://tier4.github.io/AWSIM/Introduction/CombinationWithAutoware/ (accessed 2025-02-15).
[5] OpenStreetMap, https://www.openstreetmap.org/ (accessed 2025-02-15).
[6] Y. Feng, Q. Ye, and P. Angeloudis, "Rapid procedural generation of real world environments for Autonomous Vehicle Testing," OpenReview, https://openreview.net/forum?id=qoyUO-XFFd (accessed 2025-02-15).
[7] S. F. Santonato, "A complete end-to-end simulation flow for autonomous driving frameworks," Webthesis, https://webthesis.biblio.polito.it/16703/ (accessed 2025-02-15).
[8] Q. Li, Y. Wang, Y. Wang, and H. Zhao, "HDMapNet: An online HD map construction and evaluation framework," 2022 International Conference on Robotics and Automation (ICRA), pp. 4628–4634, https://doi.org/10.1109/icra46639.2022.9812383 (accessed 2025-02-15).
[9] J. Jeong, J. Y. Yoon, H. Lee, H. Darweesh, and W. Sung, "Tutorial on high-definition map generation for automated driving in Urban Environments," Sensors, https://doi.org/10.3390/s22187056 (accessed 2025-02-15).
[10] "OSM to Pointcloud and Lanelet Conversion Process," GitHub, https://github.com/zubxxr/OSM-to-Pointcloud-and-Lanelet-Conversion-Process (accessed 2025-02-15).
[11] T. Knerr, "OSM2World create 3D models from OpenStreetMap," OSM2World, https://osm2world.org/ (accessed 2025-02-15).
[12] "Presentation," CloudCompare, https://www.cloudcompare.org/presentation.html (accessed 2025-02-15).
[13] "About," Point Cloud Library, https://pointclouds.org/about/ (accessed 2025-02-15).
[14] Vector Map Builder, https://tools.tier4.jp/vector_map_builder_ll2/ (accessed 2025-02-15).

DPS: A Novel Approach for Efficient Direction-Based Neighborhood Queries

Pedro Henrique Bergamo Bertolli and Marcela Xavier Ribeiro
Department of Computer Science
Universidade Federal de São Carlos (UFSCar)
e-mail: pbertolli@estudante.ufscar.br, marcelaxr@ufscar.br

***Abstract*—Current spatial search methods predominantly focus on distance-based metrics, while direction-based queries have emerged to address applications requiring diverse directional coverage. Existing direction-based approaches like the Direction-Based Surrounder (DBS) and Direction-Aware Nearest Neighbor (DNN) employ iterative algorithms that require examining multiple objects and their spatial relationships, leading to high computational costs particularly in dense datasets. These methods also suffer from either overly restricted results (DBS) or directionally clustered outcomes (DNN) due to their selection criteria. This paper introduces Direction Proximity Search (DPS), a novel approach that ensures directional diversity—defined as having at most one object per angular interval—while significantly reducing computational overhead. By employing geometric space partitioning to divide the search space into equal angular regions and a refinement phase that selects the nearest object per directional interval, DPS eliminates the need for extensive object-to-object comparisons. Experiments on both synthetic and real datasets show that DPS achieves processing time reductions of up to 99.9% specifically for high-density distributions (Bit and Sierpinski) with large datasets, while consistently maintaining the desired directional diversity property across all tested configurations.**

Keywords-Spatial databases; surrounding queries; efficient processing; directional diversity.

I. INTRODUCTION

Spatial queries with directional diversity are essential for critical applications where distance alone cannot guarantee accessibility. In emergency response scenarios—such as fires, floods, or traffic incidents—the nearest facilities may be unreachable, making it crucial to identify alternatives distributed across different directions. The widespread adoption of mobile devices has made spatial data processing essential in various domains, including location-based recommendations, route planning, environmental monitoring, and urban mapping. These applications rely on spatial queries to retrieve and analyze geographic information, helping users make informed decisions based on their spatial context.

Spatial query processing typically relies on Geographic Information Systems (GIS) and spatial databases. These systems manage geometric objects (points, lines, and polygons) that represent entities in the real world. For example, a restaurant can be represented as either a simple point or, more precisely, as a polygon depicting its physical boundaries. The query point in these systems could represent various entities: a mobile user's location, a point of interest, or a vehicle's projected position.

Although distance-based queries are prevalent, incorporating directional diversity has become increasingly crucial. This is particularly evident in emergency scenarios, where the nearest service point may not be the most accessible. During a fire, for example, the closest hospitals or fire stations might be inaccessible due to smoke or the spread of the fire. Similarly, during floods, nearby shelters could be in areas prone to submersion or landslides. In urban settings, traffic congestion, road closures, or construction work can render the closest facilities temporarily unreachable, highlighting the need for directionally diverse alternatives.

To address the limitations of purely distance-based approaches, nearest surrounder queries [1] were introduced as queries that consider both distance and direction of objects in relation to a query point. Subsequently, the DBS [2] and DNN [3] queries emerged as variations of this approach. These queries employ a fundamental concept called "dominance relation", which uses direction and distance properties to determine which objects should be included in the result set. While DBS applies dominance relations between pairs of objects, resulting in more restricted results, DNN considers object triplets, potentially yielding more diversity, but sometimes spatially concentrated outcomes.

In critical applications, particularly emergency planning and response, the speed of information delivery is crucial. Decision-makers need instant access to results to plan their actions and execute the necessary procedures. However, current approaches face two main limitations: computational inefficiency due to iterative processing and suboptimal result distribution that is either too restrictive or lacks sufficient directional spread.

This paper makes three key contributions: (1) a novel geometric partitioning strategy that efficiently handles direction-based queries; (2) substantial computational efficiency improvements over existing methods; and (3) comprehensive experimental evaluation that demonstrates scalability across diverse datasets. The remainder of the paper is organized as follows: Section II reviews related work in spatial queries and direction-based methods. Section III introduces our novel Direction Proximity Search (DPS) approach, detailing its partitioning, processing, and refinement phases. Section IV describes our experimental evaluation methodology and datasets. Section V discusses the performance results and comparative analysis. Finally, Section VI concludes the paper and outlines future research directions.

II. RELATED WORK

This section presents a systematic review of the literature on direction-based neighborhood queries and optimization techniques. The research was carried out in the major digital libraries (IEEE, Science Direct, Springer, ACM DL, and Google Scholar), resulting in 11 relevant studies after applying selection criteria. The analysis revealed six main categories of approaches: spatial indexing (C1), formal query definitions (C2), dominance-based algorithms (C3), computational geometry techniques (C4), visibility-based direction methods (C5), and performance testing (C6). Most works span multiple categories, demonstrating the interconnected nature of these approaches. Regarding spatial indexing (C1), Lee et al. [1] introduced direction-based neighborhood queries with the *sweep* and *ripple* algorithms using R-tree structures. Zhang et al. [4] and Chung et al. [5] expanded this approach, while Nutanong et al. [6] developed R*-Tree pruning techniques to reduce disk access. For formal query definitions (C2), Lee et al.'s work [1] established the theoretical foundations that supported subsequent studies, notably the DBS and DNN queries presented by Guo [2][3]. In dominance-based algorithms (C3), the relationship between objects determines the result set. Table I summarizes the key characteristics and computational limitations of the main direction-based query methods: DBS and DNN.

TABLE I
CHARACTERISTICS OF EXISTING DIRECTION-BASED QUERY METHODS

Method	Time Complexity (worst case)	Dominance Relation	Result Distribution
DBS	$O(n^2)$	Pairwise (2θ interval)	Sparse (uniform coverage)
DNN	$O(n^2)$	Triplet-based (relaxed criteria)	Dense (potential clustering)

As shown in Table I, the DBS algorithm [2] requires $O(n^2)$ comparisons in the worst case to examine all object pairs. Its restrictive dominance relationship, where objects dominate within a 2θ angular interval, can lead to overly limited result sets, especially with larger θ values where a single object can eliminate many candidates within its dominance range. The DNN algorithm [3] provides better directional diversity through less restrictive dominance rules but still has $O(n^2)$ worst-case complexity, making it computationally expensive for large datasets. Additionally, its relaxed dominance criteria can result in directionally close objects being returned, potentially compromising the spatial distribution consistency despite producing larger result sets.

For computational geometry techniques (C4) and visibility-based methods (C5), Lee et al. [1], Nutanong et al. [6], and Chung et al. [5] grounded the direction aspect as a visibility field. Nutanong et al. introduced the concept of minimum visible distance (MinViDist), while Chung et al. relied on angle and direction calculations. Regarding performance testing (C6), Carniel [7], [8] focused on general spatial query definitions, discussing future optimization challenges. A significant gap exists in the literature: the absence of comparative performance analyses between different algorithms, and the fundamental trade-off between computational efficiency and directional diversity in existing methods.

III. DIRECTION PROXIMITY SEARCH

This section presents the DPS method and its implementation. We detail its architecture and operation, introducing a novel direction-based neighborhood query that addresses key limitations in existing approaches.

We begin by formally defining the core concepts of DPS. The parameter θ determines the directional diversity of the result set - it ensures that returned objects are separated by at least θ degrees. For any two objects $o_i, o_j \in \mathcal{D}$ relative to query point q, their angular separation is the angle between vectors $\overrightarrow{qo_i}$ and $\overrightarrow{qo_j}$, denoted as $\angle(\overrightarrow{qo_i}, \overrightarrow{qo_j})$.

In DPS, an object o dominates an angular region R of size θ if: (i) o is the nearest object to q within R, and (ii) no closer object exists within $\theta/2$ degrees of o. This ensures directional diversity by allowing at most one object per θ interval, resulting in a maximum of $\lceil 360/\theta \rceil$ objects in the result set.

DPS employs geometric partitioning to divide the 360° space around q into $n = 360/(\theta/2)$ equal partitions. Each partition spans $\theta/2$ degrees, allowing two adjacent partitions to form a complete θ interval. This approach eliminates the $O(n^2)$ pairwise comparisons required by DBS and DNN. For a fixed θ, DPS achieves $O(n)$ time complexity, as the number of partitions $k = 360/(\theta/2)$ is constant.

A. Partitioning

The partitioning algorithm systematically divides the spatial domain around the query point into equal geometric regions. This geometric partitioning constitutes the initial phase of the DPS query, formally defined as *DPS = (t, q, θ, distMax)*, where *t* denotes the dataset, *q* represents the query point, θ specifies the angular constraint, and *distMax* determines the maximum search radius.

The number of partitions is defined by $\varphi_n = \frac{360^\circ}{\theta/2}$. Each partition has an angular interval of $\theta/2$, allowing two adjacent partitions to form a complete θ interval. The first partition φ_1 is constructed using Algorithm 1.

Algorithm 1 First Partition Construction
Require: Query point q, dataset $\mathcal{D}$, angle θ, distance $distMax$
Ensure: First partition φ_1
1: $NN \leftarrow$ FindNearestNeighbor(q, $\mathcal{D}$)
2: $NN' \leftarrow$ Project(NN, $distMax$)
3: $\vec{v} \leftarrow \overrightarrow{qNN'}$
4: $l_s \leftarrow$ Rotate($\vec{v}$, $\theta/2$)
5: $\varphi_1 \leftarrow$ CreatePolygon(q, NN', l_s)
6: **return** φ_1

To illustrate this process, we use a sample dataset with 13 points and parameters *DPS = (sample, POINT(0 0),* 90°, *200000)*. With $\theta = 90°$, we obtain $\varphi_n = 8$ partitions. The nearest neighbor to query point POINT(0,0) is point *a*.

Following Algorithm 1, we project point *a* to create NN' at distance 200000, then rotate the vector $\overrightarrow{qNN'}$ by $\theta/2$ to obtain the upper boundary l_s. The resulting polygon forms the first partition φ_1, as illustrated in Figure 1.

Subsequent partitions are created in clockwise direction using Algorithm 2, which systematically generates all φ_n partitions.

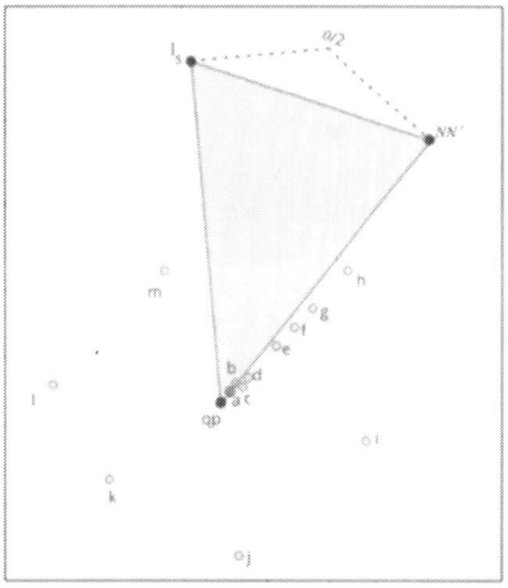

Figure 1. Construction of φ_1.

Algorithm 2 Complete Partitioning

Require: First partition φ_1, angle θ, number of partitions φ_n
Ensure: Set of partitions Φ

$\Phi \leftarrow \{\varphi_1\}$
for $i = 2$ to φ_n **do**
  $l_{prev} \leftarrow$ GetUpperBoundary(φ_{i-1})
  $l_{new} \leftarrow$ Rotate(l_{prev}, $-\theta/2$)
  $\varphi_i \leftarrow$ CreatePartition(l_{prev}, l_{new})
  $\Phi \leftarrow \Phi \cup \{\varphi_i\}$
end for
return Φ

B. Processing

This step is responsible for finding the nearest object to q within each partition. The process requires identifying all objects that intersect with each partition and determining the one closest to q. The partitioning strategy enables an optimized processing approach by confining the search to individual partitions, where only a single nearest object needs to be identified. This significantly reduces computational overhead compared to traditional methods that require multiple object comparisons to establish dominance relationships.

The processing is performed sequentially φ_n-1 times, once for each partition except the first one, which already has its Nearest Neighbor (NN) calculated during the partitioning step. Following the geometric partitioning in our example, this step identifies the nearest objects to the query point *qp* for each partition. These objects, highlighted in red in Figure 2, are accompanied by a table that presents their distances in ascending order and their directions relative to *qp*.

The key advantage of this approach is that it reduces processing to φ_n-1 sequential operations, whereas traditional methods require multiple comparisons among objects until either meeting stopping conditions or, in the worst case, examining the entire dataset.

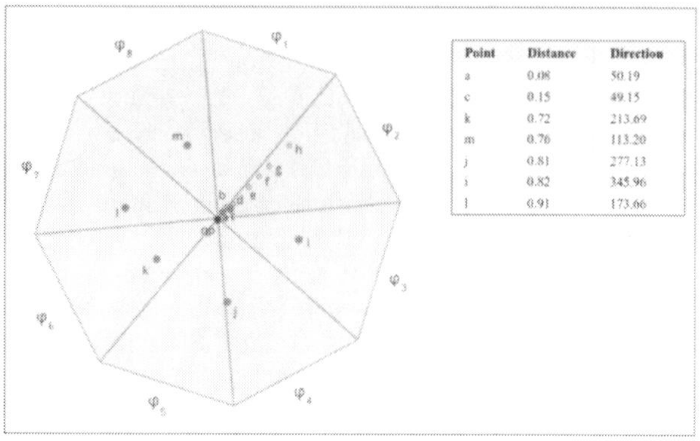

Point	Distance	Direction
a	0.08	50.19
c	0.15	49.15
k	0.72	213.69
m	0.76	113.20
j	0.81	277.13
i	0.82	345.96
l	0.91	173.66

Figure 2. Objects identified as NN for each partition and their respective directions and distances relative to *qp*.

C. Refinement

After identifying all NN of q in their respective partitions, the refinement step ensures directional diversity. Objects are considered directionally close if their angular separation is less than $\theta/2$. The refinement merges adjacent partitions into composite partitions of size θ, selecting only the nearest object from each composite partition.

To formalize the refinement process, we introduce the following definitions:

Definition 1 (Ordered Processing List): The processing result is a list of tuples containing partition identifier, NN object, and distance from q to NN, $List_p$ = ($\varphi_{i_{id}}$, NN_i, $dist(q, NN_i)$), ... ($\varphi_{n_{id}}$, NN_n, $dist(q, NN_n)$), sorted by ascending distance.

Definition 2 (Adjacent Partition): Adjacent partitions comprise predecessor and successor partitions in an ordered partition list.

Definition 3 (Ignored Partition): A partition is marked as ignored if its NN object is at an angular distance less than $\theta/2$ from the NN of a dominant partition.

The refinement algorithm (Algorithm 3) systematically processes the ordered list to determine the final result set.

Algorithm 3 DPS Refinement

Require: Ordered processing list $List_p$
Ensure: Result set R

$ignored \leftarrow \emptyset$
$R \leftarrow \emptyset$
for each $(\varphi_i, NN_i, dist_i)$ in $List_p$ **do**
  if $\varphi_i \notin ignored$ **then**
    $R \leftarrow R \cup \{NN_i\}$
    $adjacent \leftarrow$ GetAdjacentPartitions(φ_i)
    $ignored \leftarrow ignored \cup adjacent$
  end if
end for
return R

In our example, Algorithm 3 starts with partition φ_1 containing object a. Since a dominates a complete θ interval, its successor partition is marked as ignored, as shown in Figure 3.

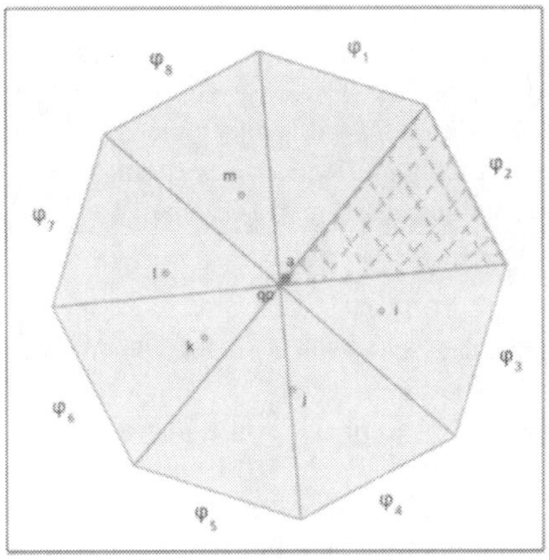

Figure 3. Ignored partition in the first iteration of the refinement step.

In the next iteration, the algorithm examines the next NN object that is not in an ignored partition. In this case, it is the point *k* in φ_6, which then marks its predecessor and successor partitions as ignored, as illustrated in Figure 4.

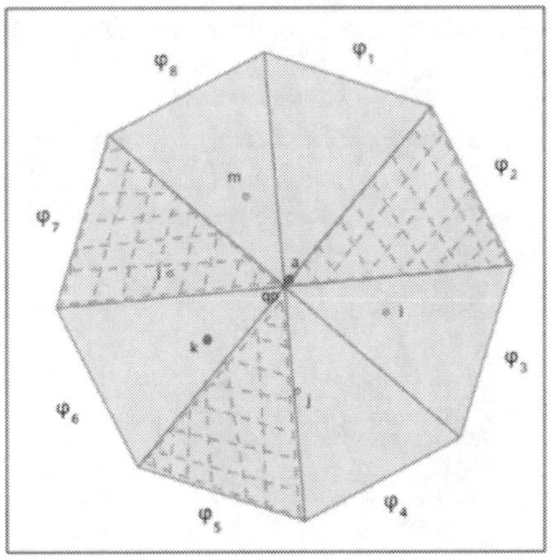

Figure 4. Adjacent partitions of φ_6 marked as ignored.

Subsequently, the object m in φ_8 does not mark any partitions as ignored, since its predecessor φ_7 was already ignored by φ_6. Being the last partition, φ_8 has no successor according to the definition of the adjacent partition. Finally, object j in φ_4 is verified and marks φ_3 as an ignored partition, as shown in Figure 5.

Definition 4 (Dominant Partition): Partitions containing the nearest object to q in an ordered processing list, not marked as ignored. These partitions contain objects for the DPS query result set.

Definition 5 (Composite Partition): A composite partition (PC) joins two consecutive partitions where k ranges from 1 to $\frac{n}{2}$:

$$\mathrm{PC}_k = (\varphi_{2k-1}, \varphi_{2k}) \tag{1}$$

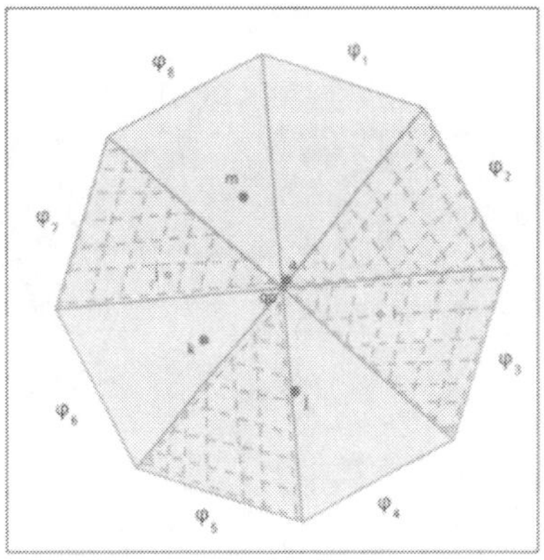

Figure 5. Final iteration of the refinement step.

From the upper limit (*ls*) of partition φ_1, we define the angular intervals (λ) for the composite partitions PC_k. For PC_1, the upper limit is as follows:

$$\mathrm{ls}_{\mathrm{PC}_1} = \overrightarrow{q\mathrm{NN}'} + \frac{\theta}{2} \tag{2}$$

The lower limit is calculated by subtracting θ from the upper limit:

$$\mathrm{li}_{\mathrm{PC}_1} = \overrightarrow{q\mathrm{ls}} - \theta \tag{3}$$

For subsequent composite partitions PCk (k > 1), the angular interval is calculated from the lower limit of the previous partition:

$$\lambda_{\mathrm{PC}_k} = \overrightarrow{q\mathrm{li}_{\mathrm{PC}_{k-1}}} - \theta \tag{4}$$

The final result set contains all NN objects from non-ignored partitions. Each object dominates the θ interval defined by a composite partition. Figure 6 shows the result set and identifies the composite partitions (PC), formed by consecutive partitions: PC_1 = φ_1 and φ_2, PC_2 = φ_3 and φ_4, PC_3 = φ_5 and φ_6, PC_4 = φ_7 and φ_8.

The refinement algorithm transforms the processing results into an ordered list, determines the dominant partitions, and combines them into composite partitions, ensuring that each object in PC_k is dominant over a complete interval θ.

IV. Experimental Evaluation

A. Datasets

To vary the distribution and complexity of spatial objects, synthetic and real datasets were constructed for the experiments.

The Spider spatial data generator [9] was used to generate synthetic data within the [0,1] interval, containing different volumes and distributions. The generated volumes were defined into three distinct categories: small, medium, and large, containing 20,000, 200,000, and 2,000,000 records, respectively.

The data distribution was generated considering the 5 types of distributions available for point objects in the generator: uniform, diagonal, Gaussian, Sierpinski, and bit. A dataset was

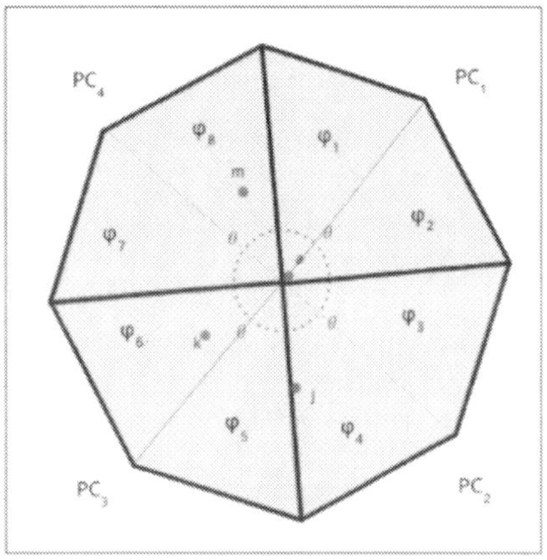

Figure 6. DPS query result with answer objects in their respective dominance intervals.

generated for each combination of volume and distribution, totaling 15 datasets.

Real-world data was collected from the OpenStreetMap platform [10], resulting in three datasets extracted from the Brazil map: a small dataset with points representing schools, a medium dataset with street intersections, and a large dataset with all point-type objects. These datasets vary in volume, representing small, medium, and large datasets.

B. Experimental Design

The experimental design was structured to comprehensively evaluate the algorithm performance under various conditions by systematically varying the query parameters. The primary parameter, θ, was tested using four distinct values: 20, 45, 60, and 90 degrees, applied consistently across all databases. Although most queries shared the same input parameters, the proposed DPS query required an additional parameter, *distMax*, which defines the maximum partition length in meters. This parameter was adjusted between real and synthetic databases to account for differences in data variation.

The experiment encompassed a total of 18 databases, 15 synthetic and 3 real. Each database was tested against four values of θ, resulting in 72 unique query scenarios. These scenarios were then doubled to compare performance between indexed and non-indexed databases, creating 144 distinct test configurations. Each configuration was evaluated using three different algorithms (DBS, DNN and DPS), culminating in 432 total test loads. Of these, 360 test loads were executed on synthetic data, while the remaining 72 were performed on real data.

C. Experimental Setup

The experiments were conducted on a physical machine with the following specifications: Intel(R) Core(TM) i7-10750H CPU @ 2.60GHz with 12 cores, 16 GB of RAM, 1 TB SSD, running Ubuntu 20.04.1 LTS (64-bit). The spatial database was implemented using PostgreSQL 12.4 with PostGIS 3.0.2 extension.

For indexed experiments, we employed the Generalized Search Tree (GiST) indexing method provided by PostGIS, which implements a variant of the R-Tree structure. All queries (DBS, DNN, and DPS) were executed systematically, with results stored in a dedicated *results* table. To ensure consistency and prevent caching effects, the system cache was cleared before each test execution using standard Linux cache clearing procedures.

D. Performance Analysis

Although statistical tests were not performed, the performance differences are substantial enough to demonstrate DPS superiority. DPS completed some queries on large datasets in under 25 seconds, while DBS and DNN were unable to complete the same queries even after 24 hours—representing a performance improvement of at least 3,456x. Such extreme differences, consistent across multiple configurations, clearly indicate algorithmic advantages beyond measurement uncertainties.

DPS query demonstrated superior efficiency in a significant portion of the test scenarios, outperforming other methods in 52.8% of cases for non-indexed databases and 61.1% of cases for indexed databases, as illustrated in Figure 7. Specifically, it achieved better performance in 38 out of 72 query scenarios for non-indexed databases and 44 out of 72 scenarios for indexed databases, indicating robust performance across both database types.

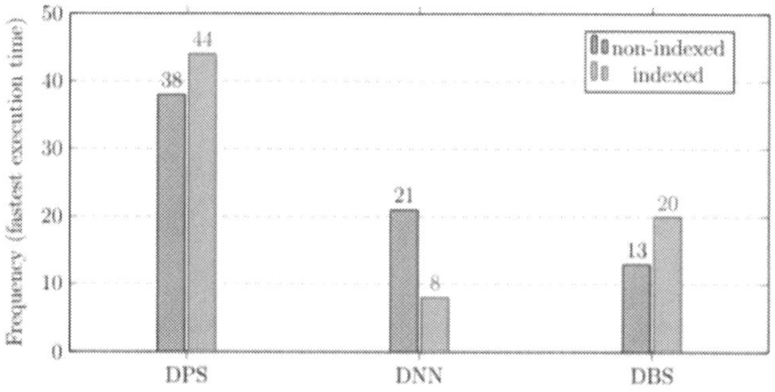

Figure 7. Frequency of algorithms (DPS, DBS, DNN) achieving fastest query execution across indexed and non-indexed databases.

Figure 8 presents a detailed breakdown of the results by data distribution, revealing significant performance patterns. The DPS algorithm demonstrated remarkable effectiveness on both synthetic and real datasets. In Bit and Sierpinski distributions, it consistently achieved optimal performance across all configurations, with a maximum frequency of 12 best results in both indexed and non-indexed scenarios. For real data, the algorithm also showed strong performance, achieving 9 and 10 best results in non-indexed and indexed configurations respectively. Although performance was more modest with the Gaussian distribution, the algorithm still maintained consistent effectiveness across diagonal and uniform distributions, demonstrating its versatility across different data patterns.

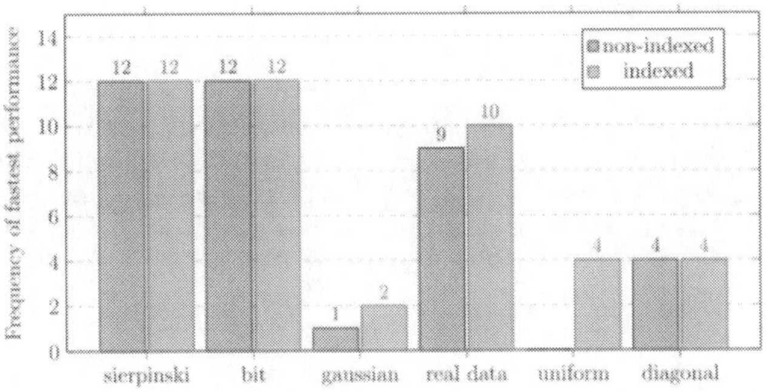

Figure 8. Frequency of DPS achieving fastest query execution across data distributions.

A deeper analysis of query execution times for Bit and Sierpinski distributions revealed significant differences among the algorithms. Both DBS and DNN algorithms encountered considerable challenges, particularly when processing large databases. In most cases involving large-scale datasets, these algorithms failed to complete execution even after 24 hours of processing time. The only exception occurred with the Sierpinski distribution, where both DBS and DNN converged to a solution in approximately 77 minutes using a θ parameter of 90°. In contrast, the DPS algorithm demonstrated remarkable efficiency. For angles of 20°, the execution time remained under 25 seconds, and for larger angles, it further decreased to less than 11 seconds. This performance improvement highlights the algorithm's scalability and optimization capabilities. To better illustrate this performance contrast, Figure 9 presents the execution time in seconds for the DPS algorithm. The graph shows results for both Bit and Sierpinski distributions in large-scale databases, comparing different values of the θ parameter across indexed and non-indexed databases.

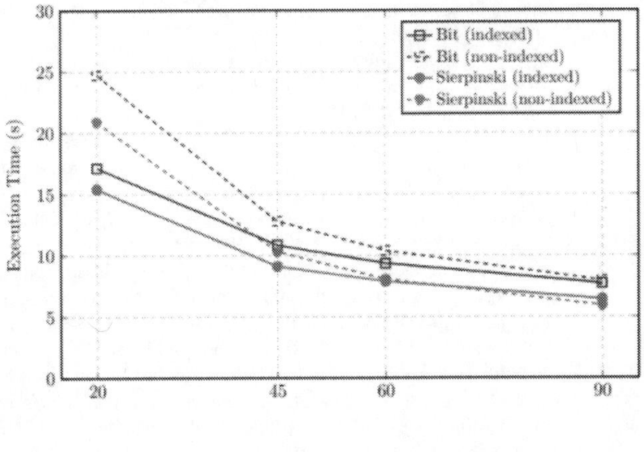

Figure 9. DPS algorithm execution time as a function of θ for larges indexed and non-indexed databases.

In the analysis of real-world data distributions, the DPS query demonstrated superior performance across most tested scenarios. The algorithm showed less favorable results for 90° angles in both indexed and non-indexed large-volume databases, as well as for 60° angles in smaller non-indexed databases. Despite these exceptions, DPS achieved excellent execution time results. Table II presents the execution times for different configurations of DBS, DNN, and DPS queries on real databases.

TABLE II
EXECUTION TIME COMPARISON BETWEEN DBS, DNN AND DPS ALGORITHMS.

Database Size	Angle	Non-Indexed			Indexed		
		DBS	DNN	DPS	DBS	DNN	DPS
Small	20°	4.37	4.36	**3.14**	4.19	4.22	**1.26**
	45°	2.18	2.13	**1.59**	2.00	2.05	**0.80**
	60°	1.25	**1.24**	1.34	1.13	1.14	**0.78**
	90°	1.28	1.18	**0.87**	1.11	1.19	**0.66**
Medium	20°	187.87	183.04	**4.51**	177.45	182.37	**5.05**
	45°	21.84	21.81	**2.39**	21.30	22.16	**2.51**
	60°	6.04	6.05	**1.92**	5.92	6.01	**2.09**
	90°	**0.78**	**0.76**	1.50	**0.71**	**0.71**	1.63
Large	20°	93.44	98.22	**37.41**	91.63	98.58	**32.13**
	45°	74.59	73.90	**19.06**	72.57	73.02	**19.44**
	60°	33.97	33.85	**15.27**	32.80	32.50	**16.75**
	90°	4.22	**3.97**	11.61	3.52	**3.49**	13.49

The analysis of the variation of the query angle, shown in Figure 10, demonstrates that DPS achieved better performance with smaller angles, particularly at $\theta = 20$. From a total of 18 queries per angle (15 on synthetic datasets and 3 on real datasets), the algorithm achieved the best 14 results on indexed bases (77.78%) and 12 on non-indexed bases (66.7%) for $\theta = 20$.

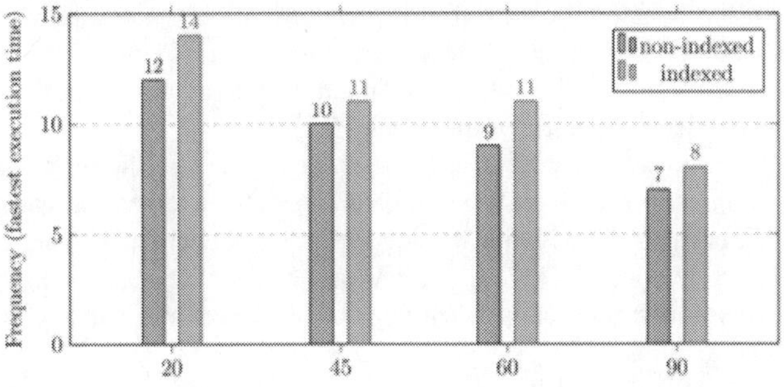

Figure 10. DPS performance comparison at different angles with and without index.

The diversity of objects returned by the DPS query reinforces this work's objective of providing consistent and homogeneous diversity in the response set, regardless of query parameters, distribution, and volume. This characteristic is demonstrated in 11, which presents a comparison of the number of objects returned in the response set among DPS, DBS, and DNN algorithms, considering only different configurations of real databases. As explained in the refinement step, if all partitions contain data, the maximum number of objects found is equal to the number of composite partitions; that is, it has a maximum of $\theta/360$ response objects.

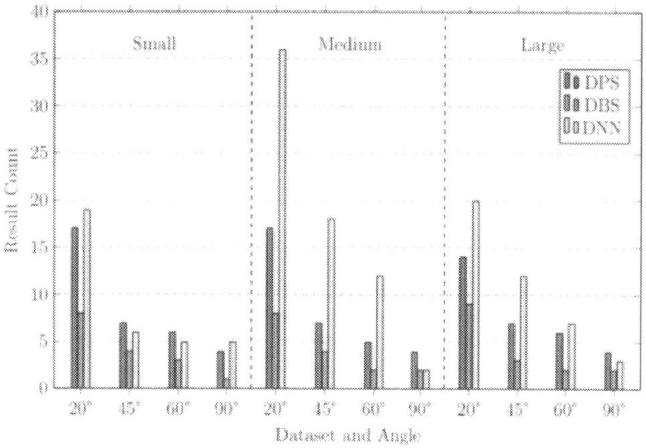

Figure 11. Comparative analysis of retrieved object counts for DPS, DBS, and DNN on real data.

V. Results Discussion

Overall, the DPS algorithm demonstrated superior performance compared to DBS and DNN algorithms, excelling in 52.8% of queries on non-indexed databases and 61.1% on indexed databases. These results demonstrate its versatility and efficiency in different application contexts.

In synthetic databases with Bit and Sierpinski distributions, DPS achieved exceptional performance, showing a 99.9% improvement in execution time for all queries on large databases. This result can be attributed to the high density of objects concentrated in specific directions, a characteristic that benefits the algorithm's geometric partitioning approach. The processing step efficiently identifies the NN point in each partition, significantly reducing the number of comparisons needed to determine the result set.

The same pattern of high object density in specific directions was observed in real-world data. This characteristic of spatial distribution explains the algorithm's excellent performance on real databases, as geometric partitioning proves to be particularly efficient when objects are concentrated in specific directions.

DPS showed better performance with smaller angle parameters, such as 20° and 45°. This behavior can be explained by the fact that smaller angles impose less strict dominance restrictions for DBS and DNN queries, meaning more objects must be evaluated before the stopping condition is reached.

Regarding the diversity of results, DPS consistently maintains that the maximum number of returned objects will be equal to $360°/\theta$, which means that there will be at most one dominant object for each θ interval.

VI. Conclusion and Future Work

This paper presented DPS, a geometric partitioning approach for direction-based queries. DPS reduces execution time by up to 99.9% compared to existing methods—completing queries in under 25 seconds that previously took over 24 hours. It also ensures directional diversity by returning at most one object per θ interval.

While our experiments focused on geographic datasets, DPS has potential applications beyond traditional GIS systems. The algorithm's ability to efficiently identify directionally diverse neighbors could benefit autonomous navigation systems when detecting surrounding obstacles, or assist IoT networks in selecting well-distributed sensor nodes. The consistent directional coverage guaranteed by DPS makes it particularly suitable for emergency response scenarios where alternative routes in different directions are critical.

Our evaluation was limited to datasets of up to 2 million points. Although DPS performed well at this scale, real-world applications with larger datasets may present additional challenges requiring further investigation.

Future research directions include:

- **Intelligent Query Selection:** Develop models to automatically choose between DPS, DBS, or DNN based on dataset characteristics and query parameters.
- **Scalability Analysis:** Evaluate DPS performance with datasets exceeding 10 million objects and identify optimization opportunities.
- **Dynamic Environments:** Adapt DPS for scenarios with frequently changing data, such as real-time traffic or mobile sensor networks.
- **Extended Domains:** Explore applications beyond spatial queries, including similarity searches in high-dimensional spaces.

These directions will help establish the practical scope and limitations of the DPS approach.

References

[1] K. C. K. Lee, W. C. Lee, and H. V. Leong, "Nearest Surrounder Queries", in *Proceedings of the 22nd International Conference on Data Engineering (ICDE)*, Atlanta, GA, USA: IEEE, Apr. 2006, pp. 85–85. DOI: 10.1109/ICDE.2006.104.

[2] X. Guo, B. Zheng, Y. Ishikawa, and Y. Gao, "Direction-based surrounder queries for mobile recommendations", *The VLDB Journal*, vol. 20, no. 5, pp. 743–766, 2011. DOI: 10.1007/s00778-011-0241-y.

[3] X. Guo and X. Yang, "Direction-aware nearest neighbor query", *IEEE Access*, vol. 7, pp. 30 285–30 301, 2019. DOI: 10.1109/ACCESS.2019.2902130.

[4] H. Zhang *et al.*, "Group Visible Nearest Surrounder Query in Obstacle Space", in *Proceedings of the 2019 IEEE International Conference on Computer Science and Educational Informatization (CSEI)*, Guangzhou, China: IEEE, 2019, pp. 345–350. DOI: 10.1109/CSEI47661.2019.8939019.

[5] J. Chung, H. J. Jang, K. H. Jung, and S. Y. Jung, "Nearest surrounder searching in mobile computing environments", *International Journal of Communication Systems*, vol. 26, no. 6, pp. 770–791, 2013. DOI: 10.1002/dac.2409.

[6] S. Nutanong, E. Tanin, and R. Zhang, "Visible Nearest Neighbor Queries", in *Proceedings of the 11th International Conference on Database Systems for Advanced Applications (DASFAA)*, Bangkok, Thailand: Springer, 2007, pp. 876–883. DOI: 10.1007/978-3-540-71703-4_73.

[7] A. C. Carniel, "Spatial Information Retrieval in Digital Ecosystems: A Comprehensive Survey", in *Proceedings of the 12th International Conference on Management of Digital EcoSystems (MEDES '20)*, New York, NY, USA: ACM, 2020, pp. 10–17. DOI: 10.1145/3415958.3433038.

[8] A. C. Carniel, "Defining and designing spatial queries: the role of spatial relationships", *Geo-spatial Information Science*, vol. 26, no. 1, pp. 1–25, 2023. DOI: 10.1080/10095020.2022.2163924.

[9] P. Katiyar, T. Vu, S. Migliorini, A. Belussi, and A. Eldawy, "SpiderWeb: A Spatial Data Generator on the Web", in *Proceedings of the 28th International Conference on Advances in Geographic Information Systems (SIGSPATIAL '20)*, Seattle, WA, USA: ACM, Nov. 2020, pp. 465–468. DOI: 10.1145/3397536.3422351.

[10] OpenStreetMap contributors, *Planet dump retrieved from https://planet.osm.org*, https://www.openstreetmap.org, 2017.